fat free

fat free

More than 320 tempting no fat, low fat and low cholesterol recipes
for every occasion, shown step by step in 1400 photographs

EDITOR
ANNE SHEASBY

LORENZ BOOKS

This edition is published by Lorenz Books
an imprint of Anness Publishing Ltd
Blaby Road, Wigston
Leicestershire LE18 4SE
info@anness.com

www.lorenzbooks.com
www.annesspublishing.com

If you like the images in this book and would like to investigate using them for publishing,
promotions or advertising, please visit our website www.practicalpictures.com for more information.

Publisher: Joanna Lorenz
Project Editor: Lucy Doncaster
Designers: Sara Kidd and Bill Mason
Photographers: Karl Adamson, Edward Allwright, Steve Baxter,
James Duncan, Amanda Heywood, Don Last, Michael Michaels,
Patrick McLeavey, Thomas Odulate and Peter Reilly
Recipes: Catherine Atkinson, Carla Capalbo, Kit Chan, Roz Denny,
Christine France, Shirley Gill, Christine Ingram, Sue Maggs,
Annie Nichols, Maggie Pannell, Laura Washburn and Stephen Wheeler
Home Economists: Kit Chan, Carla Capalbo, Kathryn Hawkins,
Wendy Lee, Jane Stevenson and Elizabeth Wolf-Cohen
Stylists: Madeleine Brehaut, Hilary Guy, Jo Harris, Blake Minton,
Thomas Odulate, Kirsty Rawlings and Fiona Tillett
Production Controller: Wendy Lawson

NOTES

Bracketed terms are intended for American readers.
For all recipes, quantities are given in both metric and imperial measures and, where appropriate, in standard cups and spoons.
Follow one set of measures, but not a mixture, because they are not interchangeable.
Standard spoon and cup measures are level. 1 tsp = 5ml, 1 tbsp = 15ml, 1 cup = 250ml/8fl oz.
Australian standard tablespoons are 20ml. Australian readers should use 3 tsp in place of 1 tbsp
for measuring small quantities.
American pints are 16fl oz/2 cups. American readers should use 20fl oz/2.5 cups in place of 1 pint when measuring liquids.
Electric oven temperatures in this book are for conventional ovens. When using a fan oven, the temperature
will probably need to be reduced by about 10–20°C/20–40°F. Since ovens vary, you should check with
your manufacturer's instruction book for guidance.

The nutritional analysis given for each recipe is
calculated per portion (i.e. serving or item), unless
otherwise stated. If the recipe gives a range, such
as Serves 4–6, then the nutritional analysis will
be for the smaller portion size, i.e. 6 servings.
The analysis does not include optional ingredients,
such as salt added to taste.
Medium (US large) eggs are used
unless otherwise stated.
Front cover shows Raspberry-Passion Fruit
Chinchillas – for recipe, see page 317.

PUBLISHER'S NOTE

CONTENTS

INTRODUCTION

Cooking and eating good food is one of life's greatest pleasures – and there's nothing wrong with enjoying good food, except that for too long 'good' often meant 'fatty'. Butter, oil, cheese and other fatty foods were considered essential for good cooking. We now know that all this fat – along with too much sugar and salt – has a huge impact on health.

Most of us eat fats in one form or another every day. In fact, we need to consume a small amount of fat to maintain a healthy and balanced diet, but almost everyone can afford to, and should, reduce their fat intake, particularly of saturated fats. Weight for weight, dietary fats supply far more energy than all the other nutrients in our diet. If you eat a diet that is high in fats and don't exercise enough to use up that energy, you will put on weight. By cutting down on fat, you can easily reduce your energy intake without affecting the other essential nutrients. And by choosing the right types of fat, using low fat and fat-free products whenever possible, and making

There are many ways of enjoying baked treats such as these Oaty Crisps without the need for high-fat mixtures.

small, simple changes to the way you cook and prepare food, you can reduce your overall fat intake quite dramatically and enjoy a much healthier diet without really noticing any difference.

As you will see, watching your fat intake doesn't have to mean dieting and deprivation. The book opens with an informative introduction about basic healthy eating guidelines – you'll find out about the five main food groups, and how, by simply choosing a variety of foods from these groups every day, you can ensure that you are eating all the nutrients you need.

One way to enjoy your favourite foods without guilt is to substitute lower fat ingredients for higher fat ones. This book will introduce you to these lower fat ingredients and show you how to use them. There are hints and tips on how to cook with fat-free and low fat ingredients; techniques for using healthy, fat-free fruit purée in place of butter or margarine in all your favourite baking recipes; suggestions for which foods to cut down on and what to try instead; easy ways to reduce fat and saturated fat

in your foods; new no fat and low fat cooking techniques, and information on the best cookware for fat-free cooking; along with a delicious section on low fat and very low fat snacks.

There are over 300 easy-to-follow recipes for delicious dishes that your whole family can enjoy. Every recipe has been developed to fit into modern nutritional guidelines, and each one has at-a-glance nutritional information so you can instantly check the calories and fat content.

The recipes are very low in fat – all contain less than five grams of fat per serving, and many contain less than one. The selection of foods included will surprise and delight you: there are barbecues and bakes, pizza and pastas, tasty sautés and stews, vegetable dishes and vegetarian main courses, fish and shellfish dishes galore, and wonderfully tempting breads, cookies and cakes – all without as much fat as traditional recipes, of course, but nevertheless packed with fantastic flavour and vitality.

Fresh vegetables (far left) and fresh fruit (left and above) make ideal choices for fat-free and low-fat cooking.

HEALTHY EATING GUIDELINES

A healthy diet is one that provides the body with all the nutrients it needs to be able to grow and repair properly. By eating the right types, balance and proportions of foods, we are more likely to feel healthy, have plenty of energy and a higher resistance to illness that will help protect our body against developing diseases such as heart disease, cancers, bowel disorders and obesity.

By choosing a variety of foods every day, you will ensure that you are supplying your body with all the essential nutrients, including vitamins and minerals, it needs. To get the balance right, it is important to know just how much of each type of food you should be eating.

There are five main food groups (see right), and it is recommended that we should eat plenty of fruit, vegetables (at least five portions a day, not including potatoes) and foods such as cereals, pasta, rice and potatoes; moderate amounts of meat, fish, poultry and dairy products; and only small amounts of foods containing fat or sugar. By choosing a good balance of foods from these groups every day, and choosing lower fat or lower sugar alternatives wherever possible, we will be supplying our bodies with all the nutrients they need for optimum health.

THE ROLE AND IMPORTANCE OF FAT IN OUR DIET

Fats shouldn't be cut out of our diets completely. We need a small amount of fat for general health and well-being – fat is a valuable source of energy, and also helps to make foods more palatable to eat. However, if you lower the fats, especially saturated fats, in your diet, you will feel healthier; it will help you lose weight and reduce the risk of developing some diseases.

THE FIVE MAIN FOOD GROUPS

- Fruit and vegetables

- Rice, potatoes, bread, pasta and other cereals

- Meat, poultry, fish and alternative proteins

- Milk and other dairy foods

- Foods which contain fat and foods which contain sugar

Aim to limit your daily intake of fats to no more than 30% of total calories. In real terms, this means that for an average intake of 2,000 calories per day, 30% of energy would come from 600 calories. Since each gram of fat provides 9 calories, your total daily intake should be no more than 66.6g fat. Your total intake of saturated fats should be no more than 10% of the total calories.

TYPES OF FAT

All fats in our foods are made up of building blocks of fatty acids and glycerol and their properties vary according to each combination.

There are two types of fat – saturated and unsaturated. The unsaturated group is divided into two types – polyunsaturated and monounsaturated fats.

There is always a combination of each of the three types of fat (saturated, polyunsaturated and monounsaturated fats) in any food, but the amount of each type varies greatly from one food to another.

Left: By choosing a variety of foods from the five main food groups, you will ensure that you are supplying your body with all the nutrients it needs.

SATURATED FATS

All fatty acids are made up of chains of carbon atoms. Each atom has one or more free "bonds" to link with other atoms and by doing so the fatty acids transport nutrients to cells throughout the body. Without these free "bonds" the atom cannot form any links, that is to say it is completely "saturated". Because of this, the body finds it hard to process the fatty acid into energy, so it simply stores it as fat.

Saturated fats are the fats which you should reduce, as they can increase the level of cholesterol in the blood, which in turn can increase the risk of developing heart disease.

The main sources of saturated fats are animal products, such as meat, and fats, such as butter and lard that are solid at room temperature. However, there are also saturated fats of vegetable origin, notably coconut and palm oils, and some margarines and oils, which are processed by changing some of the unsaturated fatty acids to saturated ones – they are labelled "hydrogenated vegetable oil" and should be avoided.

POLYUNSATURATED FATS

There are two types of polyunsaturated fats, those of vegetable or plant origin (omega 6), such as sunflower oil, soft margarine and seeds, and those from oily fish (omega 3), such as herring, mackerel and sardines. Both fats are usually liquid at room temperature. Small quantities of polyunsaturated fats are essential for good health and are thought to help reduce the level of cholesterol in the blood.

MONOUNSATURATED FATS

Monounsaturated fats are also thought to have the beneficial effect of reducing the blood cholesterol level and this could explain why in some

Above: A selection of foods containing the three main types of fat found in foods.

Mediterranean countries there is such a low incidence of heart disease. Monounsaturated fats are found in foods such as olive oil, rapeseed oil, some nuts such as almonds and hazelnuts, oily fish and avocado pears.

CUTTING DOWN ON FATS AND SATURATED FATS IN THE DIET

About one quarter of the fat we eat comes from meat and meat products, one-fifth from dairy products and margarine and the rest from cakes, cookies, pastries and other foods. It is easy to cut down on obvious sources of fat in the diet, such as butter, oils, margarine, cream, whole milk and full

fat cheese, but we also need to know about – and watch out for – "hidden" fats. Hidden fats can be found in foods such as cakes, cookies and nuts. Even lean, trimmed red meats may contain as much as 10% fat.

By being aware of foods which are high in fats and particularly saturated fats, and by making simple changes to your diet, you can reduce the total fat content of your diet quite considerably. Whenever possible, choose reduced fat or low fat alternatives to foods such as milk, cheese and salad dressings, and fill up on very low fat foods, such as fruit and vegetables, and foods that are high in carbohydrate such as pasta, rice, bread and potatoes.

EASY WAYS TO CUT DOWN FAT AND SATURATED FAT IN THE DAILY DIET

There are lots of simple no-fuss ways of reducing the fat in your diet. Just follow the simple "eat less – try instead" suggestions below to discover how easy it is.

• EAT LESS – Butter, margarine and hard fats.
• TRY INSTEAD – Low fat spread, very low fat spread or polyunsaturated margarine. If you must use butter or hard margarine, make sure they are softened at room temperature and spread them very thinly. Better still, use fat-free spreads such as low fat soft cheese, reduced sugar jams or marmalades for sandwiches and toast.

• EAT LESS – Fatty meats and high fat products such as meat pâtés, pies and sausages.
• TRY INSTEAD – Low fat meats, such as chicken, turkey and venison.
   Use only the leanest cuts of such meats as lamb, beef and pork.
   Always cut any visible fat and skin from meat before cooking.
   Choose reduced fat sausages and meat products and eat fish more often.
   Try using low fat protein products such as Quorn or tofu in place of meat in recipes.
   Make gravies using vegetable water or fat-free stock rather than using meat juices.

• EAT LESS – Full fat dairy products such as whole milk, cream, butter, hard margarine, crème fraîche, whole milk yogurts and hard cheese.
• TRY INSTEAD – Semi-skimmed (low fat) or skimmed milk and milk products, low fat yogurts, low fat fromage frais and low fat soft cheeses, reduced fat hard cheeses and reduced fat creams and crème fraîche.

• EAT LESS – Hard cooking fats, such as lard or hard margarine.
• TRY INSTEAD – Polyunsaturated or monounsaturated oils, such as olive, sunflower or corn for cooking.

• EAT LESS – Rich salad dressings like full-fat mayonnaise, salad cream or French dressing.
• TRY INSTEAD – Reduced fat or fat-free mayonnaise or dressings. Make salad dressings at home with low fat yogurt or fromage frais.

• EAT LESS – Fried foods.
• TRY INSTEAD – Fat-free cooking methods such as grilling (broiling), microwaving, steaming or baking.
   Try cooking in a non-stick wok with only a very small amount of oil.
   Always roast or grill (broil) meat or poultry on a rack.

• EAT LESS – Deep-fried chips (French fries) and sautéed potatoes.
• TRY INSTEAD – Fat-free starchy foods such as pasta, couscous and rice.
   Choose baked or boiled potatoes.

• EAT LESS – Added fat in cooking.
• TRY INSTEAD – To cook with little or no fat. Use heavy or good quality non-stick pans, so that the food doesn't stick.
   Try using a small amount of spray oil in cooking to control exactly how much fat you are using.
   Use fat-free or low fat ingredients for cooking, such as fruit juice, low fat or fat-free stock, wine or even beer.

• EAT LESS – High fat snacks such as tortilla chips, fried snacks and pastries, chocolate cakes, muffins, doughnuts, sweet pastries and cookies – especially chocolate ones!
• TRY INSTEAD – Low fat and fat-free fresh or dried fruits, breadsticks or vegetable sticks.
   Make your own home-baked low fat cakes and bakes.
   If you do buy ready-made cakes and cookies, always choose low fat and reduced fat versions.

FAT-FREE COOKING METHODS

It's very easy to cook without fat – whenever possible, grill (broil), bake, microwave or steam foods without the addition of fat, or try stir-frying without fat – use a little low fat or fat-free stock, wine or fruit juice instead.

• Choosing heavy or good quality cookware, you'll find that the amount of fat needed for cooking foods can be kept to an absolute minimum. When making casseroles or meat sauces such as bolognese, dry-fry the meat to brown it and then drain off all the excess fat before adding the other ingredients. If you do need a little fat for cooking, choose an oil which is high in unsaturates such as corn, sunflower, olive or rapeseed oil and always use as little as possible.

• When baking low fat cakes and bakes, use good quality bakeware which doesn't need greasing before use, or use non-stick baking paper and only lightly grease before lining.

• Look out for non-stick coated fabric sheet. This re-usable non-stick material is very versatile, it can be cut to size and used to line cake tins (pans), baking sheets or frying pans. Heat resistant up to 290°C/550°F and microwave safe, it will last for up to 5 years.

• When baking foods such as chicken or fish, rather than adding a bit of butter to the food, try baking the food in a loosely sealed parcel of foil or greaseproof paper and adding some wine or fruit juice and herbs or spices to the food before sealing the parcel.

• When grilling (broiling) foods, the addition of fat is often unnecessary. If the food shows signs of drying, brush with a small amount of unsaturated oil such as sunflower or corn oil.

Above: Invest in a few of these useful items of cookware for easy fat-free cooking: non-stick cookware and accurate measuring equipment are essential.

• Microwaved foods rarely need the addition of fat, so add herbs or spices for extra flavour and colour.

• Steaming or boiling are easy, fat-free ways of cooking many foods, especially vegetables, fish and chicken.

• Try poaching foods, such as chicken, fish and fruit, in stock or syrup – it is another easy, fat-free cooking method.

• Try braising vegetables in the oven in low fat or fat-free stock, wine or simply water with the addition of some herbs.

• Sauté vegetables in low fat or fat-free stock, wine or fruit juice instead of fat or oil.

• Cook vegetables in a covered pan over a low heat with a little water so they cook in their own juices.

• Marinate food such as meat or poultry in mixtures of alcohol, herbs or spices, and vinegar or fruit juice. This will help to tenderize the meat and add flavour and colour and, in addition, the marinade can be used to baste the food while it is cooking.

• When serving vegetables such as boiled potatoes, carrots or peas, resist the temptation to add a bit of butter or margarine. Instead, sprinkle the cooked vegetables with chopped fresh herbs, such as parsley, or ground spices.

COOKING WITH LOW FAT OR NON-FAT INGREDIENTS

Nowadays many foods are available in full fat and reduced fat or very low fat forms. In every supermarket you'll find a huge array of low fat dairy products, such as milk, cream, yogurt, hard and soft cheeses and fromage frais; reduced fat sweet or chocolate biscuits (cookies); reduced fat or fat-free salad dressings and mayonnaise; reduced fat snacks; low fat, half-fat or very low fat spreads; as well as such reduced fat ready-made food products as desserts.

Other foods, such as fresh fruit and vegetables, pasta, rice, potatoes and bread, naturally contain very little fat. Some foods, such as soy sauce, wine, cider, sherry, sugar, honey, syrup and jam, contain no fat at all. By combining these and other low fat foods you can create delicious dishes which contain very little fat.

Some low fat or reduced fat ingredients and products work better than others in cooking but often a simple substitution of one for another will work. The addition of low fat or non-fat ingredients, such as herbs and spices, also add plenty of extra flavour and colour to recipes.

LOW FAT SPREADS IN COOKING

There is a huge variety of low fat, reduced fat and half-fat spreads available in our supermarkets, along with some spreads that are very low in fat. Some are suitable for cooking, while others are only suitable for spreading.

Generally speaking, very low fat spreads with a fat content of around 20 per cent or less have a high water content and so are all unsuitable for cooking, as they will split, and are only suitable for spreading.

Low fat or half-fat spreads with a fat content of around 40 per cent are suitable for spreading and can be used for some cooking methods. They are suitable for recipes such as all-in-one cake and cookie recipes, all-in-one sauce recipes, sautéing vegetables, choux pastry and some cake icings.

When using these low fat spreads for cooking, the fat may behave slightly differently to full fat products such as butter or margarine.

With some recipes, the cooked result may be slightly different, but will still be very acceptable. Other recipes will be just as tasty and successful. For example, choux pastry made using half- or low fat spread is often slightly crisper and lighter in texture than traditional choux pastry, and a cheesecake cookie base made with melted half- or low fat spread combined with crushed cookie crumbs, may be slightly softer in texture and less crispy than a biscuit base made using melted butter.

When heating half- or low fat spreads, never cook them over a high heat. Always use a heavy pan over a low heat to avoid the product burning, spitting or spoiling, and stir all the time. With all-in-one sauces, the mixture should be whisked continuously over a low heat.

Half-fat or low fat spreads are not suitable for shallow or deep-fat frying, pastry making, rich fruit cakes, some cookies, shortbread, clarified butter and preserves such as lemon curd.

Remember that the keeping qualities of recipes made using half- or low fat spreads may be reduced slightly, due to the lower fat content.

Above: Almost all dairy products now come in low fat or reduced fat versions.

Another way to reduce the fat content of recipes, particularly cake recipes is to use a fruit purée in place of all or some of the fat in a recipe.

Many cake recipes work well using this method but others may not be so successful. Pastry does not work well. Breads work very well, perhaps because the amount of fat is usually relatively small, as do some cookies and bars, such as brownies and flapjacks.

To make the dried fruit purée to use in recipes, chop 115g/4oz ready-to-eat dried fruit and place in a blender or food processor with 75ml/5 tbsp water and blend to a roughly smooth purée. Then, simply substitute the same weight of this dried fruit purée for all or just some of the amount of fat in the recipe. The purée will keep in the refrigerator for up to three days.

You can use prunes, dried apricots, dried peaches, or dried apples, or substitute mashed fresh fruit, such as ripe bananas or lightly cooked apples, without the added water.

Above: A selection of cooking oils and low fat spreads. Always check the packaging of low fat spreads – for cooking, they must have a fat content of about 40 per cent.

LOW FAT AND VERY LOW FAT SNACKS

Instead of reaching for a packet of potato chips, a high fat cookie or a chocolate bar when hunger strikes, choose one of these tasty low fat snacks to fill that hungry hole.

• A piece of fresh fruit or vegetable such as an apple, banana or carrot – keep chunks or sticks wrapped in a plastic bag in the refrigerator.

• Fresh fruit or vegetable chunks – skewer them on to toothpicks or short bamboo skewers to make them into mini kebabs.

• A handful of dried fruit such as raisins, sultanas (golden raisins) or apricots. These also make a perfect addition to children's packed lunches or to school break snacks.

• A portion of canned fruit in natural fruit juice – serve with a spoonful or two of fat-free yogurt.

• One or two crisp rice cakes – delicious on their own, or topped with honey, or reduced fat cheese.

• Crackers, such as water biscuits (crackers) or crisp breads, spread with reduced sugar jam or marmalade.

• A bowl of wholewheat breakfast cereal or no-added-sugar muesli served with a little skimmed milk.

• Very low fat plain or fruit yogurt or fromage frais.

• A toasted teacake spread with reduced-sugar jam or marmalade.

• Toasted crumpet spread with yeast extract or beef extract.

THE FAT AND CALORIE CONTENTS OF FOOD

The following figures show the weight of fat (g) and the energy content per 100g/4oz of each food.

VEGETABLES

	FAT (g)	ENERGY		FAT (g)	ENERGY
Broccoli	0.9	33 Kcals/138 kJ	Onions	0.2	36 Kcals/151 kJ
Cabbage	0.4	26 Kcals/109 kJ	Peas	1.5	83 Kcals/344 kJ
Carrots	0.3	35 Kcals/146 kJ	Potatoes	0.2	75 Kcals/318 kJ
Cauliflower	0.9	34 Kcals/142 kJ	Chips (French fries), retail	12.4	239 Kcals/1001 kJ
Courgettes (zucchini)	0.4	18 Kcals/74 kJ	Chips, home-made	6.7	189 Kcals/796 kJ
Cucumber	0.1	10 Kcals/40 kJ	Oven-chips, frozen, baked	4.2	162 Kcals/687 kJ
Mushrooms	0.5	13 Kcals/55 kJ	Tomatoes	0.3	17 Kcals/73 kJ

BEANS AND PEAS

	FAT (g)	ENERGY		FAT (g)	ENERGY
Black-eyed beans (peas), cooked	1.8	116 Kcals/494 kJ	Hummus	12.6	187 Kcals/781 kJ
Butter (lima) beans, canned	0.5	77 Kcals/327 kJ	Red kidney beans, canned	0.6	100 Kcals/424 kJ
Chickpeas, canned	2.9	115 Kcals/487 kJ	Red lentils, cooked	0.4	100 Kcals/424 kJ

FISH AND SHELLFISH

	FAT (g)	ENERGY		FAT (g)	ENERGY
Cod fillets, raw	0.7	80 Kcals/337 kJ	Prawns (shrimp)	0.9	99 Kcals/418 kJ
Crab, canned	0.5	77 Kcals/326 kJ	Trout, grilled	5.4	135 Kcals/565 kJ
Haddock, raw	0.6	81 Kcals/345 kJ	Tuna, canned in brine	0.6	99 Kcals/422 kJ
Lemon sole, raw	1.5	83 Kcals/351 kJ	Tuna, canned in oil	9.0	189 Kcals/794 kJ

MEAT PRODUCTS

	FAT (g)	ENERGY		FAT (g)	ENERGY
Bacon rasher (strip), fatty	39.5	414 Kcals/1710 kJ	Chicken fillet, raw	1.1	106 Kcals/449 kJ
Turkey rasher (strip)	1.0	99 Kcals/414 kJ	Chicken, roasted	12.5	218 Kcals/910 kJ
Beef, minced (ground), raw	16.2	225 Kcals/934 kJ	Duck, meat only, raw	6.5	137 Kcals/575 kJ
Beef, minced, extra lean, raw	9.6	174 Kcals/728 kJ	Duck, roasted, meat, fat and skin	38.1	423 Kcals/1750 kJ
Rump steak, lean and fat	10.1	174 Kcals/726 kJ	Turkey, meat only, raw	1.6	105 Kcals/443 kJ
Rump steak, lean only	4.1	125 Kcals/526 kJ	Liver, lamb, raw	6.2	137 Kcals/575 kJ
Lamb chops, loin, lean and fat	23.0	277 Kcals/1150 kJ	Pork pie	27.0	376 Kcals/1564 kJ
Lamb, average, lean, raw	8.3	156 Kcals/651 kJ	Salami	45.2	491 Kcals/2031 kJ
Pork chops, loin, lean and fat	21.7	270 Kcals/1119 kJ	Sausage roll, flaky pastry	36.4	477 Kcals/1985 kJ
Pork, average, lean, raw	4.0	123 Kcals/519 kJ			

Information from *The Composition of Foods* (6th Edition 2002) is reproduced with the permission of the Royal Society of Chemistry and the Controller of Her Majesty's Stationery Office.

DAIRY, FATS AND OILS

	FAT (g)	ENERGY		FAT (g)	ENERGY
Cream, double (heavy)	48.0	449 Kcals/1849 kJ	Low fat yogurt, plain	0.8	56 Kcals/236 kJ
Cream, single (light)	19.1	198 Kcals/817 kJ	Greek yogurt	9.1	115 Kcals/477 kJ
Cream, whipping	39.3	373 Kcals/1539 kJ	Reduced fat Greek yogurt	5.0	80 Kcals/335 kJ
Crème fraîche	40.0	379 Kcals/156 kJ	Butter	81.7	737 Kcals/3031 kJ
Reduced fat crème fraîche	15.0	165 Kcals/683 kJ	Margarine	81.6	739 Kcals/3039 kJ
Reduced fat double cream	24.0	243 Kcals/1002 kJ	Low fat spread	40.5	390 Kcals/1605 kJ
Milk, skimmed	0.1	33 Kcals/130 kJ	Very low fat spread	25	273 Kcals/1128 kJ
Milk, whole	3.9	66 Kcals/275 kJ	Lard	99.0	891 Kcals/3663 kJ
Brie	26.9	319 Kcals/1323 kJ	Corn oil	99.9	899 Kcals/3696 kJ
Cheddar cheese	34.4	412 Kcals/1708 kJ	Olive oil	99.9	899 Kcals/3696 kJ
Cheddar-type, reduced fat	15.0	261 Kcals/1091 kJ	Safflower oil	99.9	899 Kcals/3696 kJ
Cream cheese	47.4	439 Kcals/1807 kJ	Eggs	10.8	147 Kcals/612 kJ
Fromage frais, plain	7.1	113 Kcals/469 kJ	Egg yolk	30.5	339 Kcals/1402 kJ
Fromage frais, very low fat	0.2	58 Kcals/247 kJ	Egg white	Trace	36 Kcals/153 kJ
Skimmed milk soft cheese	Trace	74 Kcals/313 kJ	Fat-free dressing	1.2	67 Kcals/282 kJ
Edam cheese	25.4	333 Kcals/1382 kJ	French dressing	49.4	462 Kcals/1902 kJ
Feta cheese	20.2	250 Kcals/1037 kJ	Mayonnaise	75.6	691 Kcals/2843 kJ
Parmesan cheese	32.7	452 Kcals/1880 kJ	Mayonnaise, reduced calorie	28.1	288 Kcals/1188 kJ

CEREALS, BAKING AND PRESERVES

	FAT (g)	ENERGY		FAT (g)	ENERGY
Brown rice, uncooked	2.8	357 Kcals/1518 kJ	Digestive biscuit (plain)	20.9	471 Kcals/1978 kJ
White rice, uncooked	3.6	383 Kcals/1630 kJ	Reduced fat digestive biscuits	16.4	467 Kcals/1965 kJ
Pasta, white, uncooked	1.8	342 Kcals/1456 kJ	Shortbread	26.1	498 Kcals/2087 kJ
Pasta, whole-wheat, uncooked	2.5	324 Kcal/1379 kJ	Madeira cake	16.9	393 Kcals/1652 kJ
Brown bread	2.0	218 Kcals/927 kJ	Fatless sponge cake	6.1	294 Kcals/1245 kJ
White bread	1.9	235 Kcals/1002 kJ	Doughnut, jam	14.5	336 Kcals/1414 kJ
Wholemeal (wheat) bread	2.5	215 Kcals/914 kJ	Sugar, white	0 3	94 Kcals/1680 kJ
Cornflakes	0.7	360 Kcals/1535 kJ	Chocolate, milk	30.7	520 Kcals/2177 kJ
Sultana bran	1.6	303 Kcals/1289 kJ	Chocolate, plain (semisweet)	28	510 Kcals/2157 kJ
Swiss-style muesli	5.9	363 Kcals/1540 kJ	Honey	0	288 Kcals/1229 kJ
Croissant	20.3	360 Kcals/1505 kJ	Lemon curd	5.0	283 Kcals/1198 kJ
Flapjack	26.6	484 Kcals/2028 kJ	Fruit jam	0 26	268 Kcals/1114 kJ

FRUIT AND NUTS

	FAT (g)	ENERGY		FAT (g)	ENERGY
Apples, eating	0.1	47 Kcals/199 kJ	Pears	0.1	40 Kcals/169 kJ
Avocados	19.5	190 Kcals/784 kJ	Almonds	55.8	612 Kcals/2534 kJ
Bananas	0.3	95 Kcals/403 kJ	Brazil nuts	68.2	682 Kcals/2813 kJ
Dried mixed fruit	0.4	268 Kcals/1114 kJ	Hazelnuts	63.5	650 Kcals/2685 kJ
Grapefruit	0.1	30 Kcals/126 kJ	Pine nuts	68.6	688 Kcals/2840 kJ
Oranges	0.1	37 Kcals/158 kJ	Walnuts	68.5	688 Kcals/2837 kJ
Peaches	0.1	33 Kcals/142 kJ	Peanut butter, smooth	53.7	623 Kcals/2581 kJ

SOUPS

Home-made soups are ideal served as an appetizer, a snack or a light lunch. They are filling, nutritious and low in fat, and are wonderful served with a chunk of fresh crusty bread. The wide variety of fresh vegetables available nowadays ensures that the freshest ingredients can be used to create healthy and delicious home-made soups. We include a tasty selection, including vegetable soups, chowders and bean and pasta soups. Choose from temptations such as Italian Vegetable Soup, Spicy Tomato and Lentil Soup, and Creamy Cod Chowder.

MEDITERRANEAN TOMATO SOUP

Children will love this soup – especially if you use fancy shapes of pasta such as alphabet or animal shapes.

INGREDIENTS

Serves 4
675g/1½lb ripe plum tomatoes
1 medium onion, quartered
1 celery stick
1 garlic clove
15ml/1 tbsp olive oil
450ml/¾ pint/scant 2 cups chicken stock
15ml/2 tbsp tomato purée (paste)
50g/2oz/½ cup small pasta shapes
salt and ground black pepper
fresh coriander (cilantro) or parsley,
* to garnish*

1 Place the tomatoes, onion, celery and garlic in a pan with the oil. Cover and cook over a low heat for 40–45 minutes, shaking the pan occasionally, until very soft.

2 Spoon the vegetables into a food processor or blender and process until smooth. Press though a sieve, then return to the pan.

3 Stir in the stock and tomato purée and bring to the boil. Add the pasta and simmer for about 8 minutes, or until the pasta is tender. Add salt and pepper, to taste, then sprinkle with coriander or parsley and serve hot.

NUTRITION NOTES

Per portion:	
Energy	112kcals/474kJ
Fat	3.61g
Saturated fat	0.49g
Cholesterol	0mg
Fibre	2.68g

MUSHROOM, CELERY AND GARLIC SOUP

INGREDIENTS

Serves 4
350g/12oz/4½ cups chopped mushrooms
4 celery sticks, chopped
3 garlic cloves
45ml/3 tbsp dry sherry or white wine
750ml/1¼ pints/3 cups chicken stock
30ml/2 tbsp Worcestershire sauce
5ml/1 tsp freshly grated nutmeg
salt and ground black pepper
celery leaves, to garnish

NUTRITION NOTES

Per portion:	
Energy	48kcals/200kJ
Fat	1.09g
Saturated fat	0.11g
Cholesterol	0mg
Fibre	1.64g

1 Place the mushrooms, celery and garlic in a pan and stir in the sherry or wine. Cover and cook over a low heat for 30–40 minutes, until tender.

2 Add half the stock and purée in a food processor or blender until smooth. Return to the pan and add the remaining stock, the Worcestershire sauce and nutmeg.

3 Bring to the boil, season and serve hot, garnished with celery leaves.

ITALIAN VEGETABLE SOUP

The success of this clear soup depends on the quality of the stock, so for the best results, be sure you use home-made vegetable stock rather than stock cubes.

INGREDIENTS

Serves 4

1 small carrot
1 baby leek
1 celery stick
50g/2oz green cabbage
900ml/1½ pints/3¾ cups vegetable stock
1 bay leaf
115g/4oz/1 cup cooked cannellini or
  haricot beans
25g/1oz/⅕ cup soup pasta, such as tiny
  shells, bows, stars or elbows
salt and black pepper
chopped fresh chives, to garnish

1 Cut the carrot, leek and celery into 5cm/2in long julienne strips. Slice the cabbage very finely.

NUTRITION NOTES	
Per portion:	
Energy	69Kcals/288kJ
Protein	3.67g
Fat	0.71g
Saturated fat	0.05g
Fibre	2.82g

2 Put the stock and bay leaf into a large pan and bring to the boil. Add the carrot, leek and celery, cover and simmer for 6 minutes.

3 Add the cabbage, beans and pasta shapes. Stir, then simmer uncovered for a further 4–5 minutes, or until the vegetables and pasta are tender.

4 Remove the bay leaf and season with salt and pepper to taste. Ladle into four soup bowls and garnish with chopped chives. Serve immediately.

CHICKEN AND PASTA SOUP

INGREDIENTS

Serves 4–6

900ml/1½ pints/3¾ cups chicken stock
1 bay leaf
4 spring onions (scallions), sliced
225g/8oz button (white) mushrooms, sliced
115g/4oz cooked chicken breast
50g/2oz soup pasta
150ml/¼ pint/⅔ cup dry white wine
15ml/1 tbsp chopped fresh parsley
salt and black pepper

NUTRITION NOTES

Per portion:	
Energy	126Kcals/529kJ
Fat	2.2g
Saturated fat	0.6g
Cholesterol	19mg
Fibre	1.3g

1 Put the stock and bay leaf into a pan and bring to the boil.

2 Add the sliced spring onions and mushrooms to the stock.

3 Remove the skin from the chicken and slice the meat thinly using a sharp knife. Add to the soup and season to taste. Heat through for about 2–3 minutes.

4 Add the pasta, cover and simmer for 7–8 minutes. Just before serving, add the wine and chopped parsley, heat through for 2–3 minutes, then season to taste.

BEETROOT SOUP WITH RAVIOLI

INGREDIENTS

Serves 4–6

1 quantity basic pasta dough
egg white, beaten, for brushing
flour, for dusting
1 small onion or shallot, finely chopped
2 garlic cloves, crushed
5ml/1 tsp fennel seeds
600ml/1 pint/2½ cups chicken stock
225g/8oz cooked beetroot (beets)
30ml/2 tbsp fresh orange juice
fennel or dill leaves, to garnish
crusty bread, to serve

For the filling

115g/4oz mushrooms, finely chopped
1 shallot or small onion,
    finely chopped
1–2 garlic cloves, crushed
5ml/1 tsp chopped fresh thyme
15ml/1 tbsp chopped fresh parsley
90ml/6 tbsp fresh white breadcrumbs
salt and black pepper
large pinch of ground nutmeg

1 Process all the filling ingredients and scoop into a bowl.

2 Roll the pasta dough into thin sheets. Lay one piece over a ravioli tray and put a teaspoonful of the filling into each depression. Brush around the edges of each ravioli with egg white. Cover with another sheet of pasta, press the edges well together to seal and separate the individual shapes. Transfer to a floured dish towel and rest for 1 hour before cooking.

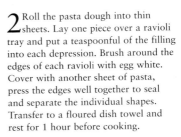

3 Cook the ravioli in a large pan of boiling, salted water for 2 minutes, in batches to stop them sticking together. Remove and drop into a bowl of cold water for 5 seconds before placing on a tray. (You can make these pasta shapes a day in advance. Cover with clear film and store in the refrigerator.)

4 Put the onion, garlic and fennel seeds into a pan with 150ml/ ¼ pint/⅔ cup of the stock. Bring to the boil, cover and simmer for 5 minutes until tender. Peel and finely dice the beetroot (reserve 60ml/4 tbsp for the garnish). Add the rest of the beetroot to the soup with the remaining stock and bring to the boil.

5 Add the orange juice and cooked ravioli and simmer for 2 minutes. Pour into shallow soup bowls and garnish with the reserved diced beetroot and fennel or dill leaves. Serve hot, with some crusty bread.

SPICY TOMATO AND LENTIL SOUP

INGREDIENTS

Serves 4

15ml/1 tbsp sunflower oil
1 onion, finely chopped
1–2 garlic cloves, crushed
2.5cm/1in piece fresh root ginger,
  peeled and finely chopped
5ml/1 tsp cumin seeds, crushed
450g/1lb ripe tomatoes, peeled, seeded
  and chopped
115g/4oz/½ cup red split lentils
1.2 litres/2 pints/5 cups vegetable or
  chicken stock
15ml/1 tbsp tomato purée (paste)
salt and black pepper
low fat natural (plain) yogurt and
  chopped fresh parsley, to garnish

1 Heat the sunflower oil in a large heavy pan and cook the chopped onion gently for 5 minutes until it is softened.

2 Stir in the garlic, ginger and cumin, followed by the tomatoes and lentils. Cook over a low heat for a further 3–4 minutes.

3 Stir in the stock and tomato purée. Bring to the boil, then lower the heat and simmer gently for about 30 minutes until the lentils are soft. Season to taste with salt and pepper.

4 Purée the soup in a blender or food processor. Return to the clean pan and reheat gently. Serve in heated bowls. If you like, garnish each portion with a swirl of yogurt and a little chopped parsley.

NUTRITION NOTES

Per portion:

Energy	165Kcals/695kJ
Fat	4g
Saturated fat	0.5g
Cholesterol	0mg

CREAMY COD CHOWDER

A delicious light version of a classic, this chowder is a tasty combination of smoked fish, vegetables, fresh herbs and milk. To cut the calories and stock even more, use vegetable or fish stock in place of the milk. Serve as a substantial appetizer or snack, or as a light main meal accompanied by warm crusty bread.

INGREDIENTS

Serves 4–6
350g/12oz smoked cod fillet
1 small onion, finely chopped
1 bay leaf
4 black peppercorns
900ml/1½ pints/3¾ cups skimmed milk
10ml/2 tsp cornflour (cornstarch)
200g/7oz canned corn kernels
15ml/1 tbsp chopped fresh parsley

1 Skin the fish and put it into a large pan with the onion, bay leaf and peppercorns. Pour over the milk.

2 Bring to the boil, then reduce the heat and simmer very gently for 12–15 minutes, or until the fish is just cooked. Do not overcook.

3 Using a slotted spoon, lift out the fish and flake into large chunks. Remove the bay leaf and peppercorns and discard.

4 Blend the cornflour with 10ml/2 tsp cold water and add to the pan. Bring to the boil and simmer for about 1 minute or until slightly thickened.

5 Drain the corn kernels and add them to the pan together with the flaked fish and parsley. Reheat gently and serve.

COOK'S TIP
The flavour of the chowder improves if it is made a day in advance. Leave to cool, then chill in the refrigerator until required. Reheat gently. Do not allow the soup to boil, or the fish will disintegrate.

NUTRITION NOTES

Per portion:
Energy	200Kcals/840kJ
Protein	24.71g
Fat	1.23g
Saturated fat	0.32g

TOMATO AND CORIANDER SOUP

This delicious soup is an ideal solution when time is short but you still want to produce a very stylish appetizer.

INGREDIENTS

Serves 4
675g/1½lb small tomatoes
30ml/2 tbsp vegetable oil
1 bay leaf
4 spring onions (scallions), cut into
   2.5cm/1in pieces
5ml/1 tsp salt
5ml/1 tsp garlic pulp
5ml/1 tsp crushed black peppercorns
30ml/2 tbsp chopped fresh
   coriander (cilantro)
750ml/1¼ pints/3 cups water
15ml/1 tbsp cornflour (cornstarch)
60ml/4 tbsp single (light) cream,
   to garnish

1 To skin the tomatoes, plunge them into very hot water for 30 seconds, then transfer to a bowl of cold water. The skin should now peel off quickly and easily. Chop the tomatoes into large chunks.

2 Heat the oil in a large pan, add the bay leaf and spring onions, then stir in the tomatoes. Cook, stirring, for a few minutes more until the tomatoes are softened.

3 Add the salt, garlic, peppercorns, coriander and water, bring to the boil, then simmer for 15 minutes.

4 Mix the cornflour to a paste with a little water. Remove the soup from the heat and press through a sieve (strainer).

5 Return the soup to the pan, add the cornflour mixture and stir over a gentle heat until boiling and thickened.

6 Ladle the soup into shallow soup plates, then swirl a tablespoon of cream into each bowl before serving.

NUTRITION NOTES	
Per portion:	
Energy	113kcals/474kJ
Fat	7.16g
Saturated fat	1.37g
Cholesterol	2.8mg

THAI-STYLE CORN SOUP

This is a very quick and easy soup, made in minutes. If you are using frozen prawns, then defrost them first before adding to the soup.

INGREDIENTS

Serves 4

2.5ml/½ tsp sesame or sunflower oil
2 spring onions (scallions), thinly sliced
1 garlic clove, crushed
600ml/1 pint/2½ cups chicken stock
425g/15oz can creamed corn
225g/8oz/1¼ cups cooked, peeled
  prawns (shrimp)
5ml/1 tsp green chilli paste or chilli
  sauce (optional)
salt and ground black pepper
fresh coriander (cilantro) leaves, to garnish

1 Heat the oil in a large, heavy pan and sauté the spring onions and garlic over a medium heat for 1 minute, until softened, but not browned.

2 Stir in the chicken stock, creamed corn, prawns and chilli paste or sauce, if using.

3 Bring the soup to the boil, stirring occasionally. Season to taste, then serve immediately, sprinkled with fresh coriander leaves to garnish.

COOK'S TIP
If creamed corn is not available, use ordinary canned corn, puréed in a food processor for a few seconds, until creamy yet with some texture left.

NUTRITION NOTES	
Per portion:	
Energy	202kcals/848kJ
Fat	3.01g
Saturated fat	0.43g
Cholesterol	45.56mg
Fibre	1.6g

SPINACH AND TOFU SOUP

This appetizing clear soup has an extremely delicate and mild flavour that can be used as a perfect counterbalance to the intense heat of a hot Thai curry.

INGREDIENTS

Serves 6

30ml/2 tbsp dried shrimps
1 litre/1¾ pints/4 cups chicken stock
225g/8oz fresh tofu, drained and cut
    into 2cm/¾in cubes
30ml/2 tbsp fish sauce
350g/12oz fresh spinach, washed
black pepper
2 spring onions (scallions), finely sliced,
    to garnish

1 Rinse and drain the dried shrimps. Combine the shrimps with the chicken stock in a large pan and bring to the boil.

2 Add the tofu and simmer for about 5 minutes. Season with fish sauce and black pepper to taste.

3 Tear the spinach leaves into bitesize pieces and add to the soup. Cook for another 1–2 minutes.

4 Remove from the heat and sprinkle with the finely sliced spring onions, to garnish.

NUTRITION NOTES	
Per portion:	
Energy	64Kcals/270kJ
Fat	225g
Saturated fat	0.26g
Cholesterol	25mg
Fibre	1.28g

COOK'S TIP
Home-made chicken stock makes the world of difference to clear soups. Accumulate enough bones to make a big batch of stock, use what you need and keep the rest in the freezer.

Put 1.5kg/3–3½lb meaty chicken bones and 450g/1lb pork bones (optional) into a large pan. Add 3 litres/5 pints/12 cups water and slowly bring to the boil. Occasionally skim off and discard any scum that rises to the surface. Add 2 slices fresh root ginger, 2 garlic cloves (optional), 2 celery sticks, 4 spring onions (scallions), 2 bruised lemon grass stalks, a few sprigs of coriander (cilantro) and 10 crushed black peppercorns. Reduce the heat to low and simmer for about 2–2½ hours.

Remove the pan from the heat and leave to cool, uncovered and undisturbed. Pour through a fine strainer, leaving the last dregs behind as they tend to cloud the soup. Leave to cool, then chill. Use as required, removing any fat that congeals on the surface.

VEGETABLE MINESTRONE

INGREDIENTS

Serves 6–8

large pinch of saffron threads
1 onion, chopped
1 leek, sliced
1 celery stick, sliced
2 carrots, diced
2–3 garlic cloves, crushed
600ml/1 pint/2½ cups chicken stock
2 x 400g/14oz cans chopped tomatoes
50g/2oz/½ cup frozen peas
50g/2oz soup pasta (anellini)
5ml/1 tsp caster (superfine) sugar
15ml/1 tbsp chopped fresh parsley
15ml/1 tbsp chopped fresh basil
salt and black pepper

1 Soak the pinch of saffron threads in 15ml/1 tbsp boiling water. Leave to stand for 10 minutes.

2 Meanwhile, put the prepared onion, leek, celery, carrots and garlic into a large pan. Add the chicken stock, bring to the boil, cover and simmer for about 10 minutes.

3 Add the canned tomatoes, the saffron with its liquid and the frozen peas. Bring back to the boil and add the soup pasta. Simmer for 10 minutes until tender.

COOK'S TIP
Saffron threads aren't essential for this soup, but they give a wonderful delicate flavour, with the bonus of a lovely rich orange-yellow colour.

4 Season with sugar, salt and pepper to taste. Stir in the chopped herbs just before serving.

NUTRITION NOTES

Per portion:	
Energy	87Kcals/367kJ
Fat	0.7g
Saturated fat	0.1g
Cholesterol	0mg
Fibre	3.3g

CORN CHOWDER WITH PASTA SHELLS

Smoked turkey rashers provide a tasty, low fat alternative to bacon in this hearty dish. If you prefer, omit the meat altogether and serve the soup as is.

INGREDIENTS

Serves 4

1 small green (bell) pepper
450g/1lb potatoes, peeled and diced
350g/12oz/2 cups canned or frozen corn
1 onion, chopped
1 celery stick, chopped
bouquet garni (bay leaf, parsley stalks and thyme)
600ml/1 pint/2½ cups chicken stock
300ml/½ pint/1¼ cups skimmed milk
50g/2oz small pasta shells
oil, for frying
150g/5oz smoked turkey rashers (strips), diced
salt and black pepper
bread sticks, to serve

NUTRITION NOTES

Per portion:

Energy	215Kcals/904kJ
Fat	1.6g
Saturated fat	0.3g
Cholesterol	13mg
Fibre	2.8g

1 Halve the green pepper, then remove the stalk and seeds. Cut the flesh into small dice, cover with boiling water and stand for 2 minutes. Drain and rinse.

2 Put the potatoes into a pan with the corn, onion, celery, green pepper, bouquet garni and stock. Bring to the boil, cover and simmer for 20 minutes until tender.

3 Add the milk and season with salt and pepper. Process half of the soup in a food processor or blender and return to the pan with the pasta shells. Simmer for 10 minutes.

4 Fry the turkey rashers in a non-stick frying pan for 2–3 minutes. Stir into the soup. Season to taste and serve with bread sticks.

RED PEPPER SOUP WITH LIME

The beautiful rich red colour of this soup makes it a very attractive first course or light lunch. For a special dinner, toast some tiny croûtons and serve sprinkled into the soup.

INGREDIENTS

Serves 4–6
1 large onion, chopped
4 red (bell) peppers, seeded and chopped
5ml/1 tsp olive oil
1 garlic clove, crushed
1 small red chilli, sliced
45ml/3 tbsp tomato purée (paste)
900ml/1½ pints/3¾ cups chicken stock
finely grated rind and juice of 1 lime
salt and ground black pepper
shreds of lime rind, to garnish

1 Cook the onion and peppers gently in the oil in a covered pan for about 5 minutes, shaking the pan occasionally, until softened.

2 Stir in the garlic, then add the chilli with the tomato purée. Stir in half the stock, then bring to the boil. Cover the pan and simmer for 10 minutes.

3 Cool slightly, then purée in a food processor or blender. Return to the pan, then add the remaining stock, the lime rind and juice, and seasoning.

4 Bring the soup back to the boil, then serve immediately with a few strips of lime rind, sprinkled into each bowl.

NUTRITION NOTES

Per portion:
Energy	87kcals/366kJ
Fat	1.57g
Saturated fat	0.12g
Cholesterol	0mg
Fibre	3.40g

CHICKEN AND COCONUT SOUP

This aromatic soup is rich with coconut milk and intensely flavoured with galangal, lemon grass and kaffir lime leaves.

1 Bring the coconut milk and chicken stock to the boil. Add the lemon grass, galangal, peppercorns and half the kaffir lime leaves. Reduce the heat and simmer gently for 10 minutes.

INGREDIENTS

Serves 4–6
750ml/1¼ pints/3 cups coconut milk
475ml/16fl oz/2 cups chicken stock
4 lemon grass stalks, bruised and chopped
2.5cm/1in section galangal, thinly sliced
10 black peppercorns, crushed
10 kaffir lime leaves, torn
300g/11oz boneless chicken, cut into thin strips
115g/4oz button (white) mushrooms
50g/2oz baby corn
60ml/4 tbsp lime juice
about 45ml/3 tbsp fish sauce
2 fresh chillies, seeded and chopped, chopped spring onions (scallions), and coriander (cilantro), to garnish

2 Strain the stock into a clean pan. Return to the heat, then add the chicken, button mushrooms and baby corn. Simmer for 5–7 minutes or until the chicken is cooked.

3 Stir in the lime juice, fish sauce to taste and the rest of the lime leaves. Serve hot, garnished with chillies, spring onions and coriander.

NUTRITION NOTES	
Per portion:	
Energy	144Kcals/609kJ
Fat	2.5g
Saturated fat	0.55g
Cholesterol	67.5mg
Fibre	0.6g

HOT AND SOUR PRAWN SOUP

This is a classic Thai shellfish soup and is probably the most popular and well known soup from Thailand.

1 Shell and devein the prawns and set aside. Rinse the prawn shells, place them in a large pan with the stock and bring to the boil.

NUTRITION NOTES	
Per portion:	
Energy	49Kcals/209kJ
Fat	0.45g
Saturated fat	0.07g
Cholesterol	78.8mg
Fibre	0.09g

INGREDIENTS

Serves 4–6
450g/1lb king prawns (jumbo shrimp)
1 litre/1¾ pints/4 cups chicken stock
3 lemon grass stalks
10 kaffir lime leaves, torn in half
225g/8oz can straw mushrooms, drained
45ml/3 tbsp fish sauce
50ml/2fl oz/¼ cup lime juice
30ml/2 tbsp chopped spring onions (scallions)
15ml/1 tbsp coriander (cilantro) leaves
4 fresh chillies, seeded and chopped
salt and black pepper

2 Bruise the lemon grass stalks with the blunt edge of a chopping knife and add them to the stock together with half the lime leaves. Simmer gently for 5–6 minutes, until the stalks change colour and the stock is fragrant.

3 Strain the stock, return to the pan and reheat. Add the mushrooms and prawns, then cook until the prawns turn pink. Stir in the fish sauce, lime juice, spring onions, coriander, chillies and the rest of the lime leaves. Taste the soup and adjust the seasoning – it should be sour, salty, spicy and hot.

RED ONION AND BEETROOT SOUP

This beautiful vivid ruby-red soup will look stunning at any dinner party.

INGREDIENTS

Serves 6

10ml/2 tsp olive oil
350g/12oz red onions, sliced
2 garlic cloves, crushed
275g/10oz cooked beetroot (beets),
*   cut into sticks*
1.2 litres/2 pints/5 cups vegetable stock
*   or water*
50g/2oz/1 cup cooked soup pasta
30ml/2 tbsp raspberry vinegar
salt and black pepper
low fat yogurt and chopped chives,
*   to garnish*

COOK'S TIP
If you prefer, try substituting cooked barley for the pasta to give extra nuttiness.

1 Heat the olive oil and add the onions and garlic.

2 Cook gently for about 20 minutes or until soft and tender.

3 Add the beetroot, stock or water, cooked pasta shapes and vinegar and heat through.

4 Adjust the seasoning to taste. Ladle the soup into bowls. Top each one with a spoonful of yogurt and sprinkle with chopped chives. Serve piping hot.

NUTRITION NOTES	
Per portion:	
Energy	76Kcals/318kJ
Fat	2.01g
Saturated fat	0.28g
Cholesterol	0.33mg
Fibre	1.83g

CAULIFLOWER AND BEAN SOUP

The sweet, liquorice flavour of the fennel seeds gives a delicious edge to this hearty soup.

INGREDIENTS

Serves 6

10ml/2 tsp olive oil
1 garlic clove, crushed
1 onion, chopped
10ml/2 tsp fennel seeds
1 cauliflower, cut into small florets
2 x 400g/14oz cans flageolet beans, drained and rinsed
1.2 litres/2 pints/5 cups vegetable stock or water
salt and black pepper
chopped fresh parsley, to garnish
toasted slices of French bread, to serve

1 Heat the olive oil. Add the garlic, onion and fennel seeds and cook gently for 5 minutes or until the onion is softened.

2 Add the cauliflower, half of the beans and all the stock or water.

3 Bring to the boil. Reduce the heat and simmer for 10 minutes or until the cauliflower is tender.

NUTRITION NOTES	
Per portion:	
Energy	194.3Kcals/822.5kJ
Fat	3.41g
Saturated fat	0.53g
Cholesterol	0mg
Fibre	7.85g

4 Pour the soup into a blender and blend until smooth. Stir in the remaining beans and season to taste. Reheat and pour into bowls. Sprinkle with chopped parsley and serve with toasted slices of French bread.

MELON AND BASIL SOUP

A deliciously refreshing, chilled fruit soup, just right for a hot summer's day. It takes next to no time to prepare, leaving you free to enjoy the sunshine and, even better, it is almost totally fat-free.

INGREDIENTS

Serves 4–6

2 Charentais or rock melons
75g/3oz/6 tbsp caster (superfine) sugar
175ml/6fl oz/³/₄ cup water
finely grated rind and juice of 1 lime
45ml/3 tbsp shredded fresh basil
fresh basil leaves, to garnish

1 Cut the melons in half across the middle. Scrape out the seeds and discard. Using a melon baller, scoop out 20–24 balls and set aside for the garnish. Scoop out the remaining flesh and place in a blender or food processor. Set aside.

2 Place the sugar, water and lime zest in a small pan over a low heat. Stir until dissolved, bring to the boil and simmer for 2–3 minutes. Remove from the heat and leave to cool slightly. Pour half the mixture into the blender or food processor with the melon flesh. Blend until smooth, adding the remaining syrup and lime juice to taste.

3 Pour the mixture into a bowl, stir in the basil and chill. Serve garnished with basil leaves and melon balls.

NUTRITION NOTES	
Per portion:	
Energy	69Kcals/293.8kJ
Fat	0.14g
Saturated fat	0g
Cholesterol	0mg
Fibre	0.47g

COOK'S TIP
Add the syrup in two stages, because the amount of sugar needed will depend on the sweetness of the melon.

CHILLED FRESH TOMATO SOUP

This effortless uncooked soup can be made in minutes.

Serves 6
1.5kg/3–3½lb ripe tomatoes, peeled
and roughly chopped
4 garlic cloves, crushed
30ml/2 tbsp balsamic vinegar
4 thick slices wholemeal (whole-
wheat) bread
black pepper
low fat fromage frais, to garnish

1 Place the tomatoes in a blender with the garlic. Blend until smooth. Pass through a sieve (strainer) to remove the seeds. Stir in balsamic vinegar and season to taste with pepper. Put in the refrigerator to chill.

2 Toast the bread lightly on both sides. While still hot, cut off the crusts and slice the toast in half horizontally. Place on a board with the uncooked sides facing down and, using a circular motion, rub to remove any doughy pieces of bread.

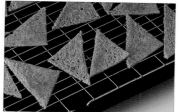

COOK'S TIP
For the best flavour, it is important to use only fully ripened, flavourful tomatoes in this soup.

3 Cut each slice into four triangles. Place on a grill (broiling) pan and toast the uncooked sides until lightly golden. Garnish each bowl of soup with a spoonful of fromage frais and serve with the Melba toast.

NUTRITION NOTES	
Per portion:	
Energy	111Kcals/475kJ
Fat	1.42g
Saturated fat	0.39g
Cholesterol	0.16mg
Fibre	4.16g

SPLIT PEA AND COURGETTE SOUP

Rich and satisfying, this tasty and nutritious soup will warm a chilly winter's day.

INGREDIENTS

Serves 4

175g/6oz/1⅞ cups yellow split peas
1 medium onion, finely chopped
5ml/1 tsp sunflower oil
2 medium courgettes (zucchini),
    finely diced
900ml/1½ pints/3¾ cups chicken stock
2.5ml/½ tsp ground turmeric
salt and ground black pepper

1 Place the split peas in a bowl, cover with cold water and leave to soak for several hours or overnight. Drain, rinse in cold water and drain again.

2 Cook the onion in the oil in a covered pan, shaking occasionally, until soft. Reserve a handful of diced courgettes and add the rest to the pan. Cook, stirring, for 2–3 minutes.

3 Add the split peas, stock and turmeric and bring to the boil. Reduce the heat, cover and simmer for 30–40 minutes, or until the split peas are tender. Adjust the seasoning.

4 When the soup is almost ready, bring a large pan of water to the boil, add the reserved diced courgettes and cook for 1 minute, then drain and add to the soup before serving hot with warm crusty bread.

> COOK'S TIP
> For a quicker alternative, use split red lentils for this soup – they need no presoaking and cook very quickly. Adjust the amount of stock, if necessary.

NUTRITION NOTES

Per portion:

Energy	174kcals/730kJ
Fat	2.14g
Saturated fat	0.54g
Cholesterol	0mg
Fibre	3.43g

CARROT AND CORIANDER SOUP

Nearly all root vegetables make excellent soups as they purée well and have an earthy flavour which complements the sharper flavours of herbs and spices. Carrots are particularly versatile, and this simple soup is elegant in both flavour and appearance.

INGREDIENTS

Serves 6

10ml/2 tsp sunflower oil
1 onion, chopped
1 celery stick, sliced, plus 2–3 leafy
  celery tops
2 small potatoes, chopped
450g/1lb carrots, preferably young and
  tender, chopped
1 litre/1¾ pints/4 cups chicken stock
10–15ml/2–3 tsp ground coriander
15ml/1 tbsp chopped fresh coriander
  (cilantro)
200ml/7fl oz/1 cup semi-skimmed milk
salt and black pepper

1 Heat the oil in a large flameproof casserole or heavy pan and fry the onion over a gentle heat for about 3–4 minutes until slightly softened but not browned. Add the celery and potato, cook for a few minutes, then add the carrot. Fry over a gentle heat for 3–4 minutes, stirring frequently, and then cover. Reduce the heat even further and cook for about 10 minutes. Shake the pan or stir occasionally so the vegetables do not stick to the base.

2 Add the stock, bring to the boil and then partially cover and simmer for a further 8–10 minutes until the carrot and potato are tender.

3 Remove 6–8 tiny celery leaves for a garnish and finely chop about 15ml/1 tbsp of the remaining celery tops. In a small pan, dry fry the ground coriander for about 1 minute, stirring constantly. Reduce the heat, add the chopped celery and fresh coriander and fry for about 1 minute. Set aside.

4 Process the soup in a food processor or blender and pour into a clean pan. Stir in the milk, coriander mixture and seasoning. Heat gently, taste and adjust the seasoning. Serve garnished with the reserved celery.

NUTRITION NOTES

Per portion:

Energy	76.5Kcals/320kJ
Fat	3.2g
Saturated fat	0.65g
Cholesterol	2.3mg
Fibre	2.2g

COOK'S TIP
For a more piquant flavour, add a little freshly squeezed lemon juice just before serving. The contrast between the orange-coloured soup and the green garnish is a feast for the eye as well as the tastebuds.

CAULIFLOWER AND WALNUT CREAM

Even though there's no cream added to this soup, the cauliflower gives it a deliciously rich, creamy texture.

INGREDIENTS

Serves 4
1 medium cauliflower
1 medium onion, roughly chopped
450ml/¾ pint/scant 2 cups chicken or
    vegetable stock
450ml/¾ pint/scant 2 cups skimmed
    milk
45ml/3 tbsp walnut pieces
salt and ground black pepper
paprika and chopped walnuts,
    to garnish

1 Trim the cauliflower of its outer leaves and break into small florets. Place the cauliflower, onion and stock in a large pan.

2 Bring to the boil, cover and simmer for about 15 minutes, or until soft. Add the milk and walnuts, then purée in a food processor until smooth.

3 Season the soup to taste, then bring to the boil. Serve sprinkled with paprika and chopped walnuts.

NUTRITION NOTES

Per portion:
Energy	166kcals/699kJ
Fat	9.02g
Saturated fat	0.88g
Cholesterol	2.25mg
Fibre	2.73g

CURRIED CARROT AND APPLE SOUP

INGREDIENTS

Serves 4
10ml/2 tsp sunflower oil
15ml/1 tbsp mild korma curry powder
500g/1¼lb carrots, chopped
1 large onion, chopped
1 cooking apple, chopped
750ml/1¼ pints/3 cups chicken stock
salt and ground black pepper
low-fat natural (plain) yogurt and
    carrot curls, to garnish

NUTRITION NOTES

Per portion:
Energy	114kcals/477kJ
Fat	3.57g
Saturated fat	0.43g
Cholesterol	0.4mg
Fibre	4.99g

1 Heat the oil and gently fry the curry powder for 2–3 minutes.

2 Add the carrots, onion and apple, stir well, then cover the pan.

3 Cook over a very low heat for about 15 minutes, shaking the pan occasionally until softened. Spoon the vegetable mixture into a food processor or blender, then add half the stock and process until smooth.

4 Return to the pan and pour in the remaining stock. Bring the soup to the boil and adjust the seasoning before serving in bowls, garnished with a swirl of yogurt and a few curls of carrot.

APPETIZERS AND SNACKS

Healthy low fat first courses provide a delicious start to a meal and are quick and easy to make. Appetizers should not be too filling as they are simply setting the scene for the low fat main course to follow. Choose from a tempting selection of recipes, including light and refreshing fruit cocktails such as Minted Melon and Grapefruit and vegetable pâtés or dips such as Guacamole with Crudités. Quick and easy snacks and light dishes are ideal served with thick slices of warm, crusty bread for a low fat, nutritious lunch or supper. We include a selection of tasty snacks, such as Pasta with Herby Scallops, Cheese and Chutney Toasties and Parma Ham and Pepper Pizzas.

MELON, PINEAPPLE AND GRAPE COCKTAIL

A light, refreshing fruit salad, with no added sugar and virtually no fat, perfect for breakfast or brunch – or any time.

INGREDIENTS

Serves 4

½ melon
225g/8oz fresh pineapple or 225g/8oz can pineapple chunks in own juice
225g/8oz seedless white grapes, halved
120ml/4fl oz/½ cup white grape juice
fresh mint leaves, to decorate (optional)

1 Remove the seeds from the melon half and use a melon baller to scoop out even-size balls.

2 Using a sharp knife, cut the skin from the pineapple and discard. Cut the fruit into bite-size chunks.

3 Combine all the fruits in a glass serving dish and pour over the juice. If you are using canned pineapple, measure the drained juice and make it up to the required quantity with the grape juice.

4 If not serving immediately, cover and chill. Serve decorated with mint leaves, if you like.

NUTRITION NOTES	
Per portion:	
Energy	95Kcals/395kJ
Fat	0.5g
Saturated fat	0g
Cholesterol	0mg

GRAPEFRUIT SALAD WITH ORANGE

The bitter-sweet flavour of Campari combines especially well with citrus fruit. Because of its alcohol content, this dish is not suitable for children.

INGREDIENTS

Serves 4
45ml/3 tbsp caster (superfine) sugar
60ml/4 tbsp Campari
30ml/2 tbsp lemon juice
4 grapefruit
5 oranges
4 sprigs fresh mint

NUTRITION NOTES

Per portion:	
Energy	196Kcals/822kJ
Fat	5.9g
Saturated fat	2.21g
Cholesterol	66.37mg
Fibre	1.6g

1 Bring 150ml/5fl oz/²/₃ cup water to the boil in a small pan, add the sugar and simmer until dissolved. Leave to cool, then add the Campari and lemon juice. Chill until ready to serve.

COOK'S TIP
When buying citrus fruit, choose brightly coloured specimens that feel heavy for their size.

2 Cut the peel from the grapefruit and oranges with a serrated knife. Segment the fruit into a bowl by slipping a small paring knife between the flesh and the membranes. Combine the fruit with the Campari syrup and chill.

3 Spoon the salad into four dishes and garnish each dish with a sprig of fresh mint.

AUBERGINE, GARLIC AND PEPPER PATE

Serve this chunky, garlicky pâté of smoky baked aubergine and red peppers on a bed of salad, accompanied by crispbreads.

INGREDIENTS

Serves 4
3 aubergines (eggplants)
2 red (bell) peppers
5 garlic cloves
7.5ml/1½ tsp pink peppercorns in brine, drained and crushed
30ml/2 tbsp chopped fresh coriander (cilantro)

NUTRITION NOTES

Per portion:
Energy	70kcals/292kJ
Fat	1.32g
Saturated fat	0g
Cholesterol	0mg
Fibre	5.96g

1 Preheat the oven to 200°C/400°F/ Gas 6. Arrange the whole aubergines, peppers and garlic cloves on a baking sheet and place in the oven. After 10 minutes remove the garlic cloves, and turn over the aubergines and peppers.

2 Carefully peel the garlic cloves and place in the bowl of a food processor or blender.

3 After a further 20 minutes remove the blistered and charred peppers from the oven and place in a plastic bag. Leave to cool.

4 After a further 10 minutes remove the aubergines from the oven. Split in half and scoop the flesh into a sieve (strainer) over a bowl. Press the flesh with a spoon to remove the bitter juices.

5 Add the aubergine flesh to the garlic in the food processor or blender, and process until smooth. Place in a large mixing bowl.

6 Peel and chop the red peppers and stir into the aubergine mixture. Mix in the peppercorns and fresh coriander, and serve immediately.

CUCUMBER AND ALFALFA TORTILLAS

Served with a crisp, fresh salsa, tortillas also make a marvellous light lunch or supper dish.

INGREDIENTS

Serves 4

225g/8oz/2 cups plain (all-purpose)
flour, sifted
pinch of salt
45ml/3 tbsp olive oil
100–150ml/4–5fl oz/½–⅔ cup
warm water
lime wedges, to garnish

For the salsa
1 red onion, finely chopped
1 red chilli, seeded and finely chopped
30ml/2 tbsp chopped fresh dill or
coriander (cilantro)
½ cucumber, peeled and chopped
175g/6oz/2 cups alfalfa sprouts

For the sauce
1 large ripe avocado, peeled and
stoned (pitted)
juice of 1 lime
15ml/1 tbsp soft goat's cheese
pinch of paprika

1 Mix all the salsa ingredients together in a bowl and set aside.

2 For the sauce, place the avocado, lime juice and goat's cheese in a food processor or blender and process until smooth. Place in a bowl and cover with clear film (plastic wrap). Dust with paprika just before serving.

3 For the tortillas, place the flour and salt in a food processor or blender, add the oil and process. Gradually add the water until a stiff dough has formed. Turn out on to a floured board and knead until smooth.

4 Divide the mixture into eight pieces. Knead each piece for a couple of minutes and form into a ball. Flatten and roll out each ball to a 23cm/9in circle.

NUTRITION NOTES

Per portion:	
Energy	395kcals/1659kJ
Fat	20.17g
Saturated fat	1.69g
Cholesterol	4.38mg
Fibre	4.15g

5 Heat a non-stick or ungreased heavy pan. Cook one tortilla at a time for about 30 seconds on each side. Place the cooked tortillas in a clean dish towel and repeat until you have made eight tortillas.

6 Spread each tortilla with a spoonful of avocado sauce, top with the salsa and roll up. Garnish with lime wedges and serve immediately.

COOK'S TIP

When peeling the avocado be sure to scrape off the bright green flesh from immediately under the skin as this gives the sauce its vivid green colour.

MINTED MELON AND GRAPEFRUIT

Melon is always a popular starter. Here the succulent flavour of the Galia melon is complemented by the refreshing taste of citrus fruit and a simple mustard and vinegar dressing. Fresh mint, used in the cocktail and as a garnish, enhances both its flavour and appearance.

INGREDIENTS

Serves 4
1 small Galia melon, weighing about
   1kg/2¼lb
2 pink grapefruit
1 yellow grapefruit
5ml/1 tsp Dijon mustard
5ml/1 tsp raspberry or sherry vinegar
5ml/1 tsp clear honey
15ml/1 tbsp chopped fresh mint
sprigs of fresh mint,
   to garnish

1 Halve the melon and remove the seeds with a teaspoon. With a melon baller, carefully scoop the flesh into balls.

NUTRITION NOTES

Per portion:	
Energy	97Kcals/409kJ
Protein	2.22g
Fat	0.63g
Saturated fat	0g
Fibre	3.05g

2 With a small sharp knife, peel the grapefruit and remove all the white pith. Remove the segments by cutting between the membranes, holding the fruit over a small bowl to catch any juices.

3 Whisk the mustard, vinegar, honey, chopped mint and grapefruit juices together in a mixing bowl. Add the melon balls together with the grapefruit and mix well. Chill for 30 minutes.

4 Ladle the fruit into four glass dishes and serve garnished with sprigs of fresh mint.

GUACAMOLE WITH CRUDITES

This fresh-tasting spicy dip is made using peas instead of the avocado pears that are traditionally associated with this dish. This version saves on both fat and calories, without compromising on taste.

INGREDIENTS

Serves 4–6
350g/12oz/2¼ cups frozen peas, defrosted
1 garlic clove, crushed
2 spring onions (scallions), chopped
5ml/1 tsp finely grated rind and juice of 1 lime
2.5ml/½ tsp ground cumin
dash of Tabasco sauce
15ml/1 tbsp reduced fat mayonnaise
30ml/2 tbsp chopped fresh coriander (cilantro) or parsley
salt and black pepper
pinch of paprika and lime slices, to garnish

For the crudités
6 baby carrots
2 celery sticks
1 red-skinned eating apple
1 pear
15ml/1 tbsp lemon or lime juice
6 baby corn

1 Put the peas, garlic clove, spring onions, lime rind and juice, cumin, Tabasco sauce, mayonnaise and salt and black pepper into a food processor or a blender for a few minutes and process until smooth.

2 Add the chopped coriander or parsley and process for a few more seconds. Spoon into a serving bowl, cover with clear film (plastic wrap) and chill in the refrigerator for 30 minutes, to let the flavours develop fully.

NUTRITION NOTES

Per portion:
Energy	110Kcals/460kJ
Protein	6.22g
Fat	2.29g
Saturated fat	0.49g
Fibre	6.73g

COOK'S TIP
Serve the guacamole dip with warmed pitta bread.

3 For the crudités, trim and peel the carrots. Halve the celery sticks lengthways and trim into sticks, the same length as the carrots. Quarter, core and thickly slice the apple and pear, then dip into the lemon or lime juice. Arrange with the baby corn on a platter.

4 Sprinkle the paprika over the guacamole and garnish with twisted lime slices.

TZATZIKI

Tzatziki is a Greek cucumber salad dressed with yogurt, mint and garlic. It is typically served with grilled lamb and chicken, but is also good served with crudités.

INGREDIENTS

Serves 4
1 cucumber
5ml/1 tsp salt
45ml/3 tbsp finely chopped fresh mint, plus a few sprigs to garnish
1 garlic clove, crushed
5ml/1 tsp caster sugar
200ml/7fl oz reduced fat Greek (US strained plain) yogurt
cucumber flower, to garnish (optional)

1 Peel the cucumber. Reserve a little of the cucumber to use as a garnish if you wish and cut the rest in half lengthways. Remove the seeds with a teaspoon and discard. Slice the cucumber thinly and combine with salt. Leave for approximately 15–20 minutes. Salt will soften the cucumber and draw out any bitter juices.

2 Combine the mint, garlic, sugar and yogurt in a bowl, reserving a few sprigs of mint as decoration.

3 Rinse the cucumber in a sieve (strainer) under cold water to flush away the salt. Drain and combine with the yogurt. Decorate with cucumber flower and/or mint. Serve cold.

NUTRITION NOTES	
Per portion:	
Energy	41.5Kcals/174.5kJ
Fat	0.51g
Saturated fat	0.25g
Cholesterol	2mg
Fibre	0.2g

CHILLI TOMATO SALSA

This universal dip is great served with absolutely anything and can be made up to 24 hours in advance.

INGREDIENTS

Serves 4
1 shallot, peeled and halved
2 garlic cloves, peeled
handful of fresh basil leaves
500g/1¼ lb ripe tomatoes
10ml/2 tsp olive oil
2 green chillies
salt and black pepper

1 Place the shallot and garlic in a food processor with the fresh basil. Whizz the shallot, garlic and basil until finely chopped.

2 Halve the tomatoes and add to the food processor. Pulse the machine until the mixture is well blended and coarsely chopped.

3 With the motor running, slowly pour in the olive oil. Add salt and pepper to taste.

NUTRITION NOTES

Per portion:
Energy	28Kcals/79kJ
Fat	0.47g
Saturated fat	0.13g
Cholesterol	0mg
Fibre	1.45g

4 Halve the chillies lengthways and remove the seeds. Finely slice the chillies widthways into tiny strips and stir into the tomato salsa. Serve at room temperature.

COOK'S TIP
The salsa is best made in the summer when tomatoes are at their best. In winter, use a drained 400g/14oz can of plum tomatoes.

CHEESE AND SPINACH PUFFS

INGREDIENTS

Serves 6
150g/5oz cooked, chopped spinach
175g/6oz/¾ cup cottage cheese
5ml/1 tsp freshly grated nutmeg
2 egg whites
30ml/2 tbsp freshly grated Parmesan cheese
salt and ground black pepper

1 Preheat the oven to 220°C/425°F/ Gas 7. Oil six ramekin dishes.

2 Mix together the spinach and cottage cheese in a small bowl, then add the nutmeg and seasoning to taste.

3 Whisk the egg whites in a separate bowl until stiff enough to hold soft peaks. Fold them evenly into the spinach mixture using a large metal spoon, then spoon the mixture into the oiled ramekins, dividing it evenly, and smooth the tops.

4 Sprinkle with the Parmesan and place on a baking sheet. Bake for 15–20 minutes, or until well risen and golden brown. Serve immediately.

NUTRITION NOTES	
Per portion:	
Energy	47kcals/195kJ
Fat	1.32g
Saturated fat	0.52g
Cholesterol	2.79mg
Fibre	0.53g

LEMONY STUFFED COURGETTES

INGREDIENTS

Serves 4
4 courgettes (zucchini), about
175g/6oz each
5ml/1 tsp sunflower oil
1 garlic clove, crushed
5ml/1 tsp ground lemon grass
finely grated rind and juice of ½ lemon
115g/4oz/1 cups cooked long
grain rice
175g/6oz cherry tomatoes, halved
30ml/2 tbsp toasted cashew nuts
salt and ground black pepper
sprigs of thyme, to garnish

NUTRITION NOTES	
Per portion:	
Energy	126kcals/530kJ
Fat	5.33g
Saturated fat	0.65g
Cholesterol	0mg
Fibre	2.31g

1 Preheat the oven to 200°C/400°F/ Gas 6. Halve the courgettes length-ways and use a teaspoon to scoop out the centres. Blanch the shells in boiling water for 1 minute, then drain well.

2 Chop the courgette flesh finely and place in a pan with the oil and garlic. Stir over medium heat until softened, but not browned.

3 Stir in the lemon grass, lemon rind and juice, rice, tomatoes and cashew nuts. Season well and spoon into the courgette shells. Place the shells in a baking tin (pan) and cover with foil.

4 Bake for 25–30 minutes or until the courgettes are tender, then serve hot, garnished with thyme sprigs.

TUNA CHILLI TACOS

Tacos are a useful, quick snack – but you will need to use both hands to eat them!

INGREDIENTS

Makes 8
8 taco shells
400g/14oz can red kidney
   beans, drained
120ml/4 fl oz/½ cup low-fat fromage
   frais or ricotta cheese
2.5ml/½ tsp chilli sauce
2 spring onions (scallions), chopped
5ml/1 tsp chopped fresh mint
½ small crisp lettuce, shredded
425g/15oz can tuna fish chunks in
   brine, drained
50g/2oz/¼ cup grated reduced-fat
   Cheddar cheese
8 cherry tomatoes, quartered
mint sprigs, to garnish

1 Warm the taco shells in a hot oven for a few minutes until crisp.

2 Mash the beans lightly with a fork, then stir in the fromage frais with the chilli sauce, spring onions and mint.

3 Fill the taco shells with the shredded lettuce, bean mixture and tuna. Top the filled shells with the cheese, and serve immediately with the tomatoes, garnished with sprigs of mint.

NUTRITION NOTES

Per portion:
Energy	147kcals/615kJ
Fat	2.42g
Saturated fat	1.13g
Cholesterol	29.69mg
Fibre	2.41g

POTATO SKINS WITH CAJUN DIP

No need to deep-fry potato skins for this treat – grilling crisps them up in no time.

INGREDIENTS

Serves 2
2 large baking potatoes
120ml/4fl oz/½ cup low-fat natural
   (plain) yogurt
1 garlic clove, crushed
5ml/1 tsp tomato purée (paste)
2.5ml/½ tsp green chilli purée (or
   ½ small green chilli, chopped)
1.5ml/¼ tsp celery salt
salt and ground black pepper

1 Bake or microwave the potatoes until tender. Cut them in half and scoop out the flesh, leaving a thin layer on the skins. Keep the scooped out potato for another meal.

2 Cut each potato in half again then place the pieces skin side down on a large baking sheet.

3 Grill (broil) for 4–5 minutes, or until crisp. Mix together the remaining ingredients and serve with the potato skins.

NUTRITION NOTES

Per portion:
Energy	202kcals/847kJ
Fat	0.93g
Saturated fat	0.34g
Cholesterol	2.3mg
Fibre	3.03g

MELON WITH WILD STRAWBERRIES

This fragrant, colourful appetizer is the perfect way to begin a rich meal as both melons and strawberries are virtually fat-free. Here several varieties are combined with strongly flavoured wild or woodland strawberries. If wild strawberries are not available, use ordinary strawberries or raspberries.

INGREDIENTS

Serves 4
1 cantaloupe or Charentais melon
1 Galia melon
900g/2lb watermelon
175g/6oz wild strawberries
4 sprigs fresh mint, to garnish

NUTRITION NOTES

Per portion:
Energy	42.5Kcals/178.6kJ
Fat	0.32g
Saturated fat	0g
Cholesterol	0mg
Fibre	1.09g

1 Using a large sharp knife, cut all three melons in half.

2 Scoop out the seeds from both the cantaloupe or Charentais and Galia melons with a spoon.

3 With a melon scoop, take out as many balls as you can from all three melons. Combine in a large bowl and chill for at least 1 hour.

4 Add the wild strawberries and mix together gently. Spoon out into four stemmed glass dishes.

5 Garnish each of the melon salads with a small sprig of mint and serve at once.

COOK'S TIP
Ripe melons should give slightly when pressed at the base, and should give off a sweet scent. Buy carefully if you plan to use the fruit on the day. If one or more varieties of melon aren't available, then substitute another, or buy two or three of the same variety – the salad might not be quite so colourful, but it will taste equally refreshing.

MUSSELS WITH THAI HERBS

Another simple dish to prepare. The lemon grass adds a refreshing tang to the mussels.

Serves 6

1kg/2¼ lb mussels, cleaned and
  beards removed
2 lemon grass stalks, finely chopped
4 shallots, chopped
4 kaffir lime leaves, roughly torn
2 red chillies, sliced
15ml/1 tbsp fish sauce
30ml/2 tbsp lime juice
2 spring onions (scallions), chopped, and
  coriander (cilantro) leaves, to garnish

1 Put all the ingredients, except the spring onions and coriander, in a large pan and stir thoroughly.

2 Cover and cook for 5–7 minutes, shaking the pan occasionally, until the mussels open. Discard any mussels that do not open.

3 Transfer the cooked mussels to a serving platter.

4 Garnish the mussels with chopped spring onions and coriander leaves. Serve immediately.

NUTRITION NOTES	
Per portion:	
Energy	56Kcals/238kJ
Fat	1.22g
Saturated fat	0.16g
Cholesterol	0.32g
Fibre	27g

PASTA WITH HERBY SCALLOPS

Low fat fromage frais, flavoured with mustard, garlic and herbs, makes a deceptively creamy sauce for pasta.

INGREDIENTS

Serves 4
120ml/4fl oz/½ cup low fat
fromage frais
10ml/2 tsp wholegrain mustard
2 garlic cloves, crushed
30–45ml/2–3 tbsp fresh lime juice
60ml/4 tbsp chopped fresh parsley
30ml/2 tbsp chopped chives
350g/12oz black tagliatelle
12 large scallops
60ml/4 tbsp white wine
150ml/¼ pint/⅔ cup fish stock
salt and black pepper
lime wedges and parsley sprigs,
to garnish

1 To make the sauce, mix the fromage frais, mustard, garlic, lime juice, parsley, chives and seasoning together in a mixing bowl.

2 Cook the pasta in a large pan of boiling salted water until *al dente*. Drain thoroughly.

3 Slice the scallops in half horizontally. Keep any coral whole. Put the wine and fish stock into a pan and heat to simmering point. Add the scallops and cook very gently for 3–4 minutes. (Don't cook for any longer, or they will toughen.)

COOK'S TIP
Black tagliatelle, made with squid ink, is available from Italian delicatessens, but other colours can be used to make this dish – try a mixture of white and green.

4 Remove the scallops. Boil the wine and stock to reduce by half and add the green sauce to the pan. Heat gently to warm, then return the scallops to the pan and cook for 1 minute. Spoon over the pasta and garnish with lime wedges and parsley.

NUTRITION NOTES
Per portion:
Energy	368Kcals/1561kJ
Fat	4.01g
Saturated fat	0.98g
Cholesterol	99mg
Fibre	1.91g

FRESH FIG, APPLE AND DATE SALAD

Sweet Mediterranean figs and dates combine especially well with crisp eating apples. A hint of almond serves to unite the flavours, but if you'd prefer to reduce the fat even more, omit the marzipan and add another 30ml/2 tbsp low fat natural yogurt or use low fat fromage frais instead.

INGREDIENTS

Serves 4
6 large eating apples
juice of ½ lemon
175g/6oz fresh dates
25g/1oz white marzipan
5ml/1 tsp orange flower water
60ml/4 tbsp low fat natural (plain) yogurt
4 green or purple figs
4 almonds, toasted

1 Core the apples. Slice thinly, then cut into fine matchsticks. Moisten with lemon juice to keep them white.

NUTRITION NOTES	
Per portion:	
Energy	255Kcals/876.5kJ
Fat	4.98g
Saturated fat	1.05g
Cholesterol	2.25mg
Fibre	1.69g

2 Remove the pits from the dates and cut the flesh into fine strips, then combine with the apple slices.

3 Soften the marzipan with orange flower water and combine with the yogurt. Mix well.

COOK'S TIP
For a slightly stronger almond flavour, add a few drops of almond essence to the yogurt mixture. When buying fresh figs, choose firm, unblemished fruit which give slightly when lightly squeezed. Avoid damaged, bruised or very soft fruit.

4 Pile the apples and dates in the centre of four plates. Remove the stem from each of the figs and divide the fruit into quarters without cutting right through the base. Squeeze the base with the thumb and forefinger of each hand to open up the fruit.

5 Place a fig in the centre of each salad. Spoon the yogurt filling on to the figs and decorate each one with a toasted almond.

CHEESE AND CHUTNEY TOASTIES

Quick cheese on toast can be made quite memorable with a few tasty additions. Serve these scrumptious toasties with a simple lettuce and cherry tomato salad.

INGREDIENTS

Serves 4
4 slices wholemeal (whole-wheat)
*   bread, thickly sliced*
85g/3¹/₂oz Cheddar cheese, grated
5ml/1 tsp dried thyme
30ml/2 tbsp chutney or relish
black pepper
salad, to serve

1 Toast the bread slices lightly on each side.

2 Mix the cheese and thyme together and season to taste with pepper.

NUTRITION NOTES

Per portion:
Energy	157.25Kcals/664.25kJ
Fat	4.24g
Saturated fat	1.99g
Cholesterol	9.25mg
Fibre	2.41g

3 Spread the chutney or relish on the toast and divide the cheese evenly between the four slices.

4 Return the toast to the grill (broiler) and cook until the cheese is browned and bubbling. Cut each slice into halves, diagonally, and serve at once with salad.

COOK'S TIP
If you prefer, use a reduced fat hard cheese, such as mature Cheddar or Red Leicester, in place of the full fat Cheddar to cut both calories and fat.

PARMA HAM AND PEPPER PIZZAS

The delicious flavours of these easy pizzas are hard to beat.

INGREDIENTS

Makes 4

½ loaf ciabatta bread
1 red and 1 yellow (bell) pepper, roasted and peeled
4 slices Parma ham, cut into thick strips
50g/2oz reduced fat mozzarella cheese
black pepper
tiny basil leaves, to garnish

NUTRITION NOTES

Per portion:	
Energy	93Kcals/395kJ
Fat	3.25g
Saturated fat	1.49g
Cholesterol	14mg
Fibre	1g

1 Cut the bread into four thick slices and toast until golden.

2 Cut the roasted peppers into thick strips and arrange on the toasted bread with the strips of Parma ham. Preheat the grill (broiler).

3 Thinly slice the mozzarella and arrange on top, then grind over plenty of black pepper. Grill (broil) for 2–3 minutes or until the cheese is bubbling.

4 Scatter the basil leaves on top and serve immediately.

CHICKEN PITTAS WITH RED COLESLAW

Pitta breads are convenient for simple snacks and packed lunches and it's easy to fill them with fresh, healthy ingredients.

INGREDIENTS

Serves 4
¼ red cabbage
1 small red onion, finely sliced
2 radishes, thinly sliced
1 red apple, peeled, cored and grated
15ml/1 tbsp lemon juice
45ml/3 tbsp low-fat fromage frais or
  ricotta cheese
1 cooked skinless chicken breast fillet,
  about 175g/6oz
4 large or 8 small pitta breads
salt and ground black pepper
chopped fresh parsley, to garnish

1 Remove the tough central spine from the cabbage leaves, then finely shred the leaves using a large sharp knife. Place the shredded cabbage in a bowl and stir in the onion, radishes, apple and lemon juice.

2 Stir the fromage frais or ricotta cheese into the shredded cabbage mixture and season to taste. Thinly slice the cooked chicken breast and stir into the mixture until well coated in fromage frais or ricotta cheese.

3 Warm the pitta breads under a hot grill (broiler), then split them along one edge using a round-bladed knife. Spoon the filling into the pitta breads, then garnish with chopped fresh parsley.

> **COOK'S TIP**
> If the filled pitta breads need to be made more than an hour in advance, line them with crisp lettuce leaves before adding the filling.

NUTRITION NOTES

Per portion:
Energy	232kcals/976kJ
Fat	2.61g
Saturated fat	0.76g
Cholesterol	24.61mg
Fibre	2.97g

SMOKED TROUT SALAD

Salads are the easy answer to fast, healthy meals. When lettuce is sweet and crisp, partner it with fillets of smoked trout, warm new potatoes and a creamy horseradish dressing.

INGREDIENTS

Serves 4

675g/1½lb new potatoes
4 smoked trout fillets
115g/4oz mixed lettuce leaves
4 slices dark rye bread, cut into fingers
salt and ground black pepper

For the dressing

60ml/4 tbsp creamed horseradish
60ml/4 tbsp groundnut (peanut) oil
15ml/1 tbsp white wine vinegar
10ml/2 tsp caraway seeds

NUTRITION NOTES

Per portion:

Energy	487kcals/2044kJ
Fat	22.22g
Saturated fat	4.1g
Cholesterol	52.1mg
Fibre	3.5g

1 Peel or scrub the potatoes. Place them in a large pan and cover with cold water. Bring to the boil and simmer for about 20 minutes.

2 Remove the skin from the trout, then pull out any little bones using your fingers or a pair of tweezers.

3 To make the dressing, place all the ingredients in a screw-top jar and shake vigorously. Season the lettuce leaves and moisten them with the prepared dressing. Divide the dressed leaves among four plates.

4 Flake the trout fillets and halve the potatoes. Sprinkle them along with the rye fingers over the salad leaves and toss to mix. Season to taste and serve.

COOK'S TIP

To save time washing lettuce leaves, buy them ready prepared from your supermarket. It is better to season the leaves rather than the dressing when making a salad.

SALMON PARCELS

Serve these little savoury parcels just as they are for a snack, or with a pool of fresh tomato sauce for a special first course.

INGREDIENTS

Makes 12
90g/3½oz can red or pink salmon
15ml/1 tbsp chopped fresh
   coriander (cilantro)
4 spring onions (scallions), finely chopped
4 sheets filo pastry, thawed if frozen
sunflower oil, for brushing
spring onions (scallions) and salad
   leaves, to serve

COOK'S TIP

When you are using filo pastry, it is important to prevent it drying out; cover any you are not using with a damp dishtowel.

---

1 Preheat the oven to 200°C/400°F/ Gas 6. Lightly oil a baking sheet. Drain the salmon, discarding any skin and bones, then place in a bowl.

2 Flake the salmon with a fork and mix with the fresh coriander and spring onions.

3 Place a single sheet of filo pastry on a work surface and brush lightly with oil. Place another sheet on top. Cut into six squares, about 10cm/4in. Repeat with the remaining pastry, to make 12 squares.

4 Place a spoonful of the salmon mixture on to each square. Brush the edges of the pastry with oil, then draw together, pressing to seal. Place the pastries on a baking sheet and bake for 12–15 minutes, until golden. Serve warm, with spring onions and salad.

NUTRITION NOTES

Per portion:
Energy	25kcals/107kJ
Fat	1.16g
Saturated fat	0.23g
Cholesterol	2.55mg
Fibre	0.05g

TOMATO CHEESE TARTS

These crisp little tartlets are easier to make than they look. Best eaten fresh from the oven.

INGREDIENTS

Serves 4
2 sheets filo pastry, thawed if frozen
1 egg white
115g/4oz/½ cup skimmed milk
   soft cheese
handful fresh basil leaves
3 small tomatoes, sliced
salt and ground black pepper

1 Preheat the oven to 200°C/400°F/ Gas 6. Brush the sheets of filo pastry lightly with egg white and cut into sixteen 10cm/4in squares.

2 Layer the squares in twos, in eight patty tins (muffin pans). Spoon the cheese into the pastry cases. Season with black pepper and top with basil leaves.

3 Arrange tomatoes on the tarts, add seasoning and bake for 10–12 minutes, until golden. Serve warm.

NUTRITION NOTES

Per portion:
Energy	50kcals/210kJ
Fat	0.33g
Saturated fat	0.05g
Cholesterol	0.29mg
Fibre	0.25g

CHINESE GARLIC MUSHROOMS

Tofu is high in protein and very low in fat, so it is a very useful food to keep handy for quick meals and snacks like this one.

INGREDIENTS

Serves 4
8 large open mushrooms
3 spring onions (scallions), sliced, plus extra strips to garnish
1 garlic clove, crushed
30ml/2 tbsp oyster sauce
275g/10oz packet marinated tofu, diced
200g/7oz can corn, drained
10ml/2 tsp sesame oil
salt and ground black pepper

1 Preheat the oven to 200°C/400°F/ Gas 6. Finely chop the mushroom stalks and mix with the spring onions, garlic and oyster sauce.

2 Stir in the diced marinated tofu and corn, season to taste with salt and ground black pepper, then spoon the filling into the mushrooms.

3 Brush the edges of the mushrooms with the sesame oil. Arrange the stuffed mushrooms in a baking dish and bake for 12–15 minutes, until golden, then garnish with spring onions and serve immediately.

COOK'S TIP
If you prefer, omit the oyster sauce and use light soy sauce instead.

NUTRITION NOTES

Per portion:
Energy	137kcals/575kJ
Fat	5.6g
Saturated fat	0.85g
Cholesterol	0mg
Fibre	1.96g

WILD RICE ROSTI WITH CARROT PUREE

Rösti is a traditional dish from Switzerland. This variation has the extra nuttiness of wild rice and a bright simple sauce as a fresh accompaniment.

INGREDIENTS

Serves 6
50g/2oz/½ cup wild rice
900g/2lb large potatoes
45ml/3 tbsp walnut oil
5ml/1 tsp yellow mustard seeds
1 onion, coarsely grated and drained
30ml/2 tbsp fresh thyme leaves
salt and ground black pepper
vegetables, to serve

For the purée
*350g/12oz carrots, peeled and
   roughly chopped*
pared rind and juice of 1 large orange

NUTRITION NOTES

Per portion:	
Energy	246kcals/1035kJ
Fat	8.72g
Saturated fat	0.78g
Cholesterol	0mg
Fibre	3.8g

1 For the purée, place the carrots in a pan, cover with cold water and add two pieces of orange rind. Bring to the boil and cook for about 10 minutes or until tender. Drain well and discard the rind.

2 Purée in a food processor or blender with 60ml/4 tbsp of the orange juice. Return to the pan.

3 Place the wild rice in a clean pan and cover with water. Bring to the boil and cook for about 30–40 minutes, until the rice is just starting to split, but still crunchy. Drain the rice.

4 Scrub the potatoes, place in a large pan and cover with cold water. Bring to the boil and cook for about 10–15 minutes until just tender. Drain well and leave to cool slightly. When the potatoes are cool, peel and coarsely grate them into a large bowl. Add the cooked rice.

5 Heat 30ml/2 tbsp of the walnut oil in a non-stick frying pan and add the mustard seeds. When they start to pop, add the onion and cook gently for about 5 minutes until soft. Add to the bowl of potato and rice, together with the thyme, and mix. Season.

6 Heat the remaining oil and add the potato mixture. Press down well and cook for about 10 minutes or until golden brown. Cover the pan with a plate and flip over, then slide the rösti back into the pan for another 10 minutes to cook the other side. Serve with the reheated carrot purée.

COOK'S TIP
Make individual rösti and serve topped with a mixed julienne of vegetables for an unusual appetizer.

AUBERGINE SUNFLOWER PATE

INGREDIENTS

Serves 4
1 large aubergine (eggplant)
1 garlic clove, crushed
15ml/1 tbsp lemon juice
30ml/2 tbsp sunflower seeds
45ml/3 tbsp low-fat natural (plain) yogurt
handful fresh coriander (cilantro)
    or parsley
ground black pepper
black olives, to garnish
vegetable sticks, to serve

1 Cut the aubergine in half and place, cut side down, on a baking sheet. Place under a hot grill (broiler) for 15–20 minutes, until the skin is blackened and the flesh is soft. Leave for a few minutes, to cool slightly.

2 Scoop the flesh of the aubergine into a food processor. Add the garlic, lemon juice, sunflower seeds and yogurt. Process until smooth.

3 Roughly chop the fresh coriander or parsley and mix in. Season, then spoon into a serving dish. Top with olives and serve with vegetable sticks.

NUTRITION NOTES

Per portion:
Energy	71kcals/298kJ
Fat	4.51g
Saturated fat	0.48g
Cholesterol	0.45mg
Fibre	2.62g

PEPPER DIPS WITH CRUDITES

Make one or both of these colourful vegetable dips – if you have time to make both they look spectacular together.

INGREDIENTS

Serves 4–6
2 medium red (bell) peppers, halved
    and seeded
2 medium yellow (bell) peppers,
    halved and seeded
2 garlic cloves
30ml/2 tbsp lemon juice
20ml/4 tsp olive oil
50g/2oz/1 cup fresh white breadcrumbs
salt and ground black pepper
fresh vegetables, for dipping

1 Place the peppers in separate pans with a peeled clove of garlic. Add just enough water to cover.

2 Bring to the boil, then cover and simmer for 15 minutes until tender. Drain, cool, then purée separately in a food processor or blender, adding half the lemon juice and olive oil to each.

3 Stir half the breadcrumbs into each and season to taste with salt and pepper. Serve the dips with a selection of fresh vegetables for dipping.

NUTRITION NOTES

Per portion:
Energy	103kcals/432kJ
Fat	3.7g
Saturated fat	0.47g
Cholesterol	0mg
Fibre	2.77g

SMOKED SALMON PANCAKES WITH PESTO

These simple pancakes are quick to prepare and are perfect for a special occasion.

INGREDIENTS

Serves 4–6
120ml/4fl oz/½ cup skimmed milk
115g/4oz/1 cup self-raising
  (self-rising) flour
1 egg
30ml/2 tbsp pesto
vegetable oil, for frying
200ml/7fl oz/scant 1 cup low-fat
  crème fraîche
75g/3oz smoked salmon
15ml/1 tbsp pine nuts, toasted
salt and ground black pepper
12–16 basil sprigs, to garnish

NUTRITION NOTES

Per portion:

Energy	116kcals/485kJ
Fat	7.42g
Saturated fat	2.4g
Cholesterol	39.58mg
Fibre	0.34g

1 Pour half of the milk into a mixing bowl. Add the flour, egg, pesto and seasoning, and mix to form a smooth batter.

2 Add the remainder of the milk and stir until evenly blended.

3 Heat the vegetable oil in a large frying pan. Spoon the pancake mixture into the heated oil in small heaps. Allow about 30 seconds for the pancakes to rise, then turn and cook briefly on the other side. Continue cooking the pancakes in batches until all the batter is used up.

4 Arrange the pancakes on a serving plate and top each one with a spoonful of crème fraîche.

5 Cut the salmon into 1cm/½ in strips and place on top of each pancake.

6 Sprinkle each pancake with pine nuts and garnish with a sprig of fresh basil before serving.

COOK'S TIP
If not serving immediately, cover the pancakes with a dish towel and keep warm in an oven pre-heated to 140°C/275°F/Gas 1.

BUCKWHEAT BLINIS

INGREDIENTS

Serves 4

5ml/1 tsp easy-blend (rapid-rise)
  dried yeast
250ml/8floz/1 cup skimmed
  milk, warmed
40g/1½oz/⅓ cup buckwheat flour
40g/1½oz/⅓ cup plain
  (all-purpose) flour
10ml/2 tsp caster (superfine) sugar
pinch of salt
1 egg, separated
oil, for frying
225g/8oz beetroot (beet), peeled
45ml/3 tbsp lime juice
chopped fresh chives, to garnish
lamb's lettuce, to serve

For the avocado cream
1 large avocado
75g/3oz/⅓ cup low-fat fromage blanc
  or ricotta cheese
juice of 1 lime
cracked black peppercorns, to garnish

1 Mix the dried yeast with the milk, then mix with the next four ingredients and the egg yolk. Cover with a dishtowel and leave to rise for about 40 minutes. Then whisk the egg white until stiff but not dry and fold into the blini mixture.

2 Heat a little oil in a non-stick frying pan and add a ladleful of batter to make a 10cm/4in pancake. Cook for about 2–3 minutes on each side. Repeat with the remaining batter mixture to make eight blinis.

3 For the avocado cream, cut the avocado in half and remove the stone (pit). Peel and place the flesh in a food processor or blender with the fromage blanc or ricotta and lime juice. Process until smooth.

4 For the pickle, shred the beetroot finely. Mix with the lime juice. To serve, top each blini with a spoonful of avocado cream and garnish with cracked peppercorns. Serve with lamb's lettuce and the pickled beetroot, garnished with chives.

NUTRITION NOTES

Per portion:

Energy	304kcals/1277kJ
Fat	16.56g
Saturated fat	2.23g
Cholesterol	56.3mg
Fibre	3.3g

COOK'S TIP
Serve with a glass of chilled vodka for a special occasion.

SPINACH AND POTATO GALETTE

Creamy layers of potato, spinach and herbs make this a warming supper dish.

INGREDIENTS

Serves 6
900g/2lb large potatoes
450g/1lb fresh spinach
2 eggs
400g/14oz/1¼ cups low-fat soft cheese
15ml/1 tbsp wholegrain mustard
50g/2oz/2 cups chopped fresh herbs
  (such as chives, parsley, chervil
  or sorrel)
salt and ground black pepper
mixed salad, to serve

1 Preheat the oven to 180°C/350°F/ Gas 4. Line a deep 23cm/9in cake tin (pan) with baking parchment. Place the potatoes in a large pan and cover with cold water. Bring to the boil and cook for about 10 minutes. Drain well and allow to cool slightly before slicing thinly.

2 Wash the spinach and place in a large pan with only the water that is clinging to the leaves. Cover and cook, stirring once, until the spinach has just wilted. Drain well in a sieve (strainer) and squeeze out the excess moisture. Chop finely.

NUTRITION NOTES

Per portion:
Energy	255kcals/1072kJ
Fat	9.13g
Saturated fat	4.28g
Cholesterol	81.82mg
Fibre	3.81g

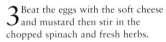

3 Beat the eggs with the soft cheese and mustard then stir in the chopped spinach and fresh herbs.

4 Place a layer of the sliced potatoes in the lined tin, arranging them in concentric circles. Top with a spoonful of the soft cheese mixture and spread out. Continue layering, seasoning with salt and pepper as you go, until all the potatoes and the soft cheese mixture are used up.

5 Cover the tin (pan) with a piece of foil and place in a roasting pan.

6 Fill the roasting pan with enough boiling water to come halfway up the sides, and cook in the oven for about 45–50 minutes. Serve hot or cold with a mixed salad.

TOMATO PESTO TOASTIES

Ready-made pesto is high in fat but, as its flavour is so powerful, it can be used in very small amounts with good effect, as in these tasty toasties.

INGREDIENTS

Serves 2
2 thick slices crusty bread
45ml/3 tbsp skimmed milk soft cheese
  or low-fat fromage frais
10ml/2 tsp red or green pesto
1 beefsteak tomato
1 red onion
salt and ground black pepper

1 Toast the bread under a hot grill (broiler) until golden brown on both sides, turning once. Leave to cool.

2 Mix together the skimmed milk soft cheese and pesto in a small bowl until well blended, then spread thickly on to the toasted bread.

3 Cut the beefsteak tomato and red onion, crossways, into thin slices using a large sharp knife.

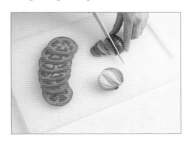

4 Arrange the slices, overlapping, on top of the toast and season with salt and pepper. Transfer the toasties to a grill (broiling) rack and cook under a hot grill until heated through, then serve immediately.

COOK'S TIP
Almost any type of crusty bread can be used for this recipe, but Italian olive oil bread and French bread will give the best flavour.

NUTRITION NOTES

Per portion:
Energy	177kcals/741kJ
Fat	2.41 g
Saturated fat	0.19g
Cholesterol	0.23mg
Fibre	2.2g

MUSHROOM CROUSTADES

The rich mushroom flavour of this filling is heightened by the addition of Worcestershire sauce.

INGREDIENTS

Serves 2–4
1 short French stick, about 25cm/10in
10ml/2 tsp olive oil
250g/9oz open cup mushrooms, quartered
10ml/2 tsp Worcestershire sauce
10ml/2 tsp lemon juice
30ml/2 tbsp skimmed milk
30ml/2 tbsp chopped fresh chives
salt and ground black pepper
chopped fresh chives, to garnish

1 Preheat the oven to 200°C/400°F/ Gas 6. Cut the French bread in half lengthways. Cut a scoop out of the soft middle of each, leaving a thick border all the way round.

2 Brush the bread with oil, place on a baking sheet and bake for about 6–8 minutes, until golden and crisp.

3 Place the mushrooms in a small pan with the Worcestershire sauce, lemon juice and milk. Simmer for about 5 minutes, or until most of the liquid is evaporated.

4 Remove from the heat, then add the chives and seasoning. Spoon into the bread croustades and serve hot, garnished with chopped chives.

NUTRITION NOTES

Per portion:	
Energy	324kcals/1361kJ
Fat	6.4g
Saturated fat	1.27g
Cholesterol	0.3mg
Fibre	3.07g

GRANARY SLTs

A quick, tasty snack or easy packed lunch with a healthy combination – sardines, lettuce and tomatoes!

INGREDIENTS

Serves 2

2 small Granary (whole-wheat)
    bread rolls
130g/4¼ oz can sardines in olive oil
4 crisp lettuce leaves
1 beefsteak tomato, sliced
juice of ½ lemon
salt and ground black pepper

1 Slice the bread rolls in half cross ways using a sharp knife. Drain off the oil from the sardines into a small bowl, then brush the cut surfaces of the rolls with a small amount of the oil.

2 Cut or break the sardines into small pieces, then fill each roll with a lettuce leaf, some sliced tomato and pieces of sardine, sprinkling the filling with a little lemon juice, and salt and pepper to taste.

3 Sandwich the rolls back together and press the lids down lightly with your hand. Serve immediately.

NUTRITION NOTES

Per portion:

Energy	248kcals/1042kJ
Fat	8.51g
Saturated fat	1.86g
Cholesterol	32.5mg
Fibre	3.01g

COOK'S TIP

If you prefer to use sardines in tomato sauce, spread the bread rolls thinly with low-fat spread before adding the filling.

SURPRISE SCOTCH 'EGGS'

This reduced-fat version of Scotch eggs is great for packed lunches or picnics. If half-fat sausage meat isn't available, buy half-fat sausages or turkey sausages and remove the skins.

INGREDIENTS

Makes 3
75ml/5 tbsp chopped parsley and chopped chives, mixed
115g/4oz/½ cup skimmed milk soft cheese
450g/1lb half-fat sausage meat (bulk sausage)
50g/2oz/scant ½ cup rolled oats
salt and ground black pepper
mixed leaf and tomato salad, to serve

1 Preheat the oven to 200°C/400°F/ Gas 6. Mix together the herbs, cheese and seasoning, then roll into three even-sized balls.

2 Divide the sausage meat into three and press each piece out to a round, about 1cm/½in thick.

3 Wrap each cheese ball in a piece of sausage meat, smoothing over all the joins to enclose the cheese completely. Spread out the rolled oats on a plate and roll the balls in the oats, using your hands to coat them evenly.

4 Place the balls on a baking sheet and bake for 30–35 minutes or until golden. Serve hot or cold, with a mixed leaf and tomato salad.

NUTRITION NOTES	
Per portion:	
Energy	352kcals/1476kJ
Fat	15.94g
Saturated fat	0.29g
Cholesterol	66.38mg
Fibre	3.82g

MIXED PEPPER PIPERADE

INGREDIENTS

Serves 4

30ml/2 tbsp olive oil
1 onion, chopped
1 red pepper
1 green pepper
4 tomatoes, peeled and chopped
1 garlic clove, crushed
4 size 2 eggs, beaten with
  15ml/1 tbsp water
ground black pepper
4 large, thick slices of wholemeal
  (whole-wheat) toast, to serve

1 Heat the oil in a large frying pan and sauté the onion gently until it becomes softened.

2 Remove the seeds from the red and green peppers and slice them thinly. Stir the pepper slices into the onion and cook together gently for 5 minutes. Add the tomatoes and garlic, season with black pepper, and cook for a further 5 minutes.

3 Pour the egg mixture over the vegetables in the frying pan and cook for 2–3 minutes, stirring until the pipérade has thickened to the consistency of lightly scrambled eggs. Serve immediately, with toast.

COOK'S TIP
Choose eggs that have been date-stamped for freshness. Do not stir the pipérade too much or the eggs may become rubbery.

NUTRITION NOTES

Per portion:
Energy	310Kcals/1300KJ
Fat	14.5g
Saturated fat	3g
Cholesterol	231mg

CHICKEN NAAN POCKETS

INGREDIENTS

Serves 4

4 small naan breads
45ml/3 tbsp low-fat natural (plain)
    yogurt
7.5ml/1½ tsp garam masala
5ml/1 tsp chilli powder
5ml/1 tsp salt
45ml/3 tbsp lemon juice
15ml/1 tbsp chopped fresh
    coriander (cilantro)
1 green chilli, chopped
450g/1lb chicken, skinned, boned
    and cubed
15ml/1 tbsp sunflower oil (optional)
8 onion rings
2 tomatoes, quartered
½ white cabbage, shredded

For the garnish
lemon wedges
2 small tomatoes, halved
mixed salad leaves
fresh coriander (cilantro) leaves

1 Cut into each naan bread to make a pocket, then set aside.

2 Mix together the yogurt, garam masala, chilli powder, salt, lemon juice, fresh coriander and chopped green chilli. Pour the marinade over the cubed chicken and leave to marinate for about 1 hour.

3 After 1 hour preheat the grill (broiler) to very hot, then lower the heat to medium. Place the chicken in a flameproof dish and grill (broil) for about 15–20 minutes until tender and cooked through, turning the chicken pieces at least twice. Baste with the oil while cooking if required.

COOK'S TIP
Use ready-made naan breads available in some supermarkets and Asian stores for speed.

4 Remove from the heat and fill each naan bread with the chicken and then with the onion rings, tomatoes and cabbage. Serve immediately with the garnish ingredients.

NUTRITION NOTES

Per portion:
Energy	364kcals/1529kJ
Fat	10.85g
Saturated fat	3.01g
Cholesterol	65.64mg

CHICKEN TIKKA

INGREDIENTS

Serves 6

450g/1lb chicken, skinned, boned and
    chopped or cubed
5ml/1 tsp grated fresh root ginger
1 garlic clove, crushed
5ml/1 tsp chilli powder
1.5ml/¼ tsp turmeric
5ml/1 tsp salt
150ml/¼ pint/⅔ cup low-fat
    natural (plain) yogurt
60ml/4 tbsp lemon juice
15ml/1 tbsp chopped fresh
    coriander (cilantro)
15ml/1 tbsp sunflower oil

For the garnish
1 small onion, cut into rings
lime wedges
mixed salad
fresh coriander (cilantro) leaves

1 In a medium bowl, mix together the chicken, ginger, garlic, chilli powder, turmeric, salt, yogurt, lemon juice and fresh coriander, and leave to marinate for at least 2 hours.

2 Place on a grill (broiling) pan or in a flameproof dish lined with foil, and baste with the oil.

3 Preheat the grill (broiler) to medium. Grill the chicken for approximately 15–20 minutes until cooked, turning and basting 2–3 times. Serve with the garnish ingredients.

COOK'S TIP
This is a quick and easy Indian first course. It can also be served as a main course for four.

NUTRITION NOTES

Per portion:
Energy	131kcals/552kJ
Fat	5.5g
Saturated fat	1.47g
Cholesterol	44.07mg

COURGETTE AND POTATO TORTILLA

INGREDIENTS

Serves 4

450g/1lb potatoes, peeled and diced
30ml/2 tbsp olive oil
1 onion, finely chopped
1 garlic clove, crushed
2 courgettes (zucchini), thinly sliced
30ml/2 tbsp chopped fresh tarragon
4 large (US extra large) eggs, beaten
salt and ground black pepper

NUTRITION NOTES

Per portion:	
Energy	265Kcals/1100KJ
Fat	14.5g
Saturated fat	3g
Cholesterol	231mg

1 Cook the potatoes in boiling, salted water for about 5 minutes.

2 Heat the oil in a large frying pan which can also be used under the grill (broiler). Add the onion and cook for 3–4 minutes until it is beginning to soften. Add the potatoes, garlic and courgettes to the pan. Cook for about 5 minutes more, shaking the pan occasionally to prevent the potatoes from sticking to the bottom, until the courgettes are softened and the potatoes are lightly browned.

3 Stir the tarragon into the eggs and season with salt and pepper. Pour the eggs over the vegetables in the pan and cook over a moderate heat until the underside of the tortilla is set. Meanwhile, preheat the grill.

4 Place the pan under the grill and cook for a few minutes more until the top of the tortilla has set. Cut into wedges and serve from the pan.

CHICKEN AND PESTO JACKETS

Although it is usually served with pasta, pesto also gives a wonderful lift to rice, bread and potato dishes – all good starchy carbohydrates. Here, it is combined with chicken and yogurt to make a low-fat topping for jacket potatoes.

INGREDIENTS

Serves 4

4 baking potatoes, pricked
2 chicken breast fillets
250ml/8fl oz/1 cup low-fat natural (plain) yogurt
15ml/1 tbsp pesto sauce
fresh basil, to garnish

1 Preheat the oven to 200°C/400°F/ Gas 6. Bake the potatoes for about 1¼ hours, or until they are soft on the inside when tested with a knife.

2 About 20 minutes before the potatoes are ready, cook the chicken, leaving the skin on, so that the flesh remains moist. Either bake the chicken in a dish alongside the potatoes in the oven, or cook it on a rack under a moderately hot grill (broiler).

3 Stir together the yogurt and pesto. When the potatoes are cooked through, cut them open. Skin the chicken fillets.

4 Slice the chicken, then fill the potatoes with the slices, top with the yogurt and garnish with basil.

NUTRITION NOTES

Per portion:	
Energy	310Kcals/1295KJ
Fat	5.5g
Saturated fat	1.5g
Cholesterol	35.5mg

PASTA, PIZZAS, PULSES AND GRAINS

Pasta, pulses and grains on their own are low in fat and
a good source of carbohydrate, but they are often
prepared with high fat ingredients and sauces. However,
recipes do not need to be high in fat to be appetizing. There
are delicious low fat recipes for pasta, such as Fusilli with
Smoked Trout and Tagliatelle with Pea and Bean Sauce.
Pulses and grains, too, are a popular choice at mealtimes,
and these recipes offer tasty and nutritious options, from
Cracked Wheat and Mint Salad to Spicy Bean Hot Pot.

TAGLIATELLE WITH MUSHROOMS

INGREDIENTS

Serves 4

1 small onion, finely chopped
2 garlic cloves, crushed
150ml/¼ pint/⅔ cup vegetable stock
225g/8oz mixed fresh mushrooms, such
  as field (portabello), chestnut, oyster
  or chanterelles
60ml/4 tbsp white or red wine
10ml/2 tsp tomato purée (paste)
15ml/1 tbsp soy sauce
5ml/1 tsp chopped fresh thyme
30ml/2 tbsp chopped fresh parsley, plus
  extra to garnish
225g/8oz fresh sun-dried tomato and
  herb tagliatelle
salt and black pepper
shavings of Parmesan cheese, to serve
  (optional)

1 Put the onion and garlic into a pan with the stock, then cover and cook for 5 minutes or until tender.

NUTRITION NOTES

Per portion:	
Energy	241Kcals/1010kJ
Fat	2.4g
Saturated fat	0.7g
Carbohydrate	45g
Fibre	3g

2 Add the mushrooms (quartered or sliced if large or left whole if small), wine, tomato purée and soy sauce. Cover and cook for 5 minutes.

3 Remove the lid from the pan and boil until the liquid has reduced by half. Stir in the chopped fresh herbs and season to taste.

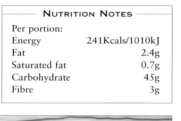

4 Cook the pasta in a large pan of boiling, salted water for 2–5 minutes until *al dente*. Drain thoroughly and toss lightly with the mushrooms. Serve, garnished with parsley and shavings of Parmesan cheese, if you like.

PASTA PRIMAVERA

You can use any mixture of fresh, young spring vegetables to make this delicately flavoured pasta dish.

INGREDIENTS

Serves 4

225g/8oz thin asparagus spears, chopped in half
115g/4oz mangetouts (snow peas), trimmed
115g/4oz baby corn
225g/8oz whole baby carrots, trimmed
1 small red pepper, seeded and chopped
8 spring onions (scallions), sliced
225g/8oz torchietti or other pasta shapes
150ml/¼ pint/⅔ cup low fat cottage cheese
150ml/¼ pint/⅔ cup low fat yogurt
15ml/1 tbsp lemon juice
15ml/1 tbsp chopped parsley
15ml/1 tbsp chopped chives
skimmed milk (optional)
salt and black pepper
sun-dried tomato bread, to serve

1 Cook the asparagus spears in a pan of boiling, salted water for 3–4 minutes. Add the mangetouts halfway through the cooking time. Drain and rinse both under cold water to stop further cooking.

2 Cook the baby corn, carrots, red pepper and spring onions in the same way until tender. Drain and rinse.

3 Cook the pasta in a large pan of boiling, salted water according to the packet instruction, until *al dente*. Drain thoroughly.

4 Put the cottage cheese, yogurt, lemon juice, parsley, chives and seasoning into a food processor or blender and process until smooth. Thin the sauce with skimmed milk, if necessary. Put into a large pan with the pasta and vegetables, heat gently and toss carefully. Serve immediately with sun-dried tomato bread.

NUTRITION NOTES	
Per portion:	
Energy	320Kcals/1344kJ
Fat	3.1g
Saturated fat	0.4g
Cholesterol	3mg
Fibre	6.2g

PENNE AND AUBERGINE WITH MINT PESTO

This splendid variation on the classic Italian pesto uses fresh mint rather than basil.

───────── INGREDIENTS ─────────

Serves 4
2 large aubergines (eggplants)
pinch of salt
450g/1lb/4 cups penne
50g/2oz/⅓ cup walnut halves

For the pesto
25g/1oz/1 cup fresh mint
15g/½oz/½ cup flat leaf parsley
40g/1½oz/¼ cup walnuts
40g/1½oz/½ cup freshly grated
   Parmesan cheese
2 garlic cloves
45ml/3 tbsp olive oil
salt and ground black pepper

───────── **NUTRITION NOTES** ─────────

Per portion:	
Energy	777kcals/2364kJ
Fat	38.11g
Saturated fat	6.29g
Cholesterol	10mg
Fibre	8.57g

1 Cut the aubergines lengthways into 1cm/½in slices.

2 Cut the slices again crossways to give short strips.

3 Layer the strips in a colander with salt and leave to stand for 30 minutes over a plate to catch any juices. Rinse well in cool water and drain.

4 For the pesto, place all the ingredients, except the oil, in a food processor or blender and blend until smooth, then gradually add the oil in a thin stream until the mixture amalgamates. Season to taste.

5 Bring a large pan of water to the boil, toss in the penne and cook for 8 minutes or until nearly cooked. Add the aubergines and cook for a further 3 minutes.

6 Drain well and mix in half of the mint pesto and walnut halves. Serve with the remaining pesto and walnut halves on top.

TAGLIATELLE WITH PEA AND BEAN SAUCE

A creamy pea sauce makes a wonderful combination with the crunchy young vegetables.

INGREDIENTS

Serves 4

15ml/1 tbsp olive oil
1 garlic clove, crushed
6 spring onions (scallions), sliced
115g/4oz/1 cup fresh or frozen baby peas, defrosted
350g/12oz fresh young asparagus
30ml/2 tbsp chopped fresh sage, plus extra leaves, to garnish
finely grated rind of 2 lemons
400ml/14fl oz/1⅔ cups vegetable stock
225g/8oz/1½ cups fresh or frozen broad (fava) beans, defrosted
450g/1lb tagliatelle
60ml/4 tbsp low-fat natural (plain) yogurt
salt and ground black pepper

NUTRITION NOTES

Per portion:	
Energy	509kcals/2139kJ
Fat	6.75g
Saturated fat	0.95g
Cholesterol	0.6mg
Fibre	9.75g

1 Heat the oil in a pan. Add the garlic and spring onions, and cook gently for about 2–3 minutes until softened.

2 Add the peas and a third of the asparagus, together with the sage, lemon rind and stock. Simmer for 10 minutes. Process in a food processor or blender until smooth.

3 Meanwhile remove the outer skins from the broad beans and discard.

4 Cut the remaining asparagus into 5cm/2in lengths, trimming off any tough fibrous stems, and blanch in boiling water for about 2 minutes.

5 Cook the tagliatelle in boiling salted water following the manufacturer's instructions until *al dente*. Drain well.

6 Add the cooked asparagus and shelled beans to the sauce, and reheat. Stir in the yogurt, season to taste, and toss into the tagliatelle. Garnish with a few extra sage leaves, and serve immediately.

COOK'S TIPS
Use fresh peas and beans when in season – they give the dish a wonderful flavour. If you don't have vegetable stock, use water.

TURKEY AND MACARONI CHEESE

A tasty low fat alternative to macaroni cheese – serve it with warm ciabatta bread and a mixed leaf salad.

NUTRITION NOTES	
Per portion:	
Energy	152Kcals/637kJ
Fat	2.8g
Saturated fat	0.7g
Cholesterol	12mg
Fibre	1.1g

INGREDIENTS

Serves 4

1 medium onion, chopped
150ml/¼ pint/⅔ cup vegetable or
  chicken stock
25g/1oz/2 tbsp low fat margarine
45ml/3 tbsp plain (all-purpose) flour
300ml/½ pint/1¼ cup skimmed milk
50g/2oz reduced fat Cheddar
  cheese, grated
5ml/1 tsp dry mustard
225g/8oz quick-cook macaroni
4 smoked turkey rashers (strips),
  cut in half
2–3 firm tomatoes, sliced
a few fresh basil leaves
15ml/1 tbsp grated Parmesan cheese
salt and black pepper

1 Put the chopped onion and stock into a non-stick frying pan. Bring to the boil, stirring occasionally and cook for 5–6 minutes or until the stock has reduced entirely and the onion is transparent.

2 Put the margarine, flour, milk and seasoning into a pan and whisk together over the heat until thickened and smooth. Draw aside and add the cheese, mustard and onion.

3 Cook the macaroni in a large pan of boiling, salted water according to the instructions on the packet. Preheat the grill (broiler). Drain thoroughly and stir into the sauce. Transfer to a shallow ovenproof dish.

4 Arrange the turkey rashers and tomatoes overlapping on top of the macaroni cheese. Tuck in the basil leaves, then sprinkle with Parmesan and grill (broil) to lightly brown the top.

PASTA WITH TOMATO AND TUNA

INGREDIENTS

Serves 6
1 medium onion, finely chopped
1 celery stick, finely chopped
1 red (bell) pepper, seeded and diced
1 garlic clove, crushed
150ml/¼ pint/⅔ cup chicken stock
400g/14oz can chopped tomatoes
15ml/1 tbsp tomato purée (paste)
10ml/2 tsp caster (superfine) sugar
15ml/1 tbsp chopped fresh basil
15ml/1 tbsp chopped fresh parsley
450g/1lb pasta shells
400g/14oz canned tuna in
  brine, drained
30ml/2 tbsp capers in vinegar, drained
salt and black pepper

1 Put the chopped onion, celery, red pepper and garlic into a pan. Add the stock, bring to the boil and cook for 5 minutes or until the stock has reduced almost completely.

2 Add the tomatoes, tomato purée, sugar and herbs. Season to taste and bring to the boil. Simmer for about 30 minutes until thick, stirring occasionally.

3 Meanwhile, cook the pasta in a large pan of boiling, salted water according to the packet instructions, until *al dente*. Drain thoroughly and transfer to a warm serving dish.

> **COOK'S TIP**
> If fresh herbs are not available, use a 400g/14oz can of chopped tomatoes with herbs and add 5–10ml/1–2 tsp mixed dried herbs, in place of the fresh herbs.

4 Flake the tuna fish into large chunks and add to the sauce with the capers. Heat gently for 1–2 minutes, pour over the pasta, toss gently and serve immediately.

NUTRITION NOTES

Per portion:	
Energy	369Kcals/1549kJ
Fat	2.1g
Saturated fat	0.4g
Cholesterol	34mg
Fibre	4g

CRAB PASTA SALAD

Low fat yogurt makes a piquant
dressing for this salad.

INGREDIENTS

Serves 6
350g/12oz pasta twists
1 small red (bell) pepper, seeded and
* finely chopped*
2 x 175g/6oz cans white crab
* meat, drained*
115g/4oz cherry tomatoes, halved
¼ cucumber, halved, seeded and sliced
* into crescents*
15ml/1 tbsp lemon juice
300ml/½ pint/1¼ cups low fat yogurt
2 celery sticks, finely chopped
10ml/2 tsp horseradish cream
2.5ml/½ tsp paprika
2.5ml/½ tsp Dijon mustard
30ml/2 tbsp sweet tomato pickle
* or chutney*
salt and black pepper
fresh basil, to garnish

1 Cook the pasta in a large pan of
boiling, salted water, according to
the instructions on the packet, until
al dente. Drain and rinse thoroughly
under cold water.

NUTRITION NOTES	
Per portion:	
Energy	305Kcals/1283kJ
Fat	2.5g
Saturated fat	0.5g
Cholesterol	43mg
Fibre	2.9g

2 Cover the chopped red pepper with
boiling water and leave to stand for
1 minute. Drain and rinse under cold
water. Pat dry on kitchen paper.

3 Drain the crab meat and pick over
carefully for pieces of shell. Put into
a bowl with the halved tomatoes and
sliced cucumber. Season with salt and
pepper and sprinkle with lemon juice.

4 To make the dressing, add the red
pepper to the yogurt, with the
celery, horseradish cream, paprika,
mustard and sweet tomato pickle or
chutney. Mix the pasta with the
dressing and transfer to a serving dish.
Spoon the crab mixture on top and
garnish with fresh basil.

FUSILLI WITH SMOKED TROUT

INGREDIENTS

Serves 4–6

2 carrots, cut in julienne sticks
1 leek, cut in julienne sticks
2 celery sticks, cut in julienne sticks
150ml/¼ pint/⅔ cup vegetable or
   fish stock
225g/8oz smoked trout fillets, skinned
   and cut into strips
200g/7oz low fat cream cheese
150ml/¼ pint/⅔ cup medium sweet
   white wine or fish stock
15ml/1 tbsp chopped fresh dill
   or fennel
225g/8oz fusilli (long, corkscrew pasta)
salt and black pepper
dill sprigs, to garnish

1 Put the carrots, leek and celery into a pan with the vegetable or fish stock. Bring to the boil and cook quickly for 4–5 minutes until the vegetables are tender and most of the stock has evaporated. Remove from the heat and add the smoked trout.

2 To make the sauce, put the cream cheese and wine or fish stock into a pan, heat and whisk until smooth. Season with salt and pepper. Add the chopped dill or fennel.

4 Return the pasta to the pan with the sauce, toss lightly and transfer to a serving bowl. Top with the cooked vegetables and trout. Serve at once garnished with dill sprigs.

NUTRITION NOTES

Per portion:

Energy	339Kcals/1422kJ
Fat	4.7g
Saturated fat	0.8g
Cholesterol	57mg
Fibre	4.1g

3 Cook the pasta according to the packet instructions in a large pan of boiling, salted water until *al dente*. Drain thoroughly.

COOK'S TIP
When making the sauce, it is important to whisk it continuously while heating, to ensure a smooth result. Smoked salmon may be used in place of the trout, for a tasty change.

TABBOULEH WITH FENNEL

A fresh salad originating in the Middle East that is perfect for a summer lunch. Serve with lettuce and pitta bread.

INGREDIENTS

Serves 4
225g/8oz/1¼ cups bulgur wheat
2 fennel bulbs
1 small red chilli, seeded and chopped
1 celery stick, finely sliced
30ml/2 tbsp olive oil
finely grated rind and juice of
    2 lemons
8 spring onions (scallions), chopped
90ml/6 tbsp chopped fresh mint
90ml/6 tbsp chopped fresh parsley
1 pomegranate, seeded
salt and ground black pepper

NUTRITION NOTES

Per portion:
Energy	188kcals/791kJ
Fat	4.67g
Saturated fat	0.62g
Cholesterol	0mg
Fibre	2.17g

1 Place the bulgur wheat in a bowl and pour over enough cold water to cover. Leave to stand for 30 minutes.

2 Drain the wheat through a sieve (strainer), pressing out any excess water using a spoon.

3 Cut the fennel bulbs in half and carefully cut into very fine slices with a sharp knife.

4 Mix all the remaining ingredients together, including the soaked bulgur wheat and fennel. Season well, cover, and set aside for 30 minutes before serving.

COOK'S TIP
Fennel has a very distinctive aniseed flavour. When you are buying fennel, choose well-rounded bulbs which are pale green to white in colour. Avoid any that are deep green.

SWEET VEGETABLE COUSCOUS

A wonderful combination of sweet vegetables and spices, this makes a substantial winter dish.

INGREDIENTS

Serves 4–6

generous pinch of saffron threads
45ml/3 tbsp boiling water
15ml/1 tbsp olive oil
1 red onion, sliced
2 garlic cloves
1–2 red chillies, seeded and
  finely chopped
2.5ml/½ tsp ground ginger
2.5ml/½ tsp ground cinnamon
400g/14oz can chopped tomatoes
300ml/½ pint/1¼ cups fresh vegetable
  stock or water
4 carrots, peeled and sliced
2 turnips, peeled and diced
450g/1lb sweet potatoes, peeled
  and diced
75g/3oz/⅔ cup raisins
2 courgettes (zucchini), sliced
400g/14oz can chickpeas, drained
  and rinsed
45ml/3 tbsp chopped fresh parsley
45ml/3 tbsp chopped fresh
  coriander (cilantro)
450g/1lb/4 cups quick-cook couscous
salt

1 Leave the saffron to infuse in the boiling water.

2 Heat the oil in a large pan or flameproof casserole. Add the onion, garlic and chillies, and cook gently for about 5 minutes.

3 Add the ground ginger and cinnamon, and gently cook for a further 1–2 minutes.

4 Add the tomatoes, stock or water, saffron and liquid, carrots, turnips, sweet potatoes and raisins, cover and simmer for a further 25 minutes.

5 Add the courgettes, chickpeas, parsley and coriander, and cook for 10 minutes more.

6 Meanwhile prepare the couscous in boiling salted water, following the manufacturer's instructions, and then serve with the prepared vegetables.

NUTRITION NOTES

Per portion:
Energy	570kcals/2393kJ
Fat	7.02g
Saturated fat	0.83g
Cholesterol	0mg
Fibre	10.04g

COOK'S TIP
Vegetable stock can be made from a variety of uncooked vegetables, including the outer leaves of cabbage, lettuce and other greens, carrot peelings, leeks, celery and parsnips.

HOT SPICY PRAWNS WITH CAMPANELLE

This low fat prawn sauce tossed with hot pasta is an ideal supper-time dish. Add less or more chilli depending on how hot you like your food.

INGREDIENTS

Serves 4–6

225g/8oz tiger prawns (jumbo shrimp), cooked and peeled
1–2 garlic cloves, crushed
finely grated rind of 1 lemon
15ml/1 tbsp lemon juice
1.5ml/¼ tsp red chilli paste or 1 large pinch of chilli powder
15ml/1 tbsp light soy sauce
150g/5oz smoked turkey rashers (strips)
1 shallot or small onion, finely chopped
60ml/4 tbsp dry white wine
225g/8oz campanelle or other pasta shapes
60ml/4 tbsp fish stock
4 firm ripe tomatoes, peeled, seeded and chopped
30ml/2 tbsp chopped fresh parsley
salt and black pepper

NUTRITION NOTES

Per portion:
Energy	331Kcals/1388kJ
Fat	2.9g
Saturated fat	0.6g
Cholesterol	64mg
Fibre	3.2g

COOK'S TIP
To save time later, the prawns and marinade ingredients can be mixed together, covered and chilled in the refrigerator overnight, until ready to use.

1 In a glass bowl, mix the prawns with the garlic, lemon rind and juice, chilli paste or powder and soy sauce. Season with salt and pepper, cover and marinate for at least 1 hour.

2 Grill the turkey rashers, then cut them into 5mm/¼in dice.

3 Put the shallot or onion and white wine into a pan, bring to the boil, cover and cook for 2–3 minutes or until they are tender and the wine has reduced by half.

4 Cook the pasta according to the packet instructions in a large pan of boiling, salted water until *al dente*. Drain thoroughly.

5 Just before serving, put the prawns with their marinade into a large frying pan, bring to the boil quickly and add the smoked turkey and fish stock. Heat through for 1 minute.

6 Add to the pasta with the chopped tomatoes and parsley, toss quickly and serve immediately.

CAMPANELLE WITH YELLOW PEPPER SAUCE

Roasted yellow peppers make a deliciously sweet and creamy sauce to serve with pasta.

INGREDIENTS

Serves 4
2 yellow (bell) peppers, halved
50g/2oz/¼ cup low-fat soft goat's cheese
115g/4oz/½ cup low-fat fromage blanc
   or crème fraîche
450g/1lb/4 cups campanelle pasta
salt and ground black pepper
50g/2oz/¼ cup flaked (sliced) almonds,
   toasted, to garnish

NUTRITION NOTES

Per portion:
Energy	529kcals/2221kJ
Fat	11.18g
Saturated fat	0.88g
Cholesterol	9.04mg
Fibre	5.69g

1 Preheat the grill (broiler). Place the yellow pepper halves under the grill until charred and blistered. Place in a plastic bag to cool. Peel and remove the seeds.

COOK'S TIP
Always cut the stalk ends from peppers and discard the midribs and seeds.

2 Place the pepper flesh in a food processor or blender with the goat's cheese and fromage blanc or crème fraîche. Process until smooth. Season with salt and lots of black pepper.

3 Cook the pasta following the manufacturer's instructions until *al dente*. Drain well.

4 Toss with the sauce and serve the dish sprinkled with the toasted flaked almonds.

GREEN LENTIL AND CABBAGE SALAD

This warm crunchy salad makes a satisfying meal if served with crusty French bread or whole-wheat rolls.

INGREDIENTS

Serves 4–6
225g/8oz/1 cups Puy lentils
1.3 litres/2¼ pints/5⅔ cups cold water
1 garlic clove
1 bay leaf
1 onion, peeled and studded with 2 cloves
15ml/1 tbsp olive oil
1 red onion, finely sliced
2 garlic cloves, crushed
15ml/1 tbsp thyme leaves
350g/12oz/3 cups finely shredded cabbage
finely grated rind and juice of 1 lemon
15ml/1 tbsp raspberry vinegar
salt and ground black pepper

NUTRITION NOTES

Per portion:
Energy	228kcals/959kJ
Fat	4.38g
Saturated fat	0.44g
Cholesterol	0mg
Fibre	8.09g

1 Rinse the lentils in cold water and place in a large pan with the water, peeled garlic clove, bay leaf and clove-studded onion. Bring to the boil and cook for about 10 minutes. Reduce the heat, cover the pan, and simmer gently for a further 15–20 minutes. Drain and remove the onion, garlic and bay leaf.

2 Heat the oil in a large pan. Add the red onion, garlic and thyme, and cook for 5 minutes until softened.

3 Add the cabbage and cook for a further 3–5 minutes until just cooked but still crunchy (al dente).

4 Stir in the cooked lentils, lemon rind and juice and the raspberry vinegar. Season to taste and serve.

COOK'S TIP
There are several varieties of cabbage available such as spring, summer, winter, white and red cabbage. White cabbage is excellent in salads. Choose one with a firm, compact head and avoid those with loose curling leaves.

LEMON AND GINGER SPICY BEANS

INGREDIENTS

Serves 4

30ml/2 tbsp roughly chopped fresh
    root ginger
3 garlic cloves, roughly chopped
250ml/8fl oz/1 cup cold water
15ml/1 tbsp sunflower oil
1 large onion, thinly sliced
1 red chilli, seeded and finely
    chopped
1.5ml/¼ tsp cayenne pepper
10ml/2 tsp ground cumin
5ml/1 tsp ground coriander
2.5ml/½ tsp ground turmeric
30ml/2 tbsp lemon juice
75g/3oz/3 cups chopped fresh
    coriander (cilantro)
400g/14oz can black-eyed beans (peas),
    drained and rinsed
400g/14oz can aduki beans,
    drained and rinsed
400g/14oz can haricot (navy) beans,
    drained and rinsed
salt and ground black pepper
crusty bread, to serve

1 Place the ginger, garlic and 60ml/4 tbsp of the cold water in a food processor or blender and process until smooth.

2 Heat the oil in a pan. Add the onion and chilli, and cook gently for about 5 minutes until softened.

3 Add the cayenne pepper, cumin, ground coriander and turmeric, and stir-fry for a further 1 minute.

4 Stir in the ginger and garlic paste from the food processor or blender and cook for a further minute.

5 Add the remaining water, lemon juice and fresh coriander, stir well and bring to the boil. Cover the pan tightly and cook for about 5 minutes.

6 Add all the beans and cook for a further 5–10 minutes, until heated through. Season with salt and pepper to taste, and serve with crusty bread.

NUTRITION NOTES

Per portion:
Energy	281kcals/1180kJ
Fat	4.3g
Saturated fat	0.42g
Cholesterol	0mg
Fibre	10.76g

SESAME NOODLE SALAD WITH PEANUTS

An Orient-inspired salad with crunchy vegetables and a light soy dressing. The hot peanuts make a surprisingly successful union with the cold noodles.

INGREDIENTS

Serves 4
350g/12oz egg noodles
2 carrots, peeled and cut into fine
    julienne strips
½ cucumber, peeled and diced
115g/4oz celeriac, peeled and cut into
    fine julienne strips
6 spring onions (scallions), finely sliced
8 canned water chestnuts, drained and
    finely sliced
175g/6oz/2 cups beansprouts
1 small green chilli, chopped
30ml/2 tbsp sesame seeds, 115g/4oz/1
    cup peanuts and extra green chillies,
    to garnish

For the dressing
15ml/1 tbsp dark soy sauce
15ml/1 tbsp light soy sauce
15ml/1 tbsp clear honey
15ml/1 tbsp rice wine or dry sherry
15ml/1 tbsp sesame oil

3 Mix the noodles with all of the prepared vegetables.

5 Place the sesame seeds and peanuts on separate baking trays and bake for 5 minutes. Remove the sesame seeds and continue to cook the peanuts for 5 minutes more, or until browned.

6 Sprinkle the sesame seeds and peanuts over each portion and serve immediately, garnished with chillies.

1 Preheat the oven to 200°C/400°F/ Gas 6. Bring a large pan of water to the boil, toss in the egg noodles and cook according to the manufacturer's instructions.

2 Drain the noodles, refresh in cold water, then drain again.

4 For the dressing, combine the ingredients in a bowl, then toss into the vegetable mixture. Divide the salad among four plates.

NUTRITION NOTES

Per portion:
Energy	634kcals/2664kJ
Fat	28.1g
Saturated fat	4.03g
Cholesterol	0mg
Fibre	5.33g

SPAGHETTI BOLOGNESE

INGREDIENTS

Serves 8

1 onion, chopped
2–3 garlic cloves, crushed
300ml/½ pint/1¼ cups beef or
* chicken stock*
450g/1lb extra-lean minced (ground)
* turkey or beef*
2 x 400g/14oz cans chopped tomatoes
5ml/1 tsp dried basil
5ml/1 tsp dried oregano
60ml/4 tbsp tomato purée (paste)
450g/1lb button (white) mushrooms,
* quartered and sliced*
150ml/¼ pint/⅔ cup red wine
450g/1lb spaghetti
salt and black pepper

NUTRITION NOTES

Per portion:	
Energy	321Kcals/1350kJ
Fat	4.1g
Saturated fat	1.3g
Cholesterol	33mg
Fibre	2.7g

1 Put the chopped onion and garlic into a non-stick pan with half of the stock. Bring to the boil and cook for 5 minutes until the onion is tender and the stock has reduced completely.

COOK'S TIP
Sautéing vegetables in fat-free stock rather than oil is an easy way of saving calories and fat. Choose fat-free stock to reduce even more.

2 Add the turkey or beef and cook for 5 minutes, breaking up the meat with a fork. Add the tomatoes, herbs and tomato purée, bring to the boil, then cover and simmer for 1 hour.

3 Meanwhile, cook the mushrooms in a non-stick pan with the wine for 5 minutes or until the wine has evaporated. Add the mushrooms to the meat with salt and pepper to taste.

4 Cook the pasta in a large pan of boiling salted water for 8–12 minutes until tender. Drain thoroughly. Serve topped with the meat sauce.

RATATOUILLE PENNE BAKE

INGREDIENTS

Serves 6

1 small aubergine (eggplant)
2 courgettes (zucchini), thickly sliced
200g/7oz firm tofu, cubed
45ml/3 tbsp dark soy sauce
1 garlic clove, crushed
10ml/2 tsp sesame seeds
1 small red pepper, seeded and sliced
1 onion, finely chopped
1–2 garlic cloves, crushed
150ml/¼ pint/⅔ cup vegetable stock
3 firm ripe tomatoes, skinned, seeded
  and quartered
15ml/1 tbsp chopped mixed herbs
225g/8oz penne or other pasta shapes
salt and black pepper
crusty bread, to serve

1 Wash the aubergine and cut into 2.5cm/1in cubes. Put into a colander with the courgettes, sprinkle with salt and leave to drain for 30 minutes.

2 Mix the tofu with the soy sauce, garlic and sesame seeds. Cover and marinate for 30 minutes.

3 Put the pepper, onion and garlic in a pan with the stock. Bring to the boil, cover and cook for 5 minutes until tender. Remove the lid and boil until all the stock has evaporated. Add the tomatoes and herbs to the pan and cook for a further 3 minutes, then add the rinsed aubergine and courgettes, and cook until tender. Season to taste.

COOK'S TIP
Tofu is a low fat protein, but it is very bland. Marinating adds plenty of flavour – make sure you leave it for the full 30 minutes.

4 Meanwhile, cook the pasta in a large pan of boiling, salted water according to the packet instructions, until *al dente*; drain thoroughly. Preheat the grill (broiler). Toss the pasta with the vegetables and tofu. Transfer to a shallow ovenproof dish and grill (broil) until lightly toasted. Serve with bread.

NUTRITION NOTES
Per portion:

Energy	208Kcals/873kJ
Fat	3.7g
Saturated fat	0.5g
Cholesterol	0mg
Fibre	3.9g

SWEET AND SOUR PEPPERS WITH PASTA

A tasty and colourful low fat dish – perfect for lunch or supper.

INGREDIENTS

Serves 4
1 red, 1 yellow and 1 orange (bell) pepper
1 garlic clove, crushed
30ml/2 tbsp capers
30ml/2 tbsp raisins
5ml/1 tsp wholegrain mustard
rind and juice of 1 lime
5ml/1 tsp clear honey
30ml/2 tbsp chopped fresh coriander
  (cilantro)
225g/8oz pasta bows
salt and black pepper
shavings of Parmesan cheese,
  to serve (optional)

1 Quarter the peppers and remove the stalks and seeds. Put the quarters into boiling water and cook for 10–15 minutes, until tender. Drain and rinse under cold water, then peel off the skin and cut the flesh into strips lengthways.

2 Put the garlic, capers, raisins, mustard, lime rind and juice, honey, coriander and seasoning into a bowl and whisk together.

3 Cook the pasta in a large pan of boiling, salted water for 10–12 minutes, until *al dente*. Drain thoroughly.

4 Return the pasta to the pan and add the pepper strips and dressing. Heat gently, tossing to mix. Transfer to a warm serving bowl and serve with a few shavings of Parmesan cheese, if using.

NUTRITION NOTES	
Per portion:	
Energy	268Kcals/1125kJ
Fat	2.0g
Saturated fat	0.5g
Cholesterol	1.3mg
Fibre	4.3g

PASTA WITH CHICKPEA SAUCE

This is a delicious, and very speedy, low fat dish. The quality of canned peas and tomatoes is so good that it is possible to transform them into a very fresh tasting pasta sauce in minutes. Choose whatever pasta shapes you like, although hollow shapes, such as penne (quills) or shells are particularly good with this sauce.

INGREDIENTS

Serves 6
450g/1lb penne or other pasta shapes
30ml/2 tsp olive oil
1 onion, thinly sliced
1 red (bell) pepper, seeded and sliced
400g/14oz can chopped tomatoes
425g/15oz can chickpeas
30ml/2 tbsp dry vermouth (optional)
5ml/1 tsp dried oregano
1 large bay leaf
30ml/2 tbsp capers
salt and black pepper
fresh oregano, to garnish

COOK'S TIP
Choose fresh or dried unfilled pasta for this dish. Whichever you choose, cook it in a large pan of water, so that the pasta keeps separate and doesn't stick together. Fresh pasta takes about 2–4 minutes to cook and dried pasta about 8–10 minutes. Cook pasta until it is *al dente* – firm and neither too hard nor too soft.

NUTRITION NOTES

Per portion:
Energy	268Kcals/1125kJ
Fat	2.0g
Saturated fat	0.5g
Cholesterol	1.3mg
Fibre	4.3g

1 Boil the pasta as instructed on the packet, then drain. Meanwhile, heat the oil in a large pan and gently fry the onion and pepper for about 5 minutes, stirring occasionally, until softened.

2 Add the tomatoes, chickpeas with their liquid, vermouth (if you like), herbs and capers and stir well.

3 Season to taste and bring to the boil, then simmer for about 10 minutes. Remove the bay leaf and mix in the pasta. Reheat and serve hot, garnished with sprigs of oregano.

PENNE WITH BROCCOLI AND CHILLI

INGREDIENTS

Serves 4

450g/1lb small broccoli florets
30ml/2 tbsp stock
1 garlic clove, crushed
1 small red chilli, sliced, or 2.5ml/½ tsp chilli sauce
60ml/4 tbsp low-fat natural (plain) yogurt
30ml/2 tbsp toasted pine nuts or cashews
350g/12oz/3 cups penne pasta
salt and ground black pepper

1 Add the pasta to a large pan of lightly salted boiling water and return to the boil. Place the broccoli in a steamer basket over the top. Cover and cook for 8–10 minutes until both are just tender. Drain.

2 Heat the stock and add the crushed garlic and chilli or chilli sauce. Stir over a low heat for 2–3 minutes.

3 Stir in the broccoli, pasta and yogurt. Adjust the seasoning, sprinkle with nuts and serve hot.

NUTRITION NOTES

Per portion:

Energy	403kcals/1695kJ
Fat	7.87g
Saturated fat	0.89g
Cholesterol	0.6mg
Fibre	5.83g

CREOLE JAMBALAYA

INGREDIENTS

Serves 6

4 skinless, boneless chicken thighs, diced
1 large green (bell) pepper, seeded and sliced
3 celery sticks, sliced
4 spring onions (scallions), sliced
about 300ml/½ pint/1¼ cups chicken stock
400g/14oz can tomatoes
5ml/1 tsp ground cumin
5ml/1 tsp ground allspice
2.5ml/½ tsp cayenne pepper
5ml/1 tsp dried thyme
300g/10oz/1½ cups long grain rice
200g/7oz cooked, peeled prawns (shrimp)
salt and ground black pepper

1 Fry the chicken in a non-stick pan without fat, turning occasionally, until golden brown.

2 Add the pepper, celery and spring onions with 15ml/1 tbsp stock. Cook for a few minutes to soften, then add the tomatoes, spices and thyme.

3 Stir in the rice and stock. Cover closely and cook for about 20 minutes, stirring occasionally, until the rice is tender. Add more stock if needed.

4 Add the prawns and heat well. Season and serve with a crisp salad.

NUTRITION NOTES

Per portion:

Energy	282kcals/1185kJ
Fat	3.37g
Saturated fat	0.85g
Cholesterol	51.33mg
Fibre	1.55g

THAI FRAGRANT RICE

A lovely, soft, fluffy rice dish, perfumed with delicious and fresh lemon grass.

INGREDIENTS

Serves 4
1 lemon grass stalk
2 limes
225g/8oz/1⅓ cups brown basmati rice
15ml/1 tbsp olive oil
1 onion, chopped
2.5cm/1in piece fresh root ginger,
* peeled and finely chopped*
7.5ml/1½ tsp coriander seeds
7.5ml/1½ tsp cumin seeds
750ml/1¼ pints/3 cups vegetable stock
60ml/4 tbsp chopped fresh
* coriander (cilantro)*
lime wedges, to garnish

> COOK'S TIP
>
> Other varieties of rice, such as white basmati or long grain, can be used for this dish but you will need to adjust the cooking times as necessary.

1 Finely chop the lemon grass and remove the rind from the limes.

2 Rinse the rice in cold water. Drain through a sieve (strainer).

3 Heat the oil in a large pan, add the onion and spices and cook gently for about 2–3 minutes.

4 Add the rice and cook for a further minute, then add the vegetable stock and bring to the boil. Reduce the heat to very low and cover the pan. Cook gently for about 30 minutes, then check the rice. If it is still crunchy, cover the pan again with the lid and leave for a further 3–5 minutes. When it is tender, remove from the heat.

5 Stir in the fresh coriander, fluff up the grains, cover and leave for 10 minutes. Garnish with lime wedges, and serve hot.

NUTRITION NOTES	
Per portion:	
Energy	259kcals/1087kJ
Fat	5.27g
Saturated fat	0.81g
Cholesterol	0mg
Fibre	1.49g

PUMPKIN AND PISTACHIO RISOTTO

This elegant combination of creamy golden rice and orange pumpkin can be made as pale or bright as you like – simply add different quantities of saffron.

INGREDIENTS

Serves 4

1.2 litres/2 pints/5 cups vegetable stock
  or water
generous pinch of saffron threads
30ml/2 tbsp olive oil
1 onion, chopped
2 garlic cloves, crushed
900g/2lb pumpkin, peeled, seeded and
  cut into 2cm/³⁄₄in cubes
450g/1lb/2¹⁄₃ cups arborio rice
200ml/7fl oz/scant 1 cup dry white wine
15ml/1 tbsp freshly grated
  Parmesan cheese
50g/2oz/¹⁄₂ cup pistachio nuts
45ml/3 tbsp chopped fresh marjoram
  or oregano, plus extra leaves,
  to garnish
salt, freshly grated nutmeg and ground
  black pepper

NUTRITION NOTES

Per portion:

Energy	630kcals/2646kJ
Fat	15.24g
Saturated fat	2.66g
Cholesterol	3.75mg
Fibre	2.59g

1 Bring the stock or water to the boil and reduce to a low simmer. Ladle a little liquid into a small bowl. Add the saffron threads and leave to infuse.

2 Heat the oil in a pan or flame-proof casserole. Add the onion and garlic, and cook gently for 5 minutes until softened. Add the pumpkin and rice and cook for a few more minutes until the rice looks transparent.

3 Pour in the wine and allow it to boil hard. When it is absorbed add a quarter of the stock or water and the infused saffron and liquid. Stir constantly until all the liquid is absorbed.

4 Gradually add a ladleful of stock or water at a time, allowing the rice to absorb the liquid before adding more, and stir constantly.

5 Cook the rice for approximately 25–30 minutes or until *al dente*. Stir in the Parmesan cheese, cover the pan and leave to stand for 5 minutes.

6 To finish, stir in the pistachio nuts and marjoram or oregano. Season to taste with a little salt, nutmeg and pepper, and sprinkle over a few extra marjoram or oregano leaves.

> COOK'S TIP
> Italian arborio rice is a special short grain rice that gives an authentic creamy consistency.

FRUITY HAM AND FRENCH BREAD PIZZA

French bread makes a great pizza base. For a really speedy recipe, use ready-prepared pizza topping instead of the tomato sauce and cook under a hot grill (broiler) for a few minutes to melt the cheese, instead of baking them in the oven.

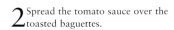

INGREDIENTS

Serves 4

2 small baguettes
300ml/¹/₂ pint/1¹/₄ cups tomato sauce
75g/3oz lean sliced cooked ham
4 canned pineapple rings, drained and chopped
¹/₂ small green (bell) pepper, seeded and cut into thin strips
50g/2oz reduced fat mature Cheddar cheese
salt and black pepper

1 Preheat the oven to 200°C/400°F/ Gas 6. Cut the baguettes in half lengthways and toast the cut sides until crisp and golden.

> **COOK'S TIP**
> If you prefer, omit the ham and substitute cooked chicken, peeled prawns (shrimp) or tuna fish.

2 Spread the tomato sauce over the toasted baguettes.

3 Cut the ham into strips and lay on the baguettes with the pineapple and green pepper. Season to taste with salt and pepper.

4 Grate the cheese and sprinkle on top. Bake for 15–20 minutes until crisp and golden.

NUTRITION NOTES	
Per portion:	
Energy	111Kcals/468.7kJ
Fat	3.31g
Saturated fat	1.63g
Cholesterol	18.25mg
Fibre	0.79g

CRACKED WHEAT AND MINT SALAD

INGREDIENTS

Serves 4

250g/9oz/1⅔ cups cracked wheat
4 tomatoes
4 small courgettes (zucchini), thinly
   sliced lengthways
4 spring onions (scallions), sliced on
   the diagonal
8 ready-to-eat dried apricots, chopped
40g/1½oz/¼ cup raisins
juice of 1 lemon
30ml/2 tbsp tomato juice
45ml/3 tbsp chopped fresh mint
1 garlic clove, crushed
salt and black pepper
sprig of fresh mint, to garnish

1 Put the cracked wheat into a large bowl. Add enough boiling water to come 2.5cm/1in above the level of the wheat. Leave to soak for 30 minutes, then drain well and squeeze out any excess water in a clean dish towel.

2 Meanwhile, plunge the tomatoes into boiling water for 1 minute and then into cold water. Slip off the skins. Halve, remove the seeds and cores and roughly chop the flesh.

3 Stir the tomatoes, courgettes, spring onions, apricots and raisins into the cracked wheat.

4 Put the lemon and tomato juice, mint, garlic clove and seasoning into a small bowl and whisk together with a fork. Pour over the salad and mix well. Chill for at least 1 hour. Serve garnished with a sprig of mint.

NUTRITION NOTES

Per portion:

Energy	293Kcals/1231.7kJ
Fat	1.69g
Saturated fat	0.28g
Fibre	2.25g

CHILLI BEAN BAKE

Contrasting textures make this
a memorable meal.

INGREDIENTS

Serves 4
225g/8oz/1¼ cups red kidney beans
1 bay leaf
1 large onion, finely chopped
1 garlic clove, crushed
2 celery sticks, sliced
5ml/1 tsp ground cumin
5ml/1 tsp chilli powder
400g/14oz can chopped tomatoes
15ml/1 tbsp tomato purée (paste)
5ml/1 tsp dried mixed herbs
15ml/1 tbsp lemon juice
1 yellow (bell) pepper, seeded and diced
salt and black pepper
mixed salad, to serve

For the cornbread topping
175g/6oz/1½ cups corn meal
*15ml/1 tbsp wholemeal (whole-
    wheat) flour*
5ml/1 tsp baking powder
1 egg, beaten
175ml/6fl oz/¾ cup skimmed milk

1 Soak the beans overnight in cold
water. Drain and rinse well. Pour
1 litre/1¾ pints/4 cups water into a
large, heavy pan, add the beans and
bay leaf and boil rapidly for 10 minutes.
Lower the heat, cover and simmer for
35–40 minutes or until the beans
are tender.

NUTRITION NOTES

Per portion:

Energy	399Kcals/1675kJ
Protein	22.86g
Fat	4.65g
Saturated fat	0.86g
Fibre	11.59g

2 Add the onion, garlic, celery, cumin,
chilli powder, chopped tomatoes,
tomato purée and dried mixed herbs.
Half cover the pan with a lid and
simmer for a further 10 minutes.

3 Stir in the lemon juice, yellow pepper
and seasoning. Simmer for a further
8–10 minutes, stirring occasionally,
until the vegetables are just tender.
Discard the bay leaf and spoon the
mixture into a large casserole.

4 Preheat the oven to 220°C/425°F/
Gas 7. To make the topping, put the
corn meal, flour, baking powder and a
pinch of salt into a bowl and mix
together. Make a well in the centre and
add the egg and milk. Mix and pour
over the bean mixture. Bake in the oven
for 20 minutes or until brown. Serve
hot with mixed salad.

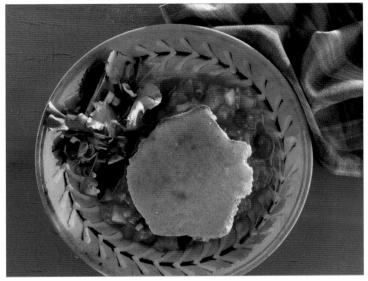

SPICY BEAN HOT POT

INGREDIENTS

Serves 4

225g/8oz/3 cups button (white)
  mushrooms
15ml/1 tbsp sunflower oil
2 onions, sliced
1 garlic clove, crushed
15ml/1 tbsp red wine vinegar
400g/14oz can chopped tomatoes
15ml/1 tbsp tomato purée (paste)
15ml/1 tbsp Worcestershire sauce
15ml/1 tbsp wholegrain mustard
15ml/1 tbsp soft dark brown sugar
250ml/8fl oz/1 cup vegetable stock
400g/14oz can red kidney beans, drained
400g/14oz can haricot (navy) or
  cannellini beans, drained
1 bay leaf
75g/3oz/¹/2 cup raisins
salt and black pepper
chopped fresh parsley, to garnish

1 Wipe the mushrooms, then cut them into small pieces. Set aside.

2 Heat the oil in a large pan or flame-proof casserole, add the onions and garlic and cook over a gentle heat for 10 minutes until soft.

3 Add all the remaining ingredients except the mushrooms and seasoning. Bring to the boil, lower the heat and simmer for 10 minutes.

4 Add the mushrooms and simmer for 5 minutes more. Stir in salt and pepper to taste. Transfer to warm plates and sprinkle with parsley.

NUTRITION NOTES

Per portion:

Energy	280Kcals/1175kJ
Fat	4.5g
Saturated fat	0.5g
Cholesterol	0mg

TOMATO RICE

This dish is delicious and is substantial enough to be eaten as a complete meal on its own.

INGREDIENTS

Serves 4
30ml/2 tbsp corn oil
2.5ml/½ tsp onion seeds
1 onion, sliced
2 tomatoes, sliced
1 orange or yellow (bell) pepper, chopped
5ml/1 tsp grated fresh root ginger
1 garlic clove, crushed
5ml/1 tsp chilli powder
*30ml/2 tbsp chopped fresh
    coriander (cilantro)*
1 potato, diced
7.5ml/1½ tsp salt
50g/2oz/½ cup frozen peas
400g/14oz/2 cups basmati rice, washed
700ml/24fl oz/2¼ cups water

NUTRITION NOTES

Per portion:
Energy	351kcals/1475kJ
Fat	6.48g
Saturated fat	0.86g
Cholesterol	0mg

1 Heat the oil and fry the onion seeds for about 30 seconds. Add the sliced onion and fry for about 5 minutes, until soft.

2 Add the next nine ingredients and stir-fry over a medium heat for a further 5 minutes.

3 Add the rice and stir-fry for about 1 minute.

4 Pour in the water and bring to the boil, then lower the heat to medium. Cover and cook for 12–15 minutes more, until the rice is tender. Leave to stand for 5 minutes, then serve.

PEA AND MUSHROOM PILAU

It is best to use whole button mushrooms and petits pois for this delectable rice dish, as they make the pilau look very attractive and appetizing.

INGREDIENTS

Serves 6
450g/1lb/2¼ cups basmati rice
30ml/2 tbsp vegetable oil
2.5ml/½ tsp black cumin seeds
2 black cardamom pods
2 cinnamon sticks
3 garlic cloves, sliced
5ml/1 tsp salt
1 tomato, sliced
50g/2oz/⅔ cup button (white) mushrooms
75g/3oz petits pois (baby peas)
750ml/1¼ pints/3 cups water

1 Wash the rice at least twice and set aside in a sieve (strainer).

NUTRITION NOTES

Per portion:
Energy	297kcals/1246kJ
Fat	4.34g
Saturated fat	0.49g
Cholesterol	0mg

2 Heat the oil in a medium pan and add the spices, garlic and salt.

3 Add the sliced tomato and button mushrooms, and stir-fry for about 2–3 minutes.

4 Add the rice and peas, and gently stir around making sure you do not break the rice.

5 Add the water and bring the mixture to the boil. Lower the heat, cover, and continue to cook for a further 15–20 minutes, until the rice is tender. Serve hot.

SPINACH AND HAZELNUT LASAGNE

A vegetarian dish which is hearty enough to satisfy meat-eaters too. Use frozen spinach if you're short of time.

INGREDIENTS

Serves 4
900g/2lb fresh spinach
300ml/½ pint/1¼ cups vegetable stock
1 medium onion, finely chopped
1 garlic clove, crushed
75g/3oz/¾ cup hazelnuts
30ml/2 tbsp chopped fresh basil
6 sheets no pre-cook lasagne
400g/14oz can chopped tomatoes
200g/7oz/1 cup low-fat fromage frais
* or crème fraîche*
salt and ground black pepper
sliced hazelnuts and chopped parsley,
* to garnish*

1 Preheat the oven to 200°C/400°F/ Gas 6. Wash the spinach and place in a pan with just the water that clings to the leaves. Cook the spinach on a fairly high heat for 2 minutes until wilted. Drain well.

2 Heat 30ml/2 tbsp of the stock in a large pan and simmer the onion and garlic until soft. Stir in the spinach, hazelnuts and basil.

3 In a large ovenproof dish, layer the spinach, lasagne and tomatoes. Season between the layers. Pour over the remaining stock. Spread the fromage frais or crème fraîche on top.

4 Bake the lasagne for about 45 minutes, or until golden brown. Serve hot, sprinkled with lines of sliced hazelnuts and chopped parsley.

> COOK'S TIP
> If you like, you can roast the hazelnuts on a baking sheet in the oven at 180°C/350°/Gas 4, or under a hot grill (broiler), until light golden.

NUTRITION NOTES

Per portion:
Energy	365kcals/1532kJ
Fat	17g
Saturated fat	1.46g
Cholesterol	0.5mg
Fibre	8.16g

CALZONE

INGREDIENTS

Makes 4
450g/1lb/4 cups plain (all-purpose)
flour
pinch of salt
1 sachet easy-blend (rapid-rise) yeast
about 350ml/12fl oz/1½ cups
warm water
skimmed milk, to glaze
salt and ground black pepper

For the filling
5ml/1 tsp olive oil
1 medium red onion, thinly sliced
3 courgettes (zucchini), sliced
2 large tomatoes, diced
150g/5oz mozzarella cheese, diced
15ml/1 tbsp chopped fresh oregano

1 To make the dough, sift the flour and salt into a bowl and stir in the yeast. Stir in just enough warm water to mix to a soft dough.

2 Knead for 5 minutes until smooth. Cover and leave in a warm place for about 1 hour, or until doubled in size.

3 Meanwhile, to make the filling, heat the oil and sauté the onion and courgettes for 3–4 minutes. Remove from the heat and add the tomatoes, cheese, oregano and seasoning.

4 Preheat the oven to 220°C/425°F/ Gas 7. Knead the dough lightly and divide into four. Roll out each piece on a lightly floured surface to a 20cm/8in round and place a quarter of the filling on one half.

5 Brush the edges with milk and fold over to enclose the filling. Press firmly to enclose. Brush with milk.

6 Bake on an oiled baking sheet for 15–20 minutes, until golden. Serve hot or cold.

NUTRITION NOTES

Per portion:
Energy	544kcals/2285kJ
Fat	10.93g
Saturated fat	5.49g
Cholesterol	24.42mg
Fibre	5.09g

BEAN PUREE WITH GRILLED CHICORY

The slightly bitter flavours of the radicchio and chicory make a wonderful marriage with the creamy bean purée. Walnut oil adds a nutty taste, but olive oil could also be used.

COOK'S TIP
Other suitable beans are haricot (navy), mung or broad (lima).

INGREDIENTS

Serves 4
400g/14oz can cannellini beans
45ml/3 tbsp low fat fromage frais
finely grated rind and juice of
 1 large orange
15ml/1 tbsp finely chopped
 fresh rosemary
4 heads of chicory
2 medium heads of radicchio
10ml/2 tbsp walnut oil
shreds of orange rind, to garnish
 (optional)

1 Drain the beans, rinse, and drain again. Purée the beans in a blender or food processor with the fromage frais, orange rind, orange juice and rosemary. Set aside.

2 Cut the heads of chicory in half lengthwise.

3 Cut each radicchio head into eight wedges. Preheat the grill (broiler).

4 Lay out the chicory and radicchio on a baking tray and brush with the walnut oil. Grill (broil) for 2–3 minutes. Serve with the purée and sprinkle over the orange shreds, if using.

NUTRITION NOTES	
Per portion:	
Energy	103Kcals/432kJ
Protein	6.22g
Fat	1.54g
Saturated fat	0.4g
Fibre	6.73g

LENTIL BOLOGNESE

A really useful sauce to serve with pasta, as a pancake stuffing or even as a protein-packed sauce for vegetables.

INGREDIENTS

Serves 6
45ml/3 tbsp olive oil
1 onion, chopped
2 garlic cloves, crushed
2 carrots, coarsely grated
2 celery sticks, chopped
115g/4oz/⅔ cup red lentils
400g/14oz can chopped tomatoes
30ml/2 tbsp tomato purée (paste)
450ml/¾ pint/2 cups stock
15ml/1 tbsp fresh marjoram, chopped,
   or 5ml/1 tsp dried marjoram
salt and black pepper

1 Heat the oil in a large pan and gently fry the onion, garlic, carrots and celery for about 5 minutes, until they are soft.

NUTRITION NOTES

Per portion:
Energy	103Kcals/432kJ
Fat	2.19g
Saturated fat	0.85g
Fibre	2.15g

2 Add the lentils, tomatoes, tomato purée, stock, marjoram and seasoning to the pan.

3 Bring the mixture to the boil, then partially cover with a lid and simmer for 20 minutes until thick and soft. Use the sauce as required.

> COOK'S TIP
> You can easily reduce the fat in this recipe by using less olive oil, or substituting a little of the stock and cooking the vegetables over a low heat in a non-stick frying pan until they are soft.

VEGETABLE BIRYANI

This exotic dish made from everyday ingredients will be appreciated by vegetarians and meat-eaters alike. It is extremely low in fat, but packed full of exciting flavours.

NUTRITION NOTES

Per portion:

Energy	175Kcals/737kJ
Protein	3.66g
Fat	0.78g
Saturated fat	0.12g
Fibre	0.58g

INGREDIENTS

Serves 4–6

175g/6oz/1 cup long grain rice
2 whole cloves
seeds of 2 cardamom pods
450ml/³⁄₄ pint/scant 2 cups vegetable
   stock
2 garlic cloves
1 small onion, roughly chopped
5ml/1 tsp cumin seeds
5ml/1 tsp ground coriander
2.5ml/¹⁄₂ tsp ground turmeric
2.5ml/¹⁄₂ tsp chilli powder
1 large potato, peeled and cut into
   2.5cm/1in cubes
2 carrots, sliced
¹⁄₂ cauliflower, broken into florets
50g/2oz French (green) beans, cut into
   2.5cm/1in lengths
30ml/2 tbsp chopped fresh coriander
   (cilantro)
30ml/2 tbsp lime juice
salt and black pepper
sprig of fresh coriander (cilantro),
   to garnish

COOK'S TIP
Substitute other vegetables, if you like. Courgettes (zucchini), broccoli, parsnips and sweet potatoes would all be good choices.

1 Put the rice, cloves and cardamom seeds into a large, heavy pan. Pour over the stock and bring to the boil.

2 Reduce the heat, cover and simmer for 20 minutes, or until all the stock has been absorbed.

3 Meanwhile put the garlic cloves, onion, cumin seeds, coriander, turmeric, chilli powder and seasoning into a blender or coffee grinder together with 30ml/2 tbsp water. Blend to a smooth paste.

4 Preheat the oven to 180°C/350°F/ Gas 4. Spoon the spicy paste into a flameproof casserole and cook over a low heat for 2 minutes, stirring occasionally.

5 Add the potato, carrots, cauliflower florets, beans and 90ml/6 tbsp water. Cover and cook over a low heat for a further 12 minutes, stirring occasionally. Add the chopped coriander.

6 Remove the cloves and spoon the rice over the vegetables. Sprinkle over the lime juice. Cover and cook in the oven for 25 minutes, or until the vegetables are tender. Fluff up the rice with a fork before serving and garnish with a sprig of fresh coriander.

COCONUT RICE

A delicious alternative to plain boiled rice, brown or white rice will both work well.

INGREDIENTS

Serves 6
450g/1lb/2 cups long grain rice
250ml/8fl oz/1 cup water
475ml/16fl oz/2 cups coconut milk
2.5ml/¹/₂ tsp salt
30ml/2 tbsp granulated sugar
fresh shredded coconut, to garnish

1 Wash the rice in cold water until it runs clear. Place the water, coconut milk, salt and sugar in a heavy pan or flameproof casserole.

COOK'S TIP
Coconut milk is available in cans, but if you cannot find it, use creamed coconut mixed with water according to the packet instructions.

2 Add the rice, cover and bring to the boil. Reduce the heat to low and simmer for about 15–20 minutes or until the rice is tender to the bite and cooked through.

3 Turn off the heat and allow the rice to rest in the pan for a further 5–10 minutes.

4 Fluff up the rice with chopsticks or a fork before serving garnished with shredded coconut.

NUTRITION NOTES	
Per portion:	
Energy	322.5Kcals/1371kJ
Fat	2.49g
Saturated fat	1.45g
Cholesterol	0mg
Fibre	0.68g

JASMINE RICE

Perfectly cooked rice makes an ideal, low fat accompaniment to many low fat dishes such as vegetable chilli and vegetable bolognese.

INGREDIENTS

Serves 6

450g/1lb/2 cups long grain rice
750ml/1¼ pints/3 cups cold water
2.5ml/½ tsp salt

NUTRITION NOTES

Per portion:

Energy	270.8Kcals/1152kJ
Fat	0.75g
Saturated fat	0g
Cholesterol	0mg
Fibre	0.37g

COOK'S TIP
An electric rice cooker both cooks the rice and keeps it warm. Different sizes and models are available. The top of the range is a non-stick version, which is expensive, but well worth the money if you eat rice a lot.

1 Rinse the rice in several changes of cold water until the water stays clear.

2 Put the rice in a heavy pan or flameproof casserole and add the water and salt. Bring the rice to a vigorous boil, uncovered, over a high heat.

3 Stir and reduce the heat to low. Cover and simmer for up to 20 minutes, or until all the water has been absorbed. Remove from the heat and leave to stand for 10 minutes.

4 Remove the lid and stir the rice gently with chopsticks or a fork to fluff up and separate the grains.

BULGUR AND LENTIL PILAF

Bulgur wheat can be used in almost any way you would normally use rice, hot or cold. Some of the finer grades need hardly any cooking, so check the pack for cooking times.

INGREDIENTS

Serves 4
5ml/1 tsp olive oil
1 large onion, thinly sliced
2 garlic cloves, crushed
5ml/1 tsp ground coriander
5ml/1 tsp ground cumin
5ml/1 tsp ground turmeric
2.5ml/½ tsp ground allspice
225g/8oz/1¼ cups bulgur wheat
about 750ml/1¼ pints/3 cups stock
    or water
115g/4oz/1½ cups button (white)
    mushrooms, sliced
115g/4oz/½ cup green lentils
salt, ground black pepper and
    cayenne pepper

1 Heat the oil in a non-stick pan and fry the onion, garlic and spices for 1 minute, stirring.

2 Stir in the bulgur wheat and cook, stirring, for about 2 minutes, until lightly browned. Add the stock or water, mushrooms and lentils.

3 Simmer over a very low heat for about 25–30 minutes, until the bulgur wheat and lentils are tender and all the liquid is absorbed. Add more stock or water, if necessary.

4 Season with salt, pepper and cayenne, and serve hot.

COOK'S TIP
Green lentils can be cooked without pre-soaking, as they cook quite quickly and keep their shape. However, if you have the time, soaking them first will shorten the cooking time slightly.

NUTRITION NOTES

Per portion:
Energy	325kcals/1367kJ
Fat	2.8g
Saturated fat	0.33g
Cholesterol	0mg
Fibre	3.61g

MINTED COUSCOUS CASTLES

Couscous is a fine semolina made from wheat grain, which is usually steamed and served plain with a meat or vegetable stew. Here it is flavoured with mint and moulded to make an unusual accompaniment to serve with any savoury dish.

INGREDIENTS

Serves 6
225g/8oz/1¼ cups couscous
475ml/16fl oz/2 cups boiling stock
15ml/1 tbsp lemon juice
2 tomatoes, diced
30ml/2 tbsp chopped fresh mint
oil, for brushing
salt and ground black pepper
mint sprigs, to garnish

1 Place the couscous in a bowl and pour over the boiling stock. Cover the bowl and leave to stand for 30 minutes, until all the stock is absorbed and the grains are tender.

2 Stir in the lemon juice with the tomatoes and chopped mint. Adjust the seasoning with salt and pepper.

3 Brush the insides of four cups or individual moulds with oil. Spoon in the couscous mixture and pack down firmly. Chill for several hours.

4 Turn out and serve cold, or cover and heat gently in a low oven or microwave, then turn out and serve hot, garnished with mint.

COOK'S TIP
Most packet couscous is now the ready-cooked variety, which can be cooked as above, but some types need steaming first, so check the pack instructions.

NUTRITION NOTES

Per portion:
Energy	95kcals/397kJ
Fat	0.53g
Saturated fat	0.07g
Cholesterol	0mg
Fibre	0.29g

CORN GRIDDLE PANCAKES

These crisp pancakes are delicious to serve as a snack lunch, or as a light supper with a crisp mixed salad.

INGREDIENTS

Serves 4, makes about 12
115g/4oz/1 cup self-raising
   (self-rising) flour
1 egg white
150ml/¼ pint/⅔ cup skimmed milk
200g/7oz can corn, drained
oil, for brushing
salt and ground black pepper
tomato chutney, to serve

2 Season the batter and add the remaining corn.

1 Place the flour, egg white and skimmed milk in a food processor or blender with half the corn, and process until smooth.

3 Heat a frying pan and brush with oil. Drop in tablespoons of batter and cook until set. Turn over the pancakes and cook the other side until golden. Serve hot with tomato chutney.

NUTRITION NOTES

Per portion:
Energy	162kcals/680kJ
Fat	0.89g
Saturated fat	0.14g
Cholesterol	0.75mg
Fibre	1.49g

BAKED POLENTA WITH TOMATOES

INGREDIENTS

Serves 4
750ml/1¼ pints/3 cups stock
175g/6oz/1⅛ cups polenta
60ml/4 tbsp chopped fresh sage
5ml/1 tsp olive oil
2 beefsteak tomatoes, sliced
15ml/1 tbsp freshly grated
   Parmesan cheese
salt and ground black pepper

1 Bring the stock to the boil in a large pan, then gradually stir in the polenta.

2 Continue stirring the polenta over a medium heat for about 5 minutes, until the mixture begins to come away from the sides of the pan. Stir in the chopped sage and season, then spoon into a lightly oiled, shallow 23 × 33cm/ 9 × 13in tin (pan) and spread evenly. Leave to cool.

3 Preheat the oven to 200°C/400°F/ Gas 6. Cut the cooled polenta into 24 squares using a sharp knife.

4 Arrange the polenta overlapping with tomato slices in a lightly oiled, shallow ovenproof dish. Sprinkle with Parmesan and bake for 20 minutes or until golden brown. Serve hot.

NUTRITION NOTES

Per portion:
Energy	200kcals/842kJ
Fat	3.8g
Saturated fat	0.77g
Cholesterol	1.88mg
Fibre	1.71g

LEMON AND HERB RISOTTO CAKE

This unusual rice dish can be served as a main course with salad, or as a satisfying side dish. It's also good served cold, and packs well for picnics.

INGREDIENTS

Serves 4
1 small leek, thinly sliced
600ml/1 pint/2½ cups chicken stock
225g/8oz/1 cup short grain rice
finely grated rind of 1 lemon
30ml/2 tbsp chopped fresh chives
30ml/2 tbsp chopped fresh parsley
75g/3oz/¾ cup grated
*   mozzarella cheese*
salt and ground black pepper
parsley and lemon wedges, to garnish

1 Preheat the oven to 200°C/400°F/ Gas 6. Lightly oil a 21cm/8½in round, loose-based cake tin (pan).

2 Cook the leek in a large pan with 45ml/3 tbsp stock, stirring over a medium heat, to soften. Add the rice and the remaining stock.

3 Bring to the boil. Cover the pan and simmer gently, stirring occasionally, for about 20 minutes, or until all the liquid is absorbed.

4 Stir in the lemon rind, herbs, cheese and seasoning. Spoon into the tin, cover with foil and bake for 30–35 minutes or until lightly browned. Turn out and serve in slices, garnished with parsley and lemon wedges.

COOK'S TIP
The best type of rice to choose for this recipe is the Italian round grain arborio rice, but if it is not available, use pudding rice instead.

NUTRITION NOTES	
Per portion:	
Energy	280kcals/1176kJ
Fat	6.19g
Saturated fat	2.54g
Cholesterol	12.19mg
Fibre	0.9g

RICE WITH SEEDS AND SPICES

A change from plain boiled rice, and a colourful accompaniment to serve with spicy curries or grilled meats. Basmati rice gives the best texture and flavour, but you can use ordinary long grain rice instead, if you prefer.

INGREDIENTS

Serves 4

5ml/1 tsp sunflower oil
2.5ml/½ tsp ground turmeric
6 cardamom pods, lightly crushed
5ml/1 tsp coriander seeds, lightly crushed
1 garlic clove, crushed
200g/7oz/1 cup basmati rice
400ml/14fl oz/1⅔ cups stock
115g/4oz/½ cup low-fat natural
   (plain) yogurt
15ml/1 tbsp toasted sunflower seeds
15ml/1 tbsp toasted sesame seeds
salt and ground black pepper
coriander (cilantro) leaves, to garnish

1 Heat the oil in a non-stick pan and fry the spices and garlic for about 1 minute, stirring all the time.

2 Add the rice and stock, bring to the boil then cover and simmer for 15 minutes or until just tender.

3 Stir in the yogurt and the toasted sunflower and sesame seeds. Adjust the seasoning and serve hot, garnished with coriander leaves.

NUTRITION NOTES

Per portion:

Energy	243kcals/1022kJ
Fat	5.5g
Saturated fat	0.73g
Cholesterol	1.15mg
Fibre	0.57g

COOK'S TIP
Seeds are rich in minerals, so they are a good addition to all kinds of dishes. Light toasting (as recipe) will improve their flavour.

MEAT AND POULTRY

Make the most of the wide range of leaner cuts of red meat available to make light and nutritious main courses that are packed with flavour. Poultry and game are mostly very low in fat, and much of the fat they do contain is unsaturated. Chicken, always a favourite choice for family meals, is versatile and economical. Turkey is now available in so many different cuts that it is interchangeable with chicken, and minced (ground) turkey can take the place of beef or lamb in bakes and pasta dishes. Game is perfect for special occasions – try Autumn Pheasant or Cider Baked Rabbit. Other tempting dishes include Fragrant Chicken Curry or Turkey Pastitsio.

THAI BEEF SALAD

Serves 6
75g/3oz lean sirloin steaks
1 red onion, finely sliced
¹/₂ cucumber, finely sliced
  into matchsticks
1 lemon grass stalk, finely chopped
30ml/2 tbsp chopped spring onions
  (scallions)
juice of 2 limes
15–30ml/1–2 tbsp fish sauce
2–4 red chillies, finely sliced, to garnish
fresh coriander (cilantro), Chinese
  mustard cress (fine curled cress) and
  mint leaves, to garnish

─── NUTRITION NOTES ───

Per portion:
Energy	101Kcals/424kJ
Fat	3.8g
Saturated fat	1.7g
Cholesterol	33.4mg
Fibre	0.28g

COOK'S TIP
Rump (round) or fillet steaks
would work just as well in this
recipe. Choose good-quality lean
steaks and remove and discard
any visible fat.

1 Grill (broil) the sirloin steaks until
they are medium-rare, then allow to
rest for 10–15 minutes.

2 When cool, thinly slice the beef and
put the slices in a large bowl.

3 Add the sliced onion, cucumber
matchsticks and lemon grass.

4 Add the spring onions. Toss and
season with lime juice and fish
sauce. Serve at room temperature or
chilled, garnished with the chillies,
coriander, mustard cress and mint.

RAGOUT OF VEAL

If you are looking for a low-calorie dish to treat yourself – or some guests – then this is perfect, and quick, too.

INGREDIENTS

Serves 4

375g/12oz veal fillet or loin
10ml/2 tsp olive oil
10–12 tiny onions, kept whole
1 yellow (bell) pepper, seeded and cut
  into eighths
1 orange or red (bell) pepper, seeded
  and cut into eighths
3 tomatoes, peeled and quartered
4 fresh basil sprigs
30ml/2 tbsp dry martini or sherry
salt and black pepper

NUTRITION NOTES

Per portion:
Energy	158Kcals/665.5kJ
Fat	4.97g
Saturated fat	1.14g
Cholesterol	63mg
Fibre	2.5g

1 Trim off any fat and cut the veal into cubes. Heat the oil in a frying pan and gently stir-fry the veal and onions until browned.

2 After a couple of minutes, add the peppers and tomatoes. Continue stir-frying for another 4–5 minutes.

COOK'S TIP
Lean beef or pork fillet may be used instead of veal, if you prefer. Shallots can replace the onions.

3 Add half the basil leaves, roughly chopped (keep some for garnish), the martini or sherry and seasoning. Cook, stirring frequently, for another 10 minutes, or until the meat is tender.

4 Sprinkle with the remaining basil leaves and serve hot.

VENISON WITH CRANBERRY SAUCE

Venison steaks are now readily available. Lean and low in fat, they make a healthy choice for a special occasion. Served with a sauce of fresh cranberries, port and ginger, they make a dish with a wonderful combination of flavours.

INGREDIENTS

Serves 4

1 orange
1 lemon
75g/3oz/1 cup fresh or frozen
  cranberries
5ml/1 tsp grated fresh root ginger
1 thyme sprig, plus extra to garnish
5ml/1 tsp Dijon mustard
60ml/4 tbsp redcurrant jelly
150ml/¼ pint/⅔ cup ruby port
10ml/2 tsp sunflower oil
4 x 90g/3½oz venison steaks
2 shallots, finely chopped
salt and black pepper
mashed potato and broccoli, to serve

NUTRITION NOTES

Per portion:	
Energy	250Kcals/1055.5kJ
Fat	4.39g
Saturated fat	1.13g
Cholesterol	50mg
Fibre	1.59g

COOK'S TIP
When frying venison, always remember: the briefer the better. Venison will turn to leather if subjected to fierce heat after it has reached the medium-rare stage. If you dislike any hint of pink, cook it to this stage, then let it rest in a low oven for a few minutes.

1 Pare the rind from half the orange and half the lemon using a vegetable peeler, then cut into very fine strips.

2 Blanch the strips in a small pan of boiling water for about 5 minutes until tender. Drain the strips and refresh under cold water.

3 Squeeze the juice from the orange and lemon, then pour into a small pan. Add the cranberries, ginger, thyme sprig, mustard, redcurrant jelly and port. Cook over a low heat until the jelly melts.

4 Bring the sauce to the boil, stirring occasionally, then cover the pan and reduce the heat. Cook gently for about 15 minutes, until the cranberries are just tender.

VARIATION
When fresh cranberries are unavailable, use redcurrants instead. Stir them into the sauce towards the end of cooking with the orange and lemon rinds.

5 Heat the oil in a heavy-based frying pan, add the venison steaks and cook over a high heat for 2–3 minutes.

6 Turn over the steaks and add the shallots to the pan. Cook the steaks on the other side for 2–3 minutes, depending on whether you like rare or medium-cooked meat.

7 Just before the end of cooking, pour in the sauce and add the strips of orange and lemon rind.

8 Leave the sauce to bubble for a few seconds to thicken slightly, then remove the thyme sprig and adjust the seasoning to taste.

9 Transfer the venison steaks to warmed plates and spoon over the sauce. Garnish with thyme sprigs and serve accompanied by mashed potato and broccoli.

PORK AND CELERY POPOVERS

Lower in fat than they look, and a good way to make the meat go further, these little popovers will be popular with children.

INGREDIENTS

Serves 4

sunflower oil, for brushing
150g/5oz plain (all-purpose) flour
1 egg white
250ml/8fl oz/1 cup skimmed milk
120ml/4fl oz/½ cup water
350g/12oz lean minced (ground) pork
2 celery sticks, finely chopped
45ml/3 tbsp rolled oats
30ml/2 tbsp chopped fresh chives
15ml/1 tbsp Worcestershire or brown sauce
salt and ground black pepper

1 Preheat the oven to 220°C/425°F/ Gas 7. Brush 12 deep patty tins (muffin pans) with a very little oil.

2 Place the flour in a bowl and make a well in the centre. Add the egg white and milk and gradually beat in the flour. Gradually add the water, beating until smooth and bubbly.

3 Place the minced pork, celery, oats, chives, Worcestershire or brown sauce and seasoning in a bowl and mix thoroughly. Mould the mixture into 12 small balls and place in the patty tins.

4 Cook for 10 minutes, remove from the oven and quickly pour the batter into the tins. Cook for a further 20–25 minutes, or until well risen and golden brown. Serve hot with thin gravy and fresh vegetables.

NUTRITION NOTES	
Per portion:	
Energy	344kcals/1443kJ
Fat	9.09g
Saturated fat	2.7g
Cholesterol	61.62mg
Fibre	2.37g

BEEF AND MUSHROOM BURGERS

It's worth making your own burgers to cut down on fat – in these the meat is extended with mushrooms for extra fibre.

INGREDIENTS

Serves 4

1 small onion, chopped
150g/5oz/2 cups mushrooms
450g/1lb lean minced (ground) beef
50g/2oz/1 cup fresh wholemeal
  (whole-wheat) breadcrumbs
5ml/1 tsp dried mixed herbs
15ml/1 tbsp tomato purée (paste)
flour, for shaping
salt and ground black pepper

1 Place the onion and mushrooms in a food processor and process until finely chopped. Add the beef, bread-crumbs, herbs, tomato purée and seasonings. Process for a few seconds, until the mixture binds together but still has some texture.

2 Divide the mixture into 8–10 pieces, then press into burger shapes using lightly floured hands.

3 Cook the burgers in a non-stick frying pan, or under a hot grill (broiler), for 12–15 minutes, turning once, until evenly cooked. Serve with relish and salad, in burger buns or pitta bread.

COOK'S TIP
The mixture is quite soft, so handle carefully and use a fish slice or metal spatula for turning to prevent the burgers from breaking up during cooking.

NUTRITION NOTES

Per portion:

Energy	196kcals/822kJ
Fat	5.9g
Saturated fat	2.21g
Cholesterol	66.37mg
Fibre	1.60g

CURRIED LAMB AND LENTILS

This colourful curry is packed with protein and low in fat.

INGREDIENTS

Serves 4
8 lean, boneless lamb leg steaks, about
    500g/1¼lb total weight
1 medium onion, chopped
2 medium carrots, diced
1 celery stick, chopped
15ml/1 tbsp hot curry paste
30ml/2 tbsp tomato purée (paste)
475ml/16fl oz/2 cups stock
175g/6oz/¾ cup green lentils
salt and ground black pepper
coriander (cilantro) leaves, to garnish
boiled rice, to serve

1 In a large, non-stick pan, fry the lamb steaks without fat until browned, turning once.

2 Add the vegetables and cook for 2 minutes, then stir in the curry paste, tomato purée, stock and lentils.

3 Bring to the boil, cover and simmer gently for 30 minutes until tender. Add more stock, if necessary. Season and serve with coriander and rice.

NUTRITION NOTES

Per portion:
Energy	375kcals/1575kJ
Fat	13.03g
Saturated fat	5.34g
Cholesterol	98.75mg
Fibre	6.11g

GOLDEN PORK AND APRICOT CASSEROLE

The rich golden colour and warm spicy flavour of this simple casserole make it ideal for chilly winter days.

INGREDIENTS

Serves 4
4 lean pork loin chops
1 medium onion, thinly sliced
2 yellow (bell) peppers, seeded and sliced
10ml/2 tsp medium curry powder
15ml/1 tbsp plain (all-purpose) flour
250ml/8fl oz/1 cup chicken stock
115g/4oz/½ cup ready-to-eat
    dried apricots
30ml/2 tbsp wholegrain mustard
salt and ground black pepper

1 Trim the excess fat from the pork and fry without fat in a large, heavy or non-stick pan until lightly browned.

2 Add the onion and peppers to the pan and stir over medium heat for 5 minutes. Stir in the curry powder and the flour.

3 Add the stock, stirring, then add the apricots and mustard. Cover and simmer for 25–30 minutes, until tender. Adjust the seasoning and serve hot, with rice or new potatoes.

NUTRITION NOTES

Per portion:
Energy	289kcals/1213kJ
Fat	10.03g
Saturated fat	3.23g
Cholesterol	82.8mg
Fibre	4.86g

STUFFED AUBERGINES WITH LAMB

INGREDIENTS

Serves 4

2 aubergines (eggplants)
30ml/2 tbsp sunflower oil
1 onion, sliced
5ml/1 tsp grated fresh root ginger
5ml/1 tsp chilli powder
1 garlic clove, crushed
1.5ml/¼ tsp turmeric
5ml/1 tsp salt
5ml/1 tsp ground coriander
1 tomato, chopped
350g/12oz lean leg of lamb,
   minced (ground)
1 green (bell) pepper, roughly chopped
1 orange (bell) pepper, roughly chopped
30ml/2 tbsp chopped fresh
   coriander (cilantro)
green salad or plain boiled rice,
   to serve

NUTRITION NOTES

Per portion:
Energy	239kcals/1003kJ
Fat	13.92g
Saturated fat	4.36g
Cholesterol	67.15mg

1 Cut the aubergines in half lengthways and cut out most of the flesh and discard. Place the aubergine shells in a lightly greased ovenproof dish.

2 In a pan, heat 15ml/1 tbsp of the oil and fry the onion until golden. Gradually stir in the ginger, chilli powder, garlic, turmeric, salt and ground coriander. Add the tomato and stir-fry for 5 minutes.

3 Preheat the oven to 180°C/350°F/ Gas 4. Add the minced lamb and stir-fry over a medium heat for a further 7–10 minutes.

4 Add the chopped peppers and fresh coriander to the lamb mixture, and stir well.

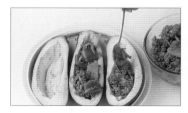

5 Spoon the lamb mixture into the aubergine shells and brush the edges of the shells with the remaining oil. Bake in the preheated oven for about 20–25 minutes until cooked through and browned on top.

6 Serve with either a green salad or plain boiled rice.

COOK'S TIP

For a special occasion, stuffed baby aubergines look particularly attractive. Use four small aubergines, leaving the stalks intact, and prepare and cook as described above. Reduce the baking time slightly, if necessary. Large tomatoes or courgettes (zucchini) also make a good alternative to aubergines.

BEEF WITH GREEN BEANS

This easy-to-cook curried dish is
a delicious variation on a
traditional Indian recipe.

INGREDIENTS

Serves 4

275g/10oz fine green beans, cut into
   2.5cm/1in pieces
30ml/2 tbsp sunflower oil
1 medium onion, sliced
5ml/1 tsp grated fresh root ginger
1 garlic clove, crushed
5ml/1 tsp chilli powder
6.5ml/1¼ tsp salt
1.5ml/¼ tsp turmeric
2 tomatoes, chopped
450g/1lb lean beef, cubed
1.2 litres/2 pints/5 cups water
1 red (bell) pepper, sliced
15ml/1 tbsp chopped fresh coriander
   (cilantro)
2 green chillies, chopped

1 Cook the green beans in a pan of
boiling salted water for about
5 minutes, then drain and set aside.

3 Mix together the ginger, garlic, chilli
powder, salt, turmeric and chopped
tomatoes. Spoon into the onions and
stir-fry for about 5–7 minutes.

4 Add the beef and stir-fry for a
further 3 minutes. Pour in the
water, bring to the boil and lower
the heat. Cover and cook for 45–60
minutes until most of the water has
evaporated and the meat is tender.

6 Finally, add the red pepper, fresh
coriander and chopped green chillies
and cook for a further 7–10 minutes,
stirring occasionally. Serve hot with
wholemeal (whole-wheat) chapatis.

2 Heat the oil in a large pan and
fry the sliced onion until golden.

5 Add the green beans and mix
everything together well.

NUTRITION NOTES	
Per portion:	
Energy	241Kcals/1012kJ
Fat	11.6g
Saturated fat	2.89g
Cholesterol	66.96mg

MEXICAN BEEFBURGERS

Nothing beats the flavour and quality of a home-made burger. This version is from Mexico and is delicately seasoned with cumin and fresh coriander.

INGREDIENTS

Makes 4

4 corn on the cob
50g/2oz/1 cup stale white breadcrumbs
90ml/6 tbsp skimmed milk
1 small onion, finely chopped
5ml/1 tsp ground cumin
2.5ml/½ tsp cayenne pepper
2.5ml/½ tsp celery salt
45ml/3 tbsp chopped fresh coriander (cilantro)
900g/2lb lean minced (ground) beef
4 sesame buns
60ml/4 tbsp reduced-calorie mayonnaise
4 tomato slices
½ iceberg lettuce or other leaves such as frisée
salt and ground black pepper
1 large packet corn chips, to serve

1 Cook the corn in a large pan of boiling water for approximately 15 minutes.

2 Combine the breadcrumbs, skimmed milk, onion, cumin, cayenne, celery salt and fresh coriander together in a large bowl.

3 Add the beef and mix by hand until the mixture is evenly blended.

4 Divide the beef mixture into four portions and flatten between sheets of clear film (plastic wrap).

5 Preheat the grill (broiler) and cook for about 10 minutes for medium, or 15 minutes for well-done burgers.

6 Split and toast the buns, spread with mayonnaise and sandwich the burgers with the tomato slices, lettuce leaves and seasoning. Serve with corn chips and the corn on the cob.

NUTRITION NOTES	
Per portion:	
Energy	563kcals/2363kJ
Fat	18.82g
Saturated fat	5.55g
Cholesterol	133.2mg

PORK STEAKS WITH GREMOLATA

Gremolata is a popular Italian dressing of garlic, lemon and parsley – it adds a hint of sharpness to the pork.

─── INGREDIENTS ───

Serves 4
30ml/2 tbsp olive oil
4 lean pork shoulder steaks, about
*   175g/6oz each*
1 onion, chopped
2 garlic cloves, crushed
30ml/2 tbsp tomato purée (paste)
400g/14oz can chopped tomatoes
150ml/¼ pint/⅔ cup dry white wine
bouquet garni
3 anchovy fillets, drained and chopped
salt and ground black pepper
salad leaves, to serve

For the gremolata
45ml/3 tbsp chopped fresh parsley
grated rind of ½ lemon
grated rind of 1 lime
1 garlic clove, chopped

1 Heat the oil in a large flameproof casserole, add the pork steaks and brown on both sides. Remove the steaks from the casserole.

2 Add the onion to the casserole and cook until soft and beginning to brown. Add the garlic and cook for about 1–2 minutes, then stir in the tomato purée, chopped tomatoes and wine. Add the bouquet garni. Bring to the boil, then boil rapidly for a further 3–4 minutes to reduce the sauce and thicken slightly.

3 Return the pork to the casserole, then cover and cook for about 30 minutes. Stir in the anchovies.

4 Cover the casserole and cook for a further 15 minutes, or until the pork is tender. For the gremolata, mix together the parsley, lemon and lime rinds and garlic.

5 Remove the pork steaks and discard the bouquet garni. Reduce the sauce over a high heat, if it is not already thick. Taste and adjust the seasoning if required.

6 Return the pork to the casserole, then sprinkle with the gremolata. Cover and cook for 5 minutes more, then serve hot with salad leaves.

─── NUTRITION NOTES ───

Per portion:
Energy	267kcals/1121kJ
Fat	13.39g
Saturated fat	3.43g
Cholesterol	69mg
Fibre	2.06g

PAN-FRIED MEDITERRANEAN LAMB

The warm summery flavours of the Mediterranean are combined for a simple weekday meal.

INGREDIENTS

Serves 4
8 lean lamb cutlets
1 medium onion, thinly sliced
2 red (bell) peppers, seeded and sliced
400g/14oz can plum tomatoes
1 garlic clove, crushed
45ml/3 tbsp chopped fresh basil leaves
30ml/2 tbsp chopped black olives
salt and ground black pepper

1 Trim any excess fat from the lamb, then fry without fat in a non-stick pan until golden brown.

2 Add the onion and peppers to the pan. Cook, stirring, for a few minutes to soften, then add the plum tomatoes, garlic and basil.

3 Cover and simmer for 20 minutes or until the lamb is tender. Stir in the olives, season and serve hot with pasta.

NUTRITION NOTES

Per portion:

Energy	224kcals/939kJ
Fat	10.17g
Saturated fat	4.32g
Cholesterol	79mg
Fibre	2.48g

BACON KOFTAS

These easy koftas are good for barbecues and summer grills, served with lots of salad.

INGREDIENTS

Serves 4
225g/8oz smoked lean back bacon,
   roughly chopped
75g/3oz/1½ cups fresh wholemeal
   (whole-wheat) breadcrumbs
2 spring onions (scallions), chopped
15ml/1 tbsp chopped fresh parsley
finely grated rind of 1 lemon
1 egg white
ground black pepper
paprika
lemon rind and fresh parsley leaves,
   to garnish

1 Place the bacon in a food processor with the breadcrumbs, spring onions, parsley, lemon rind, egg white and pepper. Process the mixture until it is finely chopped and begins to bind together. Alternatively, use a mincer.

2 Divide the bacon mixture into eight even-sized pieces and shape into long ovals around eight wooden or bamboo skewers.

3 Sprinkle the koftas with paprika and cook under a hot grill (broiler) or on a barbecue for about 8–10 minutes, turning occasionally, until browned and cooked through. Garnish with lemon rind and parsley leaves, then serve hot with lemon rice and salad.

NUTRITION NOTES

Per portion:

Energy	128kcals/538kJ
Fat	4.7g
Saturated fat	1.61g
Cholesterol	10.13mg
Fibre	1.33g

SAUSAGE BEANPOT WITH DUMPLINGS

Sausages needn't be totally banned on a low-fat diet, but choose them carefully. If you are unable to find a reduced-fat variety, choose turkey sausages instead, and always drain off any fat during cooking.

INGREDIENTS

Serves 4
450g/1lb half-fat sausages
1 medium onion, thinly sliced
1 green (bell) pepper, seeded and diced
1 small red chilli, sliced
400g/14oz can chopped tomatoes
250ml/8fl oz/1 cup beef stock
425g/15oz can red kidney
    beans, drained
salt and ground black pepper

For the dumplings
275g/10oz/2½ cups plain (all-purpose)
    flour
10ml/2 tsp baking powder
225g/8oz/1 cup cottage cheese

1 Fry the sausages without fat in a non-stick pan until brown. Add the onion and pepper. Stir in the chilli, tomatoes and stock; bring to the boil.

NUTRITION NOTES

Per portion:	
Energy	574kcals/2409kJ
Fat	13.09g
Saturated fat	0.15g
Cholesterol	52.31mg
Fibre	9.59g

2 Cover and simmer gently for about 15–20 minutes, then add the beans and bring to the boil.

3 To make the dumplings, sift the flour and baking powder together and add enough water to mix to a firm dough. Roll out thinly and stamp out 16–18 rounds using a 7.5cm/3in cutter.

4 Place a small spoonful of cottage cheese on each round and bring the edges of the dough together, pinching to enclose. Arrange the dumplings over the sausages in the pan, cover the pan and simmer for 10–12 minutes, until the dumplings are well risen. Serve hot.

SPICY SPRING LAMB ROAST

INGREDIENTS

Serves 6

1.3–1.6kg/3–3½lb lean leg
  spring lamb
5ml/1 tsp chilli powder
1 garlic clove, crushed
5ml/1 tsp ground coriander
5ml/1 tsp ground cumin
5ml/1 tsp salt
10ml/2 tsp desiccated (dry
  unsweetened shredded) coconut
10ml/2 tsp ground almonds
45ml/3 tbsp low-fat natural (plain)
  yogurt
30ml/2 tbsp lemon juice
30ml/2 tbsp sultanas (golden raisins)
30ml/2 tbsp corn oil
mixed salad leaves, fresh coriander
  (cilantro) leaves, 2 tomatoes,
  sliced, 1 large carrot, cut into
  julienne strips and lemon wedges,
  to garnish

NUTRITION NOTES

Per portion:

Energy	197Kcals/825kJ
Fat	11.96g
Saturated fat	4.7g
Cholesterol	67.38mg

1 Preheat the oven to 180°C/350°F/
Gas 4. Trim off the fat, rinse and
pat dry the leg of lamb and set aside
on a sheet of foil large enough to
enclose the whole joint.

2 In a medium bowl, mix together
the chilli powder, garlic, ground
coriander, ground cumin and salt.

3 In a food processor or blender,
process together the desiccated
coconut, ground almonds, yogurt,
lemon juice and sultanas until you
have a smooth texture.

4 Add the contents of the food
processor to the spice mixture,
together with the corn oil, and mix
everything together well. Pour this
mixture on to the leg of lamb and
rub it over the meat.

5 Enclose the meat in the foil and
place in an ovenproof dish. Cook
in the preheated oven for 1½ hours.

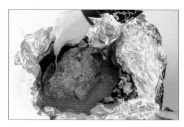

6 Remove the lamb from the oven,
open the foil and, using the back
of a spoon, spread the mixture evenly
over the meat again. Return the lamb,
uncovered, to the oven for a further
45 minutes or until it is cooked right
through and tender. Slice the meat and
serve with the garnish ingredients.

RUBY BACON CHOPS

This sweet, tangy sauce works well with lean bacon chops.

INGREDIENTS

Serves 4
1 ruby grapefruit
4 lean bacon loin chops
45ml/3 tbsp redcurrant jelly
ground black pepper

NUTRITION NOTES

Per portion:

Energy	215kcals/904kJ
Fat	8.40g
Saturated fat	3.02g
Cholesterol	20.25mg
Fibre	0.81g

1 Cut away all the peel and pith from the grapefruit, using a sharp knife, and carefully remove the segments, catching the juice in a bowl.

2 Fry the bacon chops in a non-stick frying pan without fat, turning them once, until golden and cooked.

3 Add the reserved grapefruit juice and redcurrant jelly to the pan and stir until melted. Add the grapefruit segments, then season with pepper and serve hot with fresh vegetables.

JAMAICAN BEANPOT

If pumpkin is not available, use any other type of squash, or try swede (rutabaga) instead. This recipe is a good one to double – or even treble – for a crowd.

INGREDIENTS

Serves 4
450g/1lb braising steak, diced
1 small pumpkin, about 450g/1lb
  diced flesh
1 medium onion, chopped
1 green (bell) pepper, seeded and sliced
15ml/1 tbsp paprika
2 garlic cloves, crushed
2.5cm/1in piece fresh root ginger,
  peeled and chopped
400g/14oz can chopped tomatoes
115g/4oz baby corn
250ml/8fl oz/1 cup beef stock
425g/15oz can chickpeas, drained
425g/15oz can red kidney
  beans, drained
salt and ground black pepper

1 Fry the diced beef without fat in a large flameproof casserole, stirring to seal it on all sides.

2 Stir in the pumpkin, onion and pepper, cook for 2 minutes more, then add the paprika, garlic and ginger.

3 Stir in the tomatoes, corn and stock, then bring to the boil. Cover and simmer for 40–45 minutes or until tender. Add the chickpeas and beans and heat thoroughly. Adjust the seasoning with salt and pepper to taste and serve hot with couscous or rice.

NUTRITION NOTES

Per portion:

Energy	357kcals/1500kJ
Fat	8.77g
Saturated fat	2.11g
Cholesterol	66.37mg
Fibre	10.63g

BUTTERFLIED CUMIN AND GARLIC LAMB

Ground cumin and garlic give the lamb a wonderful Middle Eastern flavour, although you may prefer a simple oil, lemon and herb marinade instead.

INGREDIENTS

Serves 6
1.8–2kg/4–4½lb lean leg of lamb
60ml/4 tbsp olive oil
30ml/2 tbsp ground cumin
4–6 garlic cloves, crushed
salt and ground black pepper
coriander (cilantro) leaves and lemon
   wedges, to garnish
toasted almond and raisin-studded rice,
   to serve

1 To butterfly the lamb, cut away the meat from the bone using a small sharp knife. Remove any excess fat and the thin, parchment-like membrane. Bat out the meat to an even thickness, then prick the fleshy side of the lamb well with the tip of a knife.

2 In a bowl, mix together the oil, cumin and garlic, and season with pepper. Spoon the mixture all over the lamb, then rub it well into the crevices. Cover and leave to marinate overnight.

3 Preheat the oven to 200°C/400°F/ Gas 6. Spread the lamb, skin side down, on a rack in a roasting pan. Season with salt, and roast for about 45–60 minutes, until crusty brown outside and pink in the centre.

4 Remove the lamb from the oven and leave it to rest for about 10 minutes. Cut into diagonal slices and garnish with coriander leaves and lemon wedges. Serve with the toasted almond and raisin-studded rice.

NUTRITION NOTES

Per portion:
Energy	387kcals/1624kJ
Fat	24.42g
Saturated fat	8.72g
Cholesterol	144.83mg
Fibre	0.14g

COOK'S TIP
The lamb may be cooked on a barbecue. Thread it on to two long skewers and cook on a hot barbecue for 20–25 minutes on each side.

SKEWERS OF LAMB WITH MINT

A delicious way to serve lamb with a Mediterranean twist. This dish could also be cooked on a barbecue and eaten *al fresco*-style in the garden.

INGREDIENTS

Serves 4
300ml/½ pint/1¼ cups low-fat natural (plain) yogurt
½ garlic clove, crushed
good pinch of saffron threads
30ml/2 tbsp chopped fresh mint
30ml/2 tbsp clear honey
45ml/3 tbsp olive oil
3 lean lamb neck fillets, about 675g/1½lb
1 aubergine (eggplant)
2 small red onions, quartered
salt and ground black pepper
small mint sprigs, to garnish
lettuce and hot pitta bread, to serve

COOK'S TIPS
If using bamboo skewers, soak them in cold water before use to prevent them burning. All lean, not-too-thick cuts of meat such as lamb or chicken grill very well on a barbecue. Meat should be marinated for several hours or overnight if at all possible.

2 Trim the lamb and cut into 2.5cm/1in cubes. Add to the marinade and stir until well coated. Leave to marinate for at least 4 hours.

4 Preheat the grill (broiler). Remove the lamb cubes from the marinade. Thread the lamb, aubergine and onion pieces alternately on to skewers. Grill (broil) for about 10–12 minutes, turning and basting occasionally with the marinade, until the lamb is tender. Serve the skewers on a bed of lettuce, garnished with mint sprigs and accompanied by hot pitta bread.

1 In a shallow dish, mix together the yogurt, garlic, saffron, mint, honey, oil and ground black pepper.

3 Cut the aubergine into 2.5cm/1in cubes and blanch in boiling salted water for 1–2 minutes. Drain well.

NUTRITION NOTES	
Per portion:	
Energy	484kcals/2032kJ
Fat	30.35g
Saturated fat	12.54g
Cholesterol	143.06mg
Fibre	2.05g

BARBECUED CHICKEN

INGREDIENTS

Serves 4 or 8

8 small chicken pieces
2 limes, cut into wedges, 2 red chillies,
    finely sliced, and 2 lemon grass
    stalks, to garnish
rice, to serve

For the marinade
2 lemon grass stalks, chopped
2.5cm/1in piece fresh root ginger
6 garlic cloves
4 shallots
$^1/_2$ bunch coriander roots
15ml/1 tbsp palm sugar
120ml/4fl oz/$^1/_2$ cup coconut milk
30ml/2 tbsp fish sauce
30ml/2 tbsp soy sauce

COOK'S TIP
Don't eat the skin of the chicken –
it's only left on to keep the flesh
moist during cooking. Coconut
milk makes a good base for a
marinade or sauce, as it is low in
calories and fat.

NUTRITION NOTES

Per portion (for 8):

Energy	106Kcals/449kJ
Fat	2.05g
Saturated fat	1.10g
Cholesterol	1.10mg
Fibre	109g

1 To make the marinade, put all the
ingredients into a food processor
and process until smooth.

2 Put the chicken pieces in a dish and
pour over the marinade. Leave in a
cool place to marinate for at least
4 hours or overnight.

3 Preheat the oven to 200°C/400°F/
Gas 6. Put the chicken pieces on
a rack on a baking tray. Brush with
marinade and bake in the oven for
about 20–30 minutes or until the
chicken is cooked and golden brown.
Turn the pieces over halfway through
and brush with more marinade.

4 Garnish with lime wedges, finely
sliced red chillies and lemon grass
stalks. Serve with rice.

TANDOORI CHICKEN KEBABS

This dish originates from the plains of the Punjab at the foot of the Himalayas, where food is traditionally cooked in clay ovens known as tandoors – hence the name.

INGREDIENTS

Serves 4

4 skinless chicken fillets (about 130g/3¹/₂oz each)
15ml/1 tbsp lemon juice
45ml/3 tbsp tandoori paste
45ml/3 tbsp low fat natural (plain) yogurt
1 garlic clove, crushed
30ml/2 tbsp chopped fresh coriander (cilantro)
1 small onion, cut into wedges and separated into layers
10ml/1 tsp oil, for brushing
salt and black pepper
coriander (cilantro) sprigs, to garnish
pilau rice and naan bread, to serve

1 Chop the chicken fillets into 2.5cm/1in cubes, put in a bowl and add the lemon juice, tandoori paste, yogurt, garlic, coriander and seasoning. Cover and leave to marinate in the refrigerator for 2–3 hours.

2 Preheat the grill (broiler) to high. Thread alternate pieces of chicken and onion on to four skewers.

COOK'S TIP
Use chopped, boned and skinned chicken thighs, or strips of turkey breast, for a cheaper and equally low fat alternative.

3 Brush the onions with a little oil, lay the skewers on a rack and cook for 10–12 minutes, turning once.

4 Garnish the kebabs with coriander and serve immediately with pilau rice and naan bread.

NUTRITION NOTES

Per portion:

Energy	215.7Kcals/911.2kJ
Fat	4.2g
Saturated fat	0.27g
Cholesterol	122mg
Fibre	0.22g

CHICKEN, CARROT AND LEEK PARCELS

These intriguing parcels may sound a bit fiddly for everyday eating, but actually they take very little time, and you can freeze them ready to cook from frozen when needed.

INGREDIENTS

Serves 4
4 chicken fillets
2 small leeks, sliced
2 carrots, grated
2 pitted black olives, chopped
1 garlic clove, crushed
4 anchovy fillets, halved lengthways
salt and black pepper
black olives and herb sprigs,
   to garnish

1 Preheat the oven to 200°C/400°F/ Gas 6. Season the chicken well.

2 Cut out four sheets of lightly greased greaseproof paper about 23cm/9in square. Divide the leeks equally among them. Put a piece of chicken on top of each.

3 Mix the carrots, olives and garlic together. Season lightly and place on top of the chicken fillets. Top each with two of the anchovy fillets.

4 Carefully wrap up each parcel, making sure the paper folds are sealed. Bake the parcels for 20 minutes and serve hot, in the paper, garnished with black olives and herb sprigs.

NUTRITION NOTES	
Per portion:	
Energy	154Kcals/651kJ
Fat	2.37g
Saturated fat	0.45g
Cholesterol	78.75mg
Fibre	2.1g

COOK'S TIP
Skinless, boneless chicken is low in fat and is an excellent source of protein. Small, skinless turkey breast fillets also work well in this recipe and make a tasty change.

THAI CHICKEN AND VEGETABLE STIR-FRY

INGREDIENTS

Serves 4

1 piece lemon grass (or the rind
   of ½ lemon)
1cm/½in piece fresh root ginger
1 large garlic clove
30ml/2 tbsp sunflower oil
275g/10oz lean chicken, thinly sliced
½ red (bell) pepper, seeded and sliced
½ green (bell) pepper, seeded and sliced
4 spring onions (scallions), chopped
2 medium carrots, cut into matchsticks
115g/4oz fine green beans
25g/1oz peanuts, lightly crushed
30 ml/2 tbsp oyster sauce
pinch of sugar
salt and black pepper
coriander (cilantro) leaves, to garnish
boiled rice, to serve

NUTRITION NOTES

Per portion:
Energy	106Kcals/449kJ
Fat	2.05g
Saturated fat	1.10g
Cholesterol	1.10mg
Fibre	109g

1 Thinly slice the lemon grass or lemon rind. Peel and chop the ginger and garlic. Heat the oil in a frying pan over a high heat. Add the lemon grass or lemon rind, ginger and garlic, and stir-fry for 30 seconds until brown.

2 Add the chicken and stir-fry for 2 minutes. Then add all the vegetables and stir-fry for 4–5 minutes, until the chicken is cooked and the vegetables are almost cooked.

3 Finally, stir in the peanuts, oyster sauce, sugar and seasoning to taste. Stir-fry for another minute to blend the flavours. Serve at once, sprinkled with the coriander leaves and accompanied by rice.

COOK'S TIP
Make this quick supper dish
a little hotter by adding more
fresh root ginger, if you like.

DUCK BREAST SALAD

Tender slices of succulent cooked duck breasts served with a salad of mixed pasta, fruit and vegetables, tossed together in a light dressing, ensure that this gourmet dish will impress friends and family alike.

INGREDIENTS

Serves 6

2 small duck breast portions, boned
5ml/1 tsp coriander seeds, crushed
350g/12oz rigatoni or penne pasta
150ml/¼ pint/⅔ cup fresh orange juice
15ml/1 tbsp lemon juice
10ml/2 tsp clear honey
1 shallot, finely chopped
1 garlic clove, crushed
1 celery stick, chopped
75g/3oz dried cherries
45ml/3 tbsp port
15ml/1 tbsp chopped fresh mint,
   plus extra to garnish
30ml/2 tbsp chopped fresh coriander
   (cilantro), plus extra to garnish
1 eating apple, diced
2 oranges, segmented
salt and black pepper

1 Remove the skin and fat from the duck portions and season with salt and pepper. Rub with coriander seeds. Preheat the grill (broiler), then grill (broil) the duck for 10 minutes on each side. Wrap in foil and leave for 20 minutes.

COOK'S TIP
Choose skinless duck breasts to reduce fat and calories. Crush your own spices, such as coriander seeds, to create fresh, aromatic, spicy flavours. Ready-ground spices lose their flavour more quickly than whole spices, which are best freshly ground just before use.

2 Cook the pasta in a large pan of boiling, salted water according to the packet instructions, until *al dente*. Drain thoroughly and rinse under cold running water. Leave to cool.

3 To make the dressing, put the orange juice, lemon juice, honey, shallot, garlic, celery, cherries, port, mint and fresh coriander into a bowl, whisk together and leave to marinate for 30 minutes.

4 Slice the duck breasts very thinly. (They should be pink in the centre.)

5 Put the pasta into a large bowl, then add the dressing, diced apple and segments of orange. Toss well to coat the pasta. Transfer the salad to a serving plate with the duck slices and garnish with the extra mint and coriander.

NUTRITION NOTES	
Per portion:	
Energy	348Kcals/1460kJ
Fat	3.8g
Saturated fat	0.9g
Cholesterol	55mg
Fibre	3g

FRAGRANT CHICKEN CURRY

In this dish, the mildly spiced sauce is thickened using lentils rather than the traditional onions fried in ghee.

INGREDIENTS

Serves 4–6
75g/3oz/¹/2 cup red lentils
30ml/2 tbsp mild curry powder
10ml/2 tsp ground coriander
5ml/1 tsp cumin seeds
475ml/16fl oz/2 cups vegetable stock
8 chicken thighs, skinned
225g/8oz fresh shredded spinach, or frozen, thawed and well drained
15ml/1 tbsp chopped fresh coriander (cilantro), plus extra sprigs to garnish
salt and black pepper
white or brown basmati rice and grilled (broiled) poppadums, to serve

1 Rinse the red lentils under cold running water. Place them in a large heavy pan with the curry powder, ground coriander, cumin seeds and vegetable stock.

2 Bring to the boil, then lower the heat. Cover and simmer gently for 10 minutes.

NUTRITION NOTES

Per portion:
Energy	152Kcals/640kJ
Fat	4.9g
Saturated fat	1.3g
Added sugar	0
Fibre	2.6g

COOK'S TIP
Lentils are an excellent source of fibre, and add colour and texture.

3 Add the chicken and spinach. Replace the cover and simmer gently for a further 40 minutes, or until the chicken has cooked.

4 Stir in the chopped coriander and season to taste. Serve garnished with fresh coriander and accompanied by the rice and grilled poppadums.

TURKEY AND PASTA BAKE

Serves 4

275g/10oz minced (ground) turkey
150g/5oz smoked turkey rashers
(strips), chopped
1–2 garlic cloves, crushed
1 onion, finely chopped
2 carrots, diced
30ml/2 tbsp tomato purée (paste)
300ml/¹/₂ pint/1¹/₄ cups chicken stock
225g/8oz rigatoni or penne pasta
30ml/2 tbsp grated Parmesan cheese
salt and black pepper

1 Brown the minced turkey in a non-stick pan, breaking up any large pieces with a wooden spoon, until well browned all over.

2 Add the chopped turkey rashers, garlic, onion, carrots, purée, stock and seasoning. Bring to the boil, cover and simmer for 1 hour until tender.

3 Preheat the oven to 180°C/350°F/ Gas 4. Cook the pasta in a large pan of boiling, salted water according to the packet instructions, until *al dente*. Drain thoroughly and mix with the turkey sauce.

COOK'S TIP
Minced (ground) chicken or extra lean minced beef work just as well in this tasty recipe.

4 Transfer to a shallow ovenproof dish and sprinkle with grated Parmesan cheese. Bake for 20–30 minutes until lightly browned on top.

NUTRITION NOTES	
Per portion:	
Energy	391Kcals/1641kJ
Fat	4.9g
Saturated fat	2.2g
Cholesterol	60mg
Fibre	3.5g

JAMBALAYA

The perfect way to use up left-over cold meat – jambalaya is a fast, easy-to-make fortifying meal for a hungry family.

INGREDIENTS

Serves 4

45ml/3 tbsp vegetable oil
1 onion, chopped
1 celery stick, chopped
½ red (bell) pepper, chopped
400g/14oz/2 cups long grain rice
1 litre/1¼ pints/4 cups chicken stock
15ml/1 tbsp tomato purée (paste)
3–4 shakes of Tabasco sauce
225g/8oz cold roast chicken, skinned and boned, or lean pork, thickly sliced
115g/4oz cooked sausage, such as chorizo or kabanos, sliced
75g/3oz/¾ cup frozen peas

1 Heat the oil in a heavy pan and add the onion, celery and pepper. Cook over a gentle heat until soft.

2 Add the rice, chicken stock, tomato purée and Tabasco sauce. Simmer uncovered for about 10 minutes.

> VARIATION
>
> Fish and shellfish are also good in a jambalaya.

3 Stir in the cold meat, sausage and peas and simmer for 5 minutes. Remove from the heat, cover and leave to stand for 5 minutes before serving.

NUTRITION NOTES	
Per portion:	
Energy	699kcals/2936kJ
Fat	25.71g
Saturated fat	7.2g
Cholesterol	65.46mg
Fibre	1.95g

GRILLED CHICKEN WITH HOT SALSA

This dish originates from Mexico. Its hot and delicious fruity flavours form the essence of Tex-Mex cooking.

INGREDIENTS

Serves 4

4 chicken breast fillets, about
175g/6oz each
pinch of celery salt and cayenne pepper
30ml/2 tbsp vegetable oil
fresh coriander (cilantro), to garnish
corn chips, to serve

For the salsa
275g/10oz watermelon
175g/6oz cantaloupe melon
1 small red onion
1–2 green chillies
30ml/2 tbsp lime juice
60ml/4 tbsp chopped fresh
coriander (cilantro)
pinch of salt

NUTRITION NOTES

Per portion:

Energy	263kcals/1106kJ
Fat	10.72g
Saturated fat	2.82g
Cholesterol	64.5mg
Fibre	0.72g

1 Preheat the grill (broiler) to medium. Slash the chicken breasts deeply to speed up the cooking time.

2 Season the chicken with celery salt and cayenne, brush with oil and grill (broil) for about 15 minutes.

3 For the salsa, remove the rind and seeds from the melons. Finely dice the flesh and put it into a bowl.

4 Finely chop the onion, split the chillies (discarding the seeds which contain most of the heat) and chop. Mix with the melon.

5 Add the lime juice and chopped coriander, and season with a pinch of salt. Mix well and turn the salsa into a small serving bowl.

6 Arrange the grilled chicken on a plate with the salsa and a handful of corn chips. Garnish with sprigs of coriander and serve.

COOK'S TIP

To capture the spirit of Tex-Mex food, cook the chicken over a barbecue and eat shaded from the hot summer sun.

MOROCCAN SPICED ROAST POUSSIN

INGREDIENTS

Serves 4
75g/3oz/1 cup cooked long grain rice
1 small onion, finely chopped
finely grated rind and juice of 1 lemon
30ml/2 tbsp chopped mint
45ml/3 tbsp chopped dried apricots
30ml/2 tbsp low-fat natural (plain) yogurt
10ml/2 tsp ground turmeric
10ml/2 tsp ground cumin
2 × 450g/1lb poussin
salt and ground black pepper
lemon slices and mint sprigs, to garnish

1 Preheat the oven to 200°C/400°F/
Gas 6. Mix together the rice, onion,
lemon rind, mint and apricots. Stir in
half each of the lemon juice, yogurt,
turmeric, cumin, and salt and pepper.

2 Stuff the poussins with the rice
mixture at the neck end only. Serve
any spare stuffing separately. Place the
poussins on a rack in a roasting pan.

3 Mix together the remaining lemon
juice, yogurt, turmeric and cumin,
then brush this over the poussins.
Cover loosely with foil and cook in
the oven for 30 minutes.

4 Remove the foil and roast for a
further 15 minutes, or until golden
brown and the juices run clear, not
pink, when pierced.

5 Cut the poussins in half with a
sharp knife or poultry shears, and
serve with the reserved rice, garnished
with lemon slices and fresh mint.

NUTRITION NOTES	
Per portion:	
Energy	219kcals/919kJ
Fat	6.02g
Saturated fat	1.87g
Cholesterol	71.55mg
Fibre	1.12g

STICKY GINGER CHICKEN

INGREDIENTS

Serves 4
30ml/2 tbsp lemon juice
30ml/2 tbsp light muscovado (brown) sugar
5ml/1 tsp grated fresh root ginger
10ml/2 tsp soy sauce
8 chicken drumsticks, skinned
ground black pepper

NUTRITION NOTES	
Per portion:	
Energy	162kcals/679kJ
Fat	5.58g
Saturated fat	1.84g
Cholesterol	73mg
Fibre	0.08g

1 Mix together the lemon juice,
sugar, ginger, soy sauce and pepper.

2 With a sharp knife, slash the chicken
drumsticks about three times
through the thickest part, then toss
the chicken in the glaze.

3 Cook the chicken on a hot grill
(broiler) or barbecue, turning
occasionally and brushing with the
glaze, until the juices run clear, not
pink, when pierced. Serve on a bed
of lettuce, with crusty bread.

CHILLI CHICKEN COUSCOUS

INGREDIENTS

Serves 4
225g/8oz/1¼ cups couscous
1 litre/1¼ pints/4 cups boiling water
5ml/1 tsp olive oil
400g/14oz chicken, skinned, boned
* and diced*
1 yellow (bell) pepper, seeded and sliced
2 large courgettes (zucchini),
* thickly sliced*
1 small green chilli, thinly sliced,
* or 5ml/1 tsp chilli sauce*
1 large tomato, diced
425g/15oz can chickpeas, drained
salt and ground black pepper
coriander (cilantro) or parsley sprigs,
* to garnish*

1 Place the couscous in a large bowl and pour over the boiling water. Cover and leave to stand for 30 minutes.

2 Heat the oil in a large, non-stick pan and stir-fry the chicken quickly to seal, then reduce the heat.

3 Stir in the pepper, courgettes and chilli or sauce. Cook for 10 minutes, until the vegetables are softened.

4 Stir in the tomato and chickpeas, then add the couscous. Adjust the seasoning and stir over a medium heat until hot. Serve garnished with sprigs of fresh coriander or parsley.

NUTRITION NOTES

Per portion:

Energy	363kcals/1525kJ
Fat	8.09g
Saturated fat	1.68g
Cholesterol	57mg
Fibre	4.38g

TURKEY BEAN BAKE

INGREDIENTS

Serves 4
1 medium aubergine (eggplant),
* thinly sliced*
15ml/1 tbsp olive oil, for brushing
450g/1lb turkey breast, diced
1 medium onion, chopped
400g/14oz can chopped tomatoes
425g/15oz can red kidney beans, drained
15ml/1 tbsp paprika
15ml/1 tbsp fresh chopped thyme, or
* 5ml/1 tsp dried*
5ml/1 tsp chilli sauce
350g/12oz/1½ cups Greek (US strained
* plain) yogurt*
2.5ml/½ tsp freshly grated nutmeg
salt and ground black pepper

1 Preheat the oven to 190°C/375°F/ Gas 5. Arrange the aubergine in a colander and sprinkle with salt.

2 Leave the aubergine for 30 minutes, then rinse and pat dry. Brush a non-stick pan with oil and fry the aubergine in batches, turning once, until golden.

3 Remove the aubergine, add the turkey and onion to the pan, then cook until lightly browned. Stir in the tomatoes, beans, paprika, thyme, chilli sauce, and salt and pepper. In a separate bowl, mix together the yogurt and grated nutmeg.

4 Layer the meat and aubergine in an ovenproof dish, finishing with aubergine. Spread over the yogurt and bake for 50–60 minutes, until golden.

NUTRITION NOTES

Per portion:

Energy	370kcals/1555kJ
Fat	13.72g
Saturated fat	5.81g
Cholesterol	66.5mg
Fibre	7.38g

SPICY MASALA CHICKEN

These chicken pieces are grilled and have a sweet-and-sour taste. They can be served cold with a salad and rice, or hot with mashed potatoes.

INGREDIENTS

Serves 6
12 skinless chicken thighs
90ml/6 tbsp lemon juice
5ml/1 tsp grated fresh root ginger
1 garlic clove, crushed
5ml/1 tsp crushed dried red chillies
5ml/1 tsp salt
5ml/1 tsp soft light brown sugar
30ml/2 tbsp clear honey
30ml/2 tbsp chopped fresh
  coriander (cilantro)
1 green chilli, finely chopped
30ml/2 tbsp sunflower oil
sliced chilli, to garnish

1 Prick the chicken thighs with a fork, rinse, pat dry and set aside in a large bowl.

2 In a large mixing bowl, mix together the lemon juice, ginger, garlic, crushed dried red chillies, salt, sugar and honey.

3 Add the chicken thighs to the spice mixture and coat well. Set aside for about 45 minutes.

4 Preheat the grill (broiler) to medium. Add the fresh coriander and chopped green chilli to the chicken thighs and place them on a flameproof dish.

5 Pour any remaining marinade over the chicken and baste with the oil, using a pastry brush.

6 Grill the chicken thighs under the preheated grill for about 15–20 minutes, turning and basting occasionally, until cooked through and browned.

7 Transfer to a serving dish and garnish with the sliced chilli.

NUTRITION NOTES	
Per portion:	
Energy	189kcals/795kJ
Fat	9.2g
Saturated fat	2.31g
Cholesterol	73mg

TANDOORI CHICKEN

This popular Indian chicken dish is traditionally cooked in a clay oven called a tandoor. Although the authentic tandoori flavour is very difficult to achieve in conventional ovens, this version still makes a very tasty dish.

INGREDIENTS

Serves 4
4 skinless chicken quarters
175ml/6fl oz/¾ cup low-fat natural
  (plain) yogurt
5ml/1 tsp garam masala
5ml/1 tsp grated fresh root ginger
1 garlic clove, crushed
7.5ml/1½ tsp chilli powder
1.5ml/¼ tsp turmeric
5ml/1 tsp ground coriander
15ml/1 tbsp lemon juice
5ml/1 tsp salt
a few drops of red food colouring
30ml/2 tbsp corn oil

For the garnish
mixed salad leaves
lime slices
chillies
tomato quarters

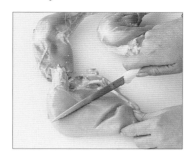

1 Rinse and pat dry the chicken quarters. Make two slits into the flesh of each piece, place in a dish and set aside.

2 Mix together the yogurt, garam masala, ginger, garlic, chilli powder, turmeric, ground coriander, lemon juice, salt, red colouring and oil, and beat so that all the ingredients are mixed together well.

3 Cover the chicken quarters with the spice mixture and leave to marinate for about 3 hours.

4 Preheat the oven to 240°C/475°F/ Gas 9. Transfer the chicken pieces to an ovenproof dish.

5 Bake in the preheated oven for about 20–25 minutes or until the chicken is cooked right through and browned on top.

6 Remove from the oven, transfer to a serving dish, and garnish with the salad leaves, lime slices, chillies and tomato quarters.

NUTRITION NOTES	
Per portion:	
Energy	242kcals/1018kJ
Fat	10.64g
Saturated fat	2.74g
Cholesterol	81.9mg

TURKEY PASTITSIO

This is just as tasty as the traditional Greek pastitsio, made with beef.

INGREDIENTS

Serves 4–6

450g/1lb lean minced (ground) turkey
1 large onion, finely chopped
60ml/4 tbsp tomato purée (paste)
250ml/8fl oz/1 cup red wine or stock
5ml/1 tsp ground cinnamon
300g/11oz/2¾ cups macaroni
300ml/½ pint/1¼ cups skimmed milk
25g/1oz/2 tbsp sunflower margarine
25g/1oz/¼ cup plain (all-purpose) flour
5ml/1 tsp freshly grated nutmeg
2 tomatoes, sliced
60ml/4 tbsp wholemeal (whole-wheat) breadcrumbs
salt and ground black pepper
green salad, to serve

1 Preheat the oven to 220°C/425°F/ Gas 7. Fry the turkey and onion in a non-stick pan without fat, stirring until lightly browned.

2 Stir in the tomato purée, red wine or stock and cinnamon. Season, then cover and simmer for 5 minutes.

3 Cook the macaroni in salted boiling water until just tender, then drain. Layer with the meat mixture in a wide ovenproof dish.

4 Place the milk, margarine and flour in a pan and whisk over a medium heat until thickened and smooth. Add the nutmeg, and salt and pepper to taste.

5 Pour the sauce evenly over the pasta and meat. Arrange the tomato slices on top and sprinkle lines of breadcrumbs over the surface.

6 Bake for 30–35 minutes, or until golden brown and bubbling. Serve hot with a green salad.

NUTRITION NOTES

Per portion:

Energy	566kcals/2382kJ
Fat	8.97g
Saturated fat	1.76g
Cholesterol	57.06mg
Fibre	4.86g

TUSCAN CHICKEN

This simple peasant casserole has all the flavours of traditional Tuscan ingredients.

INGREDIENTS

Serves 4
8 skinless chicken thighs
5ml/1 tsp olive oil
1 medium onion, sliced thinly
2 red (bell) peppers, seeded and sliced
1 garlic clove, crushed
300ml/½ pint/1¼ cups passata
* (bottled strained tomatoes)*
150ml/¼ pint/⅔ cup dry white wine
a large sprig fresh of oregano,
* or 5ml/1 tsp dried oregano*
400g/14oz can cannellini beans, drained
45ml/3 tbsp fresh breadcrumbs
salt and ground black pepper

1 Fry the chicken in the oil in a non-stick or heavy pan until golden brown. Remove and keep hot. Add the onion and peppers to the pan and gently sauté until softened, but not brown. Stir in the garlic.

2 Add the chicken, passata, wine and oregano. Season well, bring to the boil then cover the pan tightly.

NUTRITION NOTES

Per portion:
Energy	248kcals/1045kJ
Fat	7.53g
Saturated fat	2.06g
Cholesterol	73mg
Fibre	4.03g

3 Lower the heat and simmer gently, stirring occasionally, for 30–35 minutes or until the chicken is tender and the juices run clear, not pink, when pierced with the point of a knife.

4 Stir in the cannellini beans and simmer for a further 5 minutes until heated through. Sprinkle with the breadcrumbs and cook under a hot grill (broiler) until golden brown.

TURKEY SPIRALS

Here's a simple way to make
turkey more interesting.

INGREDIENTS

Serves 4

4 thin turkey breast steaks, about
90g/3 ½oz each
20ml/4 tsp tomato purée (paste)
15g/½oz/½ cup large basil leaves
1 garlic clove, crushed
15ml/1 tbsp skimmed milk
30ml/2 tbsp wholemeal
(whole-wheat) flour
salt and black pepper
passata (bottled strained tomatoes)
or fresh tomato sauce and pasta with
fresh basil, to serve

1 Place the turkey steaks on a board
and flatten them slightly by beating
with a rolling pin.

2 Spread each turkey breast steak
with tomato purée, then top with
a few leaves of basil, a little crushed
garlic, and salt and pepper.

3 Roll up firmly around the filling
and secure with a cocktail stick
(toothpick). Brush with milk and
sprinkle with flour to coat lightly.

4 Place the spirals on a foil-lined
grill (broiling) pan. Cook under a
medium hot grill (broiler) for 15–20
minutes, turning occasionally, until
thoroughly cooked. Serve hot, sliced
with a spoonful or two of passata or
fresh tomato sauce and pasta, sprinkled
with basil.

COOK'S TIP
When flattening the steaks with a
rolling pin, place between two
sheets of clear film (plastic wrap).

NUTRITION NOTES

Per portion:	
Energy	123kcals/518kJ
Fat	1.21g
Saturated fat	0.36g
Cholesterol	44.17mg
Fibre	0.87g

CARIBBEAN CHICKEN KEBABS

These kebabs have a rich, Caribbean sunshine flavour and the marinade keeps them moist without the need for oil. Serve with a colourful salad and rice.

INGREDIENTS

Serves 4
500g/1¼lb skinless chicken breast fillets
finely grated rind of 1 lime
30ml/2 tbsp lime juice
15ml/1 tbsp rum or sherry
15ml/1 tbsp light muscovado
  (brown) sugar
5ml/1 tsp ground cinnamon
2 mangoes, peeled and cubed
rice and salad, to serve

1 Cut the chicken into bitesize chunks and place in a bowl with the lime rind and juice, rum or sherry, sugar and cinnamon. Toss well, cover and leave to stand for 1 hour.

2 Save the juices and thread the chicken on to four wooden skewers, alternating with the mango cubes.

3 Cook the skewers under a hot grill (broiler) or on a barbecue for 8–10 minutes, turning occasionally and basting with the juices, until the chicken is tender and golden brown. Serve at once with rice and salad.

COOK'S TIP
The rum or sherry adds a lovely rich flavour, but it can be omitted if you prefer to make the dish more economical.

NUTRITION NOTES	
Per portion:	
Energy	218kcals/918kJ
Fat	4.17g
Saturated fat	1.33g
Cholesterol	53.75mg
Fibre	2.26g

AUTUMN PHEASANT

Pheasant is worth buying as it is low in fat, full of flavour and never dry when cooked like this.

INGREDIENTS

Serves 4

1 oven-ready pheasant
2 small onions, quartered
3 celery sticks, thickly sliced
2 red eating apples, thickly sliced
120ml/4fl oz/½ cup stock
15ml/1 tbsp clear honey
30ml/2 tbsp Worcestershire sauce
5ml/1 tsp freshly grated nutmeg
30ml/2 tbsp chopped toasted hazelnuts
salt and ground black pepper

1 Preheat the oven to 180°C/350°F/ Gas 4. Fry the pheasant without fat in a non-stick pan, turning occasionally until golden. Remove and keep hot.

2 Fry the onions and celery in the pan to brown lightly. Spoon into a casserole and place the pheasant on top. Tuck the apple slices around it.

3 Spoon over the stock, honey and Worcestershire sauce. Sprinkle with nutmeg, salt and pepper, cover and bake for 1¼–1½ hours or until tender. Sprinkle with nuts and serve hot.

NUTRITION NOTES

Per portion:

Energy	387kcals/1624kJ
Fat	16.97g
Saturated fat	4.28g
Cholesterol	126mg
Fibre	2.72g

CIDER BAKED RABBIT

Rabbit is a low-fat meat and an economical choice for family meals. Chicken joints may be used as an alternative.

INGREDIENTS

Serves 4

450g/1lb rabbit joints
15ml/1 tbsp plain (all-purpose) flour
5ml/1 tsp mustard powder
3 medium leeks, thickly sliced
250ml/8fl oz/1 cup dry cider
2 sprigs fresh rosemary
salt and black pepper
fresh rosemary, to garnish

1 Preheat the oven to 180°C/350°F/ Gas 4. Place the rabbit joints in a bowl and sprinkle over the flour and mustard powder. Toss to coat evenly.

2 Arrange the rabbit in one layer in a wide casserole. Blanch the leeks in boiling water, then drain and add to the casserole.

3 Add the cider, rosemary and seasoning, cover, then bake for 1–1¼ hours, or until the rabbit is tender. Garnish with fresh rosemary and serve with baked potatoes and vegetables.

NUTRITION NOTES

Per portion:

Energy	162kcals/681kJ
Fat	4.22g
Saturated fat	1.39g
Cholesterol	62.13mg
Fibre	1.27g

FISH AND SHELLFISH

The range of fresh fish available in our supermarkets
is impressive, and fish is always a good choice for a
healthy low fat diet. Most fish, particularly white fish, is low
in fat and is an excellent source of protein. Oily fish contains
more fat than white fish, but contains high levels of essential
fatty acids which are vital for good health. Fish is quick and
easy to prepare and cook and is ideal for serving with fresh
seasonal vegetables as part of a healthy low fat meal.
Try Cajun-style Cod, Herby Fishcakes with Lemon Sauce,
Mediterranean Fish Cutlets or Curried Prawns in Coconut
Milk – just some of the delicious, low fat recipes
included in this chapter.

CAJUN-STYLE COD

This recipe works equally well with any firm-fleshed fish – choose low fat fish, such as haddock or monkfish.

NUTRITION NOTES

Per portion:

Energy	137Kcals/577kJ
Protein	28.42g
Fat	1.75g
Saturated fat	0.26g
Fibre	0.06g

INGREDIENTS

Serves 4

4 cod steaks, each weighing about
 175g/6oz
30ml/2 tbsp low fat natural
 (plain) yogurt
15ml/1 tbsp lime or lemon juice
1 garlic clove, crushed
5ml/1 tsp ground cumin
5ml/1 tsp paprika
5ml/1 tsp mustard powder
2.5ml/¹/₂ tsp cayenne pepper
2.5ml/¹/₂ tsp dried thyme
2.5ml/¹/₂ tsp dried oregano
non-stick cooking spray
lemon slices, to garnish
new potatoes and mixed salad, to serve

1 Pat the fish dry on kitchen paper. Mix together the yogurt and lime or lemon juice and brush lightly over both sides of the fish.

2 Mix together the crushed garlic, spices and herbs. Coat both sides of the fish with the seasoning mix, rubbing in well.

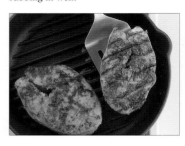

3 Spray a ridged griddle pan or heavy frying pan with non-stick cooking spray. Heat until very hot. Add the fish and cook over a high heat for 4 minutes, or until the undersides are well browned.

4 Turn the steaks over and cook for a further 4 minutes, or until cooked through. Serve immediately, garnished with lemon and accompanied by new potatoes and a mixed salad.

PLAICE PROVENCAL

INGREDIENTS

Serves 4

4 large plaice fillets
2 small red onions
120ml/4fl oz/½ cup vegetable stock
60ml/4 tbsp dry red wine
1 garlic clove, crushed
2 courgettes (zucchini), sliced
1 yellow (bell) pepper, seeded and sliced
400g/14oz can chopped tomatoes
15ml/1 tbsp chopped fresh thyme
salt and black pepper
potato gratin, to serve

1 Preheat the oven to 180°C/350°F/
Gas 4. Lay the plaice skin-side
down and, holding the tail end, push a
sharp knife between the skin and flesh
in a sawing movement. Hold the knife
at a slight angle with the blade towards
the skin.

2 Cut each onion into eight wedges.
Put into a heavy pan with the stock.
Cover and simmer for 5 minutes.
Uncover and continue to cook, stirring
occasionally, until the stock has
reduced entirely. Add the wine and
garlic clove to the pan and continue to
cook until the onions are soft.

3 Add the courgettes, yellow pepper,
tomatoes and thyme and season to
taste. Simmer for 3 minutes. Spoon the
sauce into a large casserole.

COOK'S TIP
Skinless white fish fillets such as
plaice are low in fat and make
an ideal tasty and nutritious basis
for many low fat recipes such as
this one.

4 Fold each fillet in half and put on
top of the sauce. Cover and cook in
the oven for 15–20 minutes, until the
fish is opaque and flakes easily. Serve
with a potato gratin.

NUTRITION NOTES	
Per portion:	
Energy	191Kcals/802kJ
Protein	29.46g
Fat	3.77g
Saturated fat	0.61g
Fibre	1.97g

PRAWNS WITH VEGETABLES

This is a light and nutritious dish. It is excellent served either on a bed of lettuce leaves, with plain boiled rice or wholemeal (whole-wheat) chapatis.

INGREDIENTS

Serves 4

30ml/2 tbsp chopped fresh
   coriander (cilantro)
5ml/1 tsp salt
2 green chillies, seeded if required
45ml/3 tbsp lemon juice
30ml/2 tbsp vegetable oil
20 cooked king prawns (jumbo
   shrimp), peeled
1 courgette (zucchini), thickly sliced
1 onion, cut into 8 chunks
8 cherry tomatoes
8 baby corn, halved
mixed salad leaves, to serve

NUTRITION NOTES

Per portion:
Energy	109kcals/458kJ
Fat	6.47g
Saturated fat	0.85g
Cholesterol	29.16mg

1 Place the chopped coriander, salt, green chillies, lemon juice and oil in a food processor or blender and process for a few seconds.

2 Remove the paste from the processor and transfer to a mixing bowl.

3 Add the peeled prawns to the paste and stir to make sure that all the prawns are well coated. Set aside to marinate for about 30 minutes.

4 Preheat the grill (broiler) to very hot, then turn the heat down to medium.

5 Arrange the vegetables and prawns alternately on four skewers. When all the skewers are ready place them under the preheated grill for about 5–7 minutes until cooked and browned.

6 Serve immediately on a bed of mixed salad leaves.

COOK'S TIP

King prawns are a luxury, but worth choosing for a very special dinner party. For a more economical variation, replace the king prawns with 450g/1lb/2½ cups peeled prawns (shrimp).

GRILLED FISH FILLETS

This deliciously spicy dish is perfect served with a simple green salad and plain boiled rice or new potatoes.

INGREDIENTS

Serves 4

4 flatfish fillets, such as plaice, sole or
*   flounder, about 115g/4oz each*
1 garlic clove, crushed
5ml/1 tsp garam masala
5ml/1 tsp chilli powder
1.5ml/¼ tsp turmeric
2.5ml/½ tsp salt
15ml/1 tbsp finely chopped fresh
*   coriander (cilantro)*
15ml/1 tbsp vegetable oil
30ml/2 tbsp lemon juice

1 Line a flameproof dish or grill (broiling) tray with foil. Rinse and pat dry the fish fillets and put them on the foil-lined dish or tray.

2 In a small bowl, mix together the garlic, garam masala, chilli powder, turmeric, salt, fresh coriander, oil and lemon juice.

3 Using a pastry brush, baste the fish fillets evenly all over with the spice and lemon juice mixture.

COOK'S TIP
Although frozen fish can be used for this dish always try to buy fresh. It is more flavoursome.

4 Preheat the grill (broiler) to very hot, then lower the heat to medium. Grill (broil) the fillets for about 10 minutes, turning as necessary and basting occasionally, until they are cooked right through.

5 Serve immediately with an attractive garnish. This could include grated carrot, tomato quarters and lime slices, if you wish.

NUTRITION NOTES

Per portion:
Energy	143kcals/599kJ
Fat	5.63g
Saturated fat	0.84g
Cholesterol	47.25mg

MONKFISH AND MUSSEL SKEWERS

Skinless white fish such as monkfish is a good source of protein whilst also being low in calories and fat. These attractive shellfish kebabs, flavoured with a light marinade, are excellent grilled or barbecued and served with herby boiled rice and a mixed leaf salad.

INGREDIENTS

Serves 4
450g/1lb monkfish, skinned and boned
5ml/1 tsp olive oil
30ml/2 tbsp lemon juice
5ml/1 tsp paprika
1 garlic clove, crushed
4 turkey rashers (strips)
8 cooked mussels
8 raw prawns (shrimp)
15ml/1 tbsp chopped fresh dill
salt and black pepper
lemon wedges, to garnish
salad leaves and long grain and wild
rice, to serve

1 Cut the monkfish into 2.5cm/1in cubes and place in a shallow glass dish. Mix together the oil, lemon juice, paprika and garlic clove and season.

2 Pour the marinade over the fish and toss to coat evenly. Cover and leave in a cool place for 30 minutes.

3 Cut the turkey rashers in half and wrap each strip around a mussel. Thread on to skewers, alternating with the fish cubes and raw prawns. Preheat the grill (broiler) to high.

4 Cook the kebabs for 7–8 minutes, turning once and basting with the marinade. Sprinkle with chopped dill and salt. Garnish with lemon wedges and serve with salad and rice.

NUTRITION NOTES

Per portion:

Energy	133Kcals/560kJ
Protein	25.46g
Fat	3.23g
Saturated fat	0.77g
Fibre	0.12g

LEMON SOLE BAKED IN A PAPER CASE

INGREDIENTS

Serves 4

4 lemon sole fillets, each weighing
 about 150g/5oz
½ small cucumber, sliced
4 lemon slices
60ml/4 tbsp dry white wine
sprigs of fresh dill, to garnish
potatoes and braised celery, to serve

For the yogurt hollandaise
150ml/¼ pint low fat plain yogurt
5ml/1 tsp lemon juice
2 egg yolks
5ml/1 tsp Dijon mustard
salt and black pepper

1 Preheat the oven to 180°C/350°F/
Gas 4. Cut out four heart shapes
from non-stick baking paper, each
about 20 x 15cm/8 x 6in.

2 Place a sole fillet on one side of each
paper heart. Arrange the cucumber
and lemon slices on top of each fillet.
Sprinkle with the wine and close the
parcels by turning the edges of the
paper and twisting to secure. Put on
a baking tray and cook in the oven for
15 minutes.

3 Meanwhile make the hollandaise.
Beat together the yogurt, lemon
juice and egg yolks in a double boiler
or bowl placed over a pan. Cook over
simmering water, stirring for about
15 minutes, or until thickened. (The
sauce will become thinner after
10 minutes, but will thicken again.)

COOK'S TIP
Make sure that the paper parcels
are well sealed, so that none of the
delicious juices can escape.

4 Remove from the heat and stir in
the mustard. Season to taste with
salt and pepper. Open the fish parcels,
garnish with a sprig of dill and serve
accompanied with the sauce, new
potatoes and braised celery.

NUTRITION NOTES	
Per portion:	
Energy	185Kcals/779kJ
Protein	29.27g
Fat	4.99g
Saturated fat	1.58g
Fibre	0.27g

CRUNCHY-TOPPED COD

Colourful and quick to cook, this is ideal for weekday meals.

INGREDIENTS

Serves 4

4 pieces cod fillet, about 115g/4oz each, skinned
2 medium tomatoes, sliced
50g/2oz/1 cup fresh wholemeal (whole-wheat) breadcrumbs
30ml/2 tbsp chopped fresh parsley
finely grated rind and juice of ½ lemon
5ml/1 tsp sunflower oil
salt and ground black pepper

1 Preheat the oven to 200°C/400°F/ Gas 6. Arrange the cod fillets in a wide, ovenproof dish.

2 Arrange the tomato slices on top. Mix together the breadcrumbs, fresh parsley, lemon rind and juice and the oil with seasoning to taste.

3 Spoon the crumb mixture evenly over the fish, then bake for 15–20 minutes, until tender. Serve hot.

NUTRITION NOTES

Per portion:

Energy	130kcals/546kJ
Fat	2.06g
Saturated fat	0.32g
Cholesterol	52.9mg
Fibre	1.4g

SPECIAL FISH PIE

This fish pie is colourful, healthy and, best of all, very easy to make. For a more economical version, omit the prawns and replace with more fish fillet.

INGREDIENTS

Serves 4

350g/12oz haddock fillet, skinned
30ml/2 tbsp cornflour (cornstarch)
115g/4oz cooked, peeled prawns (shrimp)
200g/7oz can corn, drained
75g/3oz/¾ cup frozen peas
150ml/¼ pint/⅔ cup skimmed milk
150g/5oz/⅔ cup low-fat fromage frais or crème fraîche
75g/3oz/1½ cups fresh wholemeal (whole-wheat) breadcrumbs
40g/1½oz/scant ½ cup grated reduced fat Cheddar cheese
salt and ground black pepper

1 Preheat the oven to 190°C/375°F/ Gas 5. Cut the haddock into bitesize pieces and toss in cornflour to coat evenly.

2 Place the fish, prawns, corn and peas in an ovenproof dish. Beat together the milk, fromage frais or crème fraîche and seasonings, then add to the dish.

3 Mix together the breadcrumbs and grated cheese, then spoon evenly over the top. Bake for 25–30 minutes, or until golden brown. Serve hot with fresh vegetables.

NUTRITION NOTES

Per portion:

Energy	290kcals/1218kJ
Fat	4.87g
Saturated fat	2.1g
Cholesterol	63.91mg
Fibre	2.61g

HADDOCK AND BROCCOLI CHOWDER

A warming main-course soup for
hearty appetites.

INGREDIENTS

Serves 4

4 spring onions (scallions), sliced
450g/1lb new potatoes, diced
300ml/½ pint/1¼ cups fish stock
  or water
300ml/½ pint/1¼ cups skimmed milk
1 bay leaf
225g/8oz/2 cups broccoli florets, sliced
450g/1lb smoked haddock
  fillets, skinned
200g/7oz can corn, drained
salt and ground black pepper

1 Place the spring onions and potatoes
in a large pan and add the stock
or water, milk and bay leaf. Bring to
the boil, then cover the pan and
simmer for 10 minutes.

2 Add the broccoli to the pan. Cut the
fish into bitesize chunks and add
to the pan with the corn.

3 Season the soup to taste with salt
and pepper, then cover the pan and
simmer for a further 5 minutes, or until
the fish is cooked through. Remove the
bay leaf and serve the soup hot, with
crusty bread.

COOK'S TIP
When new potatoes are not
available, other ones can be used,
but choose a waxy variety which
will not disintegrate.

NUTRITION NOTES

Per portion:
Energy	268kcals/1124kJ
Fat	2.19g
Saturated fat	0.27g
Cholesterol	57.75mg
Fibre	3.36g

MOROCCAN FISH TAGINE

Tagine is actually the name of the large Moroccan cooking pot used for this type of cooking, but you can use an ordinary casserole intead.

INGREDIENTS

Serves 4

2 garlic cloves, crushed
30ml/2 tbsp ground cumin
30ml/2 tbsp paprika
1 small red chilli (optional)
30ml/2 tbsp tomato purée (paste)
60ml/4 tbsp lemon juice
4 cutlets of whiting or cod, about 175g/6oz each
350g/12oz tomatoes, sliced
2 green (bell) peppers, seeded and thinly sliced
salt and ground black pepper
chopped fresh coriander (cilantro) or parsley, to garnish

1 Mix together the garlic, cumin, paprika, chilli, if using, tomato purée and lemon juice. Spread this mixture over the fish, then cover and chill for 30 minutes.

2 Preheat the oven to 200°C/400°F/ Gas 6. Arrange half the tomatoes and peppers in a baking dish.

3 Cover with the fish, in one layer, then arrange the remaining tomatoes and pepper on top. Cover the baking dish with foil and bake for about 45 minutes, until the fish is tender. Sprinkle with chopped coriander or parsley and serve.

COOK'S TIP
If you are preparing this dish for a dinner party, it can be assembled completely and stored in the refrigerator, ready for baking when needed.

NUTRITION NOTES

Per portion:
Energy	203kcals/855kJ
Fat	3.34g
Saturated fat	0.29g
Cholesterol	80.5mg
Fibre	2.48g

HERBY FISHCAKES WITH LEMON SAUCE

The wonderful flavour of fresh herbs makes these fishcakes the catch of the day.

INGREDIENTS

Serves 4
350g/12oz potatoes, roughly chopped
75ml/5 tbsp skimmed milk
350g/12oz haddock or hoki
fillets, skinned
15ml/1 tbsp lemon juice
15ml/1 tbsp creamed horseradish sauce
30ml/2 tbsp chopped fresh parsley
flour, for dusting
115g/4oz/2 cups fresh wholemeal
(whole-wheat) breadcrumbs
salt and black pepper
flat leaf parsley sprigs, to garnish
mangetouts (snow peas) or sugar snap
peas, and a sliced tomato and onion
salad, to serve

For the lemon and chive sauce
thinly pared rind and juice of
½ small lemon
120ml/4fl oz/½ cup dry white wine
2 thin slices of fresh root ginger
10ml/2 tsp cornflour (cornstarch)
30ml/2 tbsp chopped fresh chives

NUTRITION NOTES

Per portion:	
Energy	232Kcals/975kJ
Protein	19.99g
Fat	1.99g
Saturated fat	0.26g
Fibre	3.11g

COOK'S TIP
Dry white wine is a tasty fat-free basis for this herby sauce. Try using cider as an alternative to wine, for a change.

1 Cook the potatoes in a large pan of boiling water for 15–20 minutes. Drain and mash with the milk and season to taste.

2 Purée the fish together with the lemon juice and horseradish sauce in a blender or food processor. Mix with the potatoes and parsley.

3 With floured hands, shape the mixture into eight fishcakes and coat with the breadcrumbs. Chill in the refrigerator for 30 minutes.

4 Preheat the grill (broiler) to medium and cook the fishcakes for 5 minutes on each side, until browned.

5 To make the sauce, cut the lemon rind into julienne strips and put into a large pan together with the lemon juice, wine and ginger. Season to taste with salt and pepper.

6 Simmer, uncovered, for about 6 minutes. Blend the cornflour with 15ml/1 tbsp of cold water, add to the pan and simmer until clear. Stir in the chives immediately before serving.

7 Serve the sauce hot with the fishcakes, garnished with parsley and accompanied by mangetouts and a tomato and onion salad.

STEAMED FISH WITH CHILLI SAUCE

Steaming is one of the lowest fat methods of cooking fish.

INGREDIENTS

Serves 6
1 large or 2 medium, firm fish such as
* bass or grouper, scaled and cleaned*
a fresh banana leaf or large piece of foil
30ml/2 tbsp rice wine
3 red chillies, seeded and finely sliced
2 garlic cloves, finely chopped
2cm/³⁄₄in piece of fresh root ginger,
* finely shredded*
2 lemon grass stalks, crushed and chopped
2 spring onions (scallions), chopped
30ml/2 tbsp fish sauce
juice of 1 lime

For the chilli sauce
10 red chillies, seeded and chopped
4 garlic cloves, chopped
60ml/4 tbsp fish sauce
15ml/1 tbsp sugar
75ml/5 tbsp lime juice

NUTRITION NOTES

Per portion:
Energy	170Kcals/721kJ
Fat	3.46g
Saturated fat	0.54g
Cholesterol	106mg
Fibre	0.35g

1 Rinse the fish under cold running water. Pat dry with kitchen paper. With a sharp knife, slash the skin of the fish a few times on both sides.

2 Place the fish on the banana leaf or foil. Mix together the remaining ingredients and spread over the fish.

3 Place a small upturned plate in the bottom of a wok or large frying pan, and add about 5cm/2in boiling water. Lay the banana leaf or foil with the fish on top on the plate and cover with a lid.

4 Steam for about 10–15 minutes or until the fish is cooked.

5 Meanwhile, put all the chilli sauce ingredients in a food processor and process until smooth. You may need to add a little cold water.

6 Serve the fish hot on the banana leaf, with the sweet chilli sauce.

BAKED COD WITH TOMATOES

For the very best flavour, use firm sun-ripened tomatoes for the sauce, and make sure it is thick before spooning it over the cod.

INGREDIENTS

Serves 4

10ml/2 tsp olive oil
1 onion, chopped
2 garlic cloves, finely chopped
450g/1lb tomatoes, peeled, seeded
   and chopped
5ml/1 tsp tomato purée (paste)
60ml/4 tbsp dry white wine
60ml/4 tbsp chopped flat leaf parsley
4 cod cutlets
30ml/2 tbsp dried breadcrumbs
salt and black pepper
new potatoes and green salad, to serve

NUTRITION NOTES

Per portion:

Energy	151Kcals/647kJ
Fat	1.5g
Saturated fat	0.2g
Cholesterol	55.2mg
Fibre	2.42g

1 Preheat the oven to 190°C/375°F/ Gas 5. Heat the oil in a pan and fry the onion for about 5 minutes. Add the garlic, tomatoes, tomato purée, wine and seasoning.

2 Bring the sauce just to the boil, then reduce the heat slightly and cook, uncovered, for 15–20 minutes until thick. Stir in the parsley.

3 Grease an ovenproof dish, put in the cod cutlets and spoon an equal quantity of the tomato sauce on to each. Sprinkle the dried breadcrumbs over the top.

4 Bake for 20–30 minutes, basting the fish occasionally with the sauce, until the fish is tender and cooked through, and the breadcrumbs are golden and crisp. Serve hot with new potatoes and a green salad.

COOK'S TIP

For extra speed, use a 400g/14oz can of chopped tomatoes in place of fresh and 5–10ml/1–2 tsp ready-minced (ground) garlic in place of the garlic cloves.

SHELLFISH PILAF

This all-in-one-pan main course is a satisfying meal for any day of the week. For a special meal, substitute dry white wine for the orange juice.

INGREDIENTS

Serves 4
10ml/2 tsp olive oil
250g/9oz/1¼ cups long grain rice
5ml/1 tsp ground turmeric
1 red (bell) pepper, seeded and diced
1 small onion, finely chopped
2 medium courgettes (zucchini), sliced
150g/5oz/2 cups button (white)
  mushrooms, halved
350ml/12 fl oz/1½ cups fish or
  chicken stock
150ml/¼ pint/⅔ cup orange juice
350g/12oz white fish fillets
12 fresh mussels in the shell, cleaned
  (or cooked shelled mussels)
salt and ground black pepper
grated rind of 1 orange, to garnish

1 Heat the oil in a large, non-stick pan and fry the rice and turmeric over a low heat for 1 minute, stirring.

2 Add the pepper, onion, courgettes, and mushrooms. Stir in the stock and orange juice. Bring to the boil.

3 Reduce the heat and add the fish. Cover and simmer gently for about 15 minutes, until the rice is tender and the liquid absorbed. Stir in the mussels and heat thoroughly. Discard any mussels that do not open, season, sprinkle with orange rind and serve.

NUTRITION NOTES

Per portion:
Energy	370kcals/1555kJ
Fat	3.84g
Saturated fat	0.64g
Cholesterol	61.25mg
Fibre	2.08g

SALMON PASTA WITH PARSLEY SAUCE

INGREDIENTS

Serves 4
450g/1lb salmon fillet, skinned
225g/8oz/2 cups pasta, such as penne
  or twists
175g/6oz cherry tomatoes, halved
150ml/¼ pint/⅔ cup low-fat
  crème fraîche
45ml/3 tbsp finely chopped parsley
finely grated rind of ½ orange
salt and ground black pepper

NUTRITION NOTES

Per portion:
Energy	452kcals/1902kJ
Fat	17.4g
Saturated fat	5.36g
Cholesterol	65.63mg
Fibre	2.56g

1 Cut the salmon into bitesize pieces, arrange on a heatproof plate and cover with foil.

2 Bring a large pan of salted water to the boil, add the pasta and return to the boil. Place the plate of salmon on top and simmer for 10–12 minutes, until the pasta and salmon are cooked.

3 Drain the pasta and toss with the tomatoes and salmon. Mix together the crème fraîche, parsley, orange rind and pepper to taste, then toss into the salmon and pasta and serve hot or cold.

MEDITERRANEAN FISH CUTLETS

These wonderfully low fat
fish cutlets are very well
complemented by boiled
potatoes, broccoli and carrots.

INGREDIENTS

Serves 4
4 white fish cutlets, about
150g/5oz each
about 150ml/¹/4 pint/²/3 cup fish stock
or dry white wine (or a mixture
of the two), for poaching
1 bay leaf, a few black peppercorns
and a strip of pared lemon rind,
for flavouring
chopped fresh parsley, to garnish

For the tomato sauce
400g/14oz can chopped tomatoes
1 garlic clove, crushed
15ml/1 tbsp pastis or other
aniseed-flavoured liqueur
15ml/1 tbsp drained capers
12–16 pitted black olives
salt and black pepper

1 To make the sauce, place the
tomatoes, garlic, pastis or liqueur,
capers and olives in a pan. Season with
salt and pepper, and cook over a low
heat for about 15 minutes, stirring.

NUTRITION NOTES

Per portion:	
Energy	165Kcals/685kJ
Fat	3.55g
Saturated fat	0.5g
Cholesterol	69mg

2 Place the fish in a frying pan, pour
over the stock and/or wine and add
the bay leaf, peppercorns and lemon
rind. Cover and simmer for 10 minutes
or until it flakes easily.

3 Using a slotted spoon, transfer the
fish into a heated dish. Strain the
stock into the tomato sauce and boil
to reduce the liquid slightly. Season
the sauce, pour it over the fish and
serve immediately, sprinkled with
the chopped fresh parsley.

BAKED FISH IN BANANA LEAVES

Fish that is prepared in this way is particularly succulent and flavourful. Fillets are used here, rather than whole fish, which is easier for those who don't like to mess about with bones. It is a great dish for a barbecue.

INGREDIENTS

Serves 4

250ml/8fl oz/1 cup coconut milk
30ml/2 tbsp red curry paste
45ml/3 tbsp fish sauce
30ml/2 tbsp caster (superfine) sugar
5 kaffir lime leaves, torn
4 x 175g/6oz fish fillets, such
  as snapper
175g/6oz mixed vegetables, such as
  carrots or leeks, finely shredded
4 banana leaves or pieces of foil
30ml/2 tbsp shredded spring onions
  (scallions), to garnish
2 red chillies, finely sliced, to garnish

NUTRITION NOTES

Per portion:

Energy	258Kcals/1094kJ
Fat	4.31g
Saturated fat	0.7g
Cholesterol	64.75mg
Fibre	1.23g

COOK'S TIP
Coconut milk is low in calories and fat and so makes an ideal basis for a low fat marinade or sauce. Choose colourful mixed vegetables such as carrots, leeks and red (bell) pepper, to make the dish more attractive and appealing.

1 Combine the coconut milk, curry paste, fish sauce, sugar and kaffir lime leaves in a shallow dish.

2 Marinate the fish in this mixture for about 15–30 minutes. Preheat the oven to 200°C/400°F/Gas 6.

3 Mix the vegetables together and lay a portion on top of a banana leaf or piece of foil. Place a piece of fish on top with a little of its marinade.

4 Wrap the fish up by turning in the sides and ends of the leaf and secure with cocktail sticks (toothpicks). (With foil, just crumple the edges together.) Repeat with the rest of the fish.

5 Bake for 20–25 minutes or until the fish is cooked. Alternatively, cook under the grill (broiler) or on a barbecue. Just before serving, garnish the fish with a sprinkling of spring onions and sliced red chillies.

STUFFED PLAICE ROLLS

Plaice fillets are a good choice for families because they are economical, easy to cook and free of bones. If you prefer, the skin can be removed first.

INGREDIENTS

Serves 4
1 medium courgette (zucchini), grated
2 medium carrots, grated
60ml/4 tbsp fresh wholemeal
*   (whole-wheat) breadcrumbs*
15ml/1 tbsp lime or lemon juice
4 plaice or flounder fillets
salt and ground black pepper

1 Preheat the oven to 200°C/400°F/ Gas 6. Mix together the carrots and courgettes. Stir in the breadcrumbs, lime juice and seasoning.

2 Lay the fish fillets skin side up and divide the stuffing between them, spreading it evenly.

3 Roll up to enclose the stuffing and place in an ovenproof dish. Cover and bake for about 30 minutes, or until the fish flakes easily. Serve hot with new potatoes.

COOK'S TIP
This recipe creates its own delicious juices, but for an extra sauce, stir chopped fresh parsley into a little low-fat crème fraîche and serve with the fish.

NUTRITION NOTES	
Per portion:	
Energy	158kcals/665kJ
Fat	3.22g
Saturated fat	0.56g
Cholesterol	50.4mg
Fibre	1.94g

MACKEREL KEBABS WITH PARSLEY DRESSING

Oily fish such as mackerel are ideal for grilling as they cook quickly and need no extra oil.

INGREDIENTS

Serves 4
450g/1lb mackerel fillets
finely grated rind and juice of 1 lemon
45ml/3 tbsp chopped fresh parsley
12 cherry tomatoes
8 black olives, pitted
salt and ground black pepper

1 Cut the fish into 4cm/1½in chunks and place in a bowl with half the lemon rind and juice, half the parsley and seasoning. Mix well, cover and leave to marinate for 30 minutes.

2 Thread the chunks of fish on to eight long wooden or metal skewers, alternating them with the cherry tomatoes and olives. Cook the kebabs under a hot grill (broiler) for 3–4 minutes, turning the kebabs occasionally, until the fish is cooked.

3 Mix the remaining lemon rind and juice with the remaining parsley in a small bowl, then season to taste with salt and pepper. Spoon the dressing over the kebabs and serve hot with plain boiled rice or noodles and a leafy green salad.

COOK'S TIP
When using wooden or bamboo kebab skewers, soak them first in a bowl of cold water for a few minutes to help prevent them burning.

NUTRITION NOTES

Per portion:
Energy	268kcals/1126kJ
Fat	19.27g
Saturated fat	4.5g
Cholesterol	61.88mg
Fibre	1g

PINEAPPLE CURRY WITH SHELLFISH

The delicate sweet and sour flavour of this curry comes from the pineapple, and although it seems an odd combination, it is delicious.

INGREDIENTS

Serves 4

600ml/1 pint/2¹⁄₂ cups coconut milk
30ml/2 tbsp red curry paste
30ml/2 tbsp fish sauce
15ml/1 tbsp sugar
225g/8oz king prawns (jumbo shrimp),
  shelled and deveined
450g/1lb mussels, cleaned and
  beards removed
175g/6oz fresh pineapple, finely
  crushed or chopped
5 kaffir lime leaves, torn
2 red chillies, chopped, and coriander
  (cilantro) leaves, to garnish

1 In a large pan, bring half the coconut milk to the boil and heat, stirring, until it separates.

2 Add the red curry paste and cook until fragrant. Add the fish sauce and sugar and continue to cook for a few moments.

3 Stir in the rest of the coconut milk and bring back to the boil. Add the king prawns, mussels, pineapple and kaffir lime leaves.

4 Reheat until boiling and then simmer for 3–5 minutes, until the prawns are cooked and the mussels have opened. Remove any mussels that have not opened and discard. Serve garnished with chillies and coriander.

NUTRITION NOTES	
Per portion:	
Energy	187Kcals/793kJ
Fat	3.5g
Saturated fat	0.53g
Cholesterol	175.5mg
Fibre	0.59g

CURRIED PRAWNS IN COCONUT MILK

A curry-like dish where the prawns are cooked in a spicy coconut gravy with sweet and sour flavours from the tomatoes.

INGREDIENTS

Serves 4

600ml/1 pint/2¹⁄₂ cups coconut milk
30ml/2 tbsp Thai curry paste
15ml/1 tbsp fish sauce
2.5ml/¹⁄₂ tsp salt
5ml/1 tsp sugar
450g/1lb shelled king prawns (jumbo
  shrimp), tails left intact and deveined
225g/8oz cherry tomatoes
1 chilli, seeded and chopped
juice of ¹⁄₂ lime, to serve
chilli and coriander (cilantro), to garnish

1 Put half the coconut milk into a pan or wok and bring to the boil.

2 Add the curry paste to the coconut milk, stir until it disperses, then simmer for about 10 minutes.

3 Add the fish sauce, salt, sugar and remaining coconut milk. Simmer for another 5 minutes.

NUTRITION NOTES	
Per portion:	
Energy	184Kcals/778kJ
Fat	3.26g
Saturated fat	0.58g
Cholesterol	315mg
Fibre	0.6g

4 Add the prawns, cherry tomatoes and chilli. Simmer gently for about 5 minutes until the prawns are pink and tender.

5 Serve sprinkled with lime juice and garnish with sliced chilli and chopped coriander leaves.

FISH FILLETS WITH A CHILLI SAUCE

Fish fillets, marinated with fresh coriander and lemon juice, then cooked and served with a chilli sauce, are delicious accompanied with saffron rice.

INGREDIENTS

Serves 4

4 flatfish fillets, such as plaice, sole or flounder, about 115g/4oz each
30ml/2 tbsp lemon juice
15ml/1 tbsp finely chopped fresh coriander (cilantro)
15ml/1 tbsp vegetable oil
lime wedges and coriander (cilantro) leaves, to garnish

For the sauce

5ml/1 tsp grated fresh root ginger
30ml/2 tbsp tomato purée (paste)
5ml/1 tsp sugar
5ml/1 tsp salt
15ml/1 tbsp chilli sauce
15ml/1 tbsp malt vinegar
300ml/½ pint/1¼ cups water

1 Rinse, pat dry and place the fish fillets in a medium bowl. Add the lemon juice, fresh coriander and oil and rub into the fish. Leave to marinate for at least 1 hour. The flavour will improve if you can leave it for longer.

2 To make the sauce, mix together all the sauce ingredients, pour into a small pan and simmer over a low heat for about 6 minutes, stirring occasionally.

3 Preheat the grill (broiler) to medium. Cook the fillets under the grill for about 5–7 minutes.

4 When the fillets are cooked, remove and arrange them on a warmed serving dish.

5 The chilli sauce should now be fairly thick – about the consistency of a thick chicken soup.

6 Spoon the sauce over the fillets, garnish with the lime wedges and coriander leaves, and serve with rice.

NUTRITION NOTES

Per portion:

Energy	140kcals/586kJ
Fat	5.28g
Saturated fat	0.78g
Cholesterol	47.25mg

STEAMING MUSSELS WITH A SPICY SAUCE

INGREDIENTS

Serves 4
2 French loaves
1.8kg/4lb live mussels
75ml/5 tbsp dry white wine

For the dipping sauce
75ml/5 tbsp red lentils
30ml/2 tbsp sunflower oil
1 small onion, finely chopped
½ celery stick, finely chopped
1 large garlic clove, crushed
5ml/1 tsp medium-hot curry paste

1 Soak the lentils in a bowl filled with plenty of cold water until they are required. Preheat the oven to 150°C/300°F/Gas 2 and put the bread in to warm. Clean the mussels in plenty of cold water and pull off any beards. Discard any of the mussels that are damaged or do not close when tapped.

2 Place the mussels in a large pan or flameproof casserole. Add the white wine, cover and steam the mussels for about 8 minutes.

3 Transfer the mussels to a colander over a bowl to collect the juices. Keep warm until required.

4 For the dipping sauce, heat the sunflower oil in a second pan, add the onion and celery, and cook for about 3–4 minutes to soften without colouring. Strain the mussel juices into a jug (pitcher) to remove any sand or grit.

Cook's Tip
Always buy mussels from a reputable supplier and ensure that the shells are tightly closed. After cooking, discard any mussels that remain closed. Atlantic blue shell mussels are the most common. Small mussels are preferred for their tenderness and sweet flavour.

5 Add the mussel juices to the pan, then add the garlic, curry paste and drained lentils. Bring to the boil and simmer for a further 10–12 minutes or until the lentils have fallen apart.

6 Place the mussels on four serving plates and serve with the dipping sauce, the warm French bread and a bowl to put the empty shells in.

NUTRITION NOTES
Per portion:	
Energy	627kcals/2634kJ
Fat	12.68g
Saturated fat	2.24g
Cholesterol	135mg
Fibre	3.85g

OATY HERRINGS WITH RED SALSA

Herrings are one of the most economical and nutritious fish. If you buy them ready filleted, they're much easier to eat than the whole fish.

INGREDIENTS

Serves 4
30ml/2 tbsp skimmed milk
10ml/2 tsp Dijon mustard
50g/2oz/²⁄₃ cup rolled oats
2 large herrings, filleted
salt and ground black pepper

For the salsa
1 small red (bell) pepper, seeded
4 medium tomatoes
1 spring onion (scallion), chopped
15ml/1 tbsp lime juice
5ml/1 tsp caster (superfine) sugar

1 Preheat the oven to 200°C/400°F/ Gas 6. To make the salsa, place the pepper, tomatoes, spring onion, lime juice, sugar and seasoning in a food processor. Process until finely chopped.

2 Mix the milk and mustard, and the oats and pepper. Dip the fillets into the mustard mixture, then oats to coat.

3 Place on a baking sheet, then bake for 20 minutes. Serve with the salsa.

NUTRITION NOTES
Per portion:

Energy	261kcals/1097kJ
Fat	15.56g
Saturated fat	3.17g
Cholesterol	52.65mg
Fibre	2.21g

SPICED RAINBOW TROUT

Farmed rainbow trout are very good value and cook quickly on a grill or barbecue. Herring and mackerel can be cooked in this way too.

INGREDIENTS

Serves 4
4 large rainbow trout fillets, about 150g/5oz each
15ml/1 tbsp ground coriander
1 garlic clove, crushed
30ml/2 tbsp finely chopped fresh mint
5ml/1 tsp paprika
175g/6oz/³⁄₄ cup low-fat natural (plain) yogurt
salad and pitta bread, to serve

1 With a sharp knife, slash the flesh of the fish fillets through the skin fairly deeply at intervals.

2 Mix together the coriander, garlic, mint, paprika and yogurt. Spread this mixture evenly over the fish and leave to marinate for about an hour.

3 Cook the fish under a medium heat grill (broiler) or on a barbecue, turning occasionally, for about 8–10 minutes, until crisp and golden. Serve hot with salad and pitta bread.

> COOK'S TIP
> If you are using the grill, it is best to line the grill (broiler) pan with foil before cooking the trout.

NUTRITION NOTES
Per portion:

Energy	188kcals/792kJ
Fat	5.66g
Saturated fat	1.45g
Cholesterol	110.87mg
Fibre	0.05g

HOKI BALLS IN TOMATO SAUCE

These fish balls are popular with children and adults alike.

INGREDIENTS

Serves 4
450g/1lb hoki or other white fish
   fillets, skinned
60ml/4 tbsp fresh wholemeal
   (whole-wheat) breadcrumbs
30ml/2 tbsp chopped chives or spring
   onion (scallion)
400g/14oz can chopped tomatoes
50g/2oz/¼ cup button (white)
   mushrooms, sliced
sliced chives, to garnish
steamed vegetables, to serve
salt and ground black pepper

1 Cut the fish fillets into large chunks and place in a food processor. Add the wholemeal breadcrumbs and chives or spring onion. Season to taste with salt and pepper and process until the fish is finely chopped, but still has some texture left.

2 Divide the fish mixture into about 16 even-sized pieces, then mould them into balls with your hands.

3 Place the tomatoes and mushrooms in a wide pan and bring to the boil over a medium heat. Add the fish balls, cover and simmer for about 10 minutes, until cooked. Transfer to a serving dish, sprinkle with chives, and serve with steamed vegetables.

> **COOK'S TIPS**
> Hoki is a good choice for this dish but if it's not available, use cod, haddock or whiting instead. For a spicy flavour, add a little chilli sauce.

NUTRITION NOTES
Per portion:

Energy	138kcals/580kJ
Fat	1.38g
Saturated fat	0.24g
Cholesterol	51.75mg
Fibre	1.89g

TUNA AND CORN FISHCAKES

These economical little tuna fishcakes are quick to make, especially if using some potatoes left over from a previous meal.

INGREDIENTS

Serves 4

300g/11oz/3¼ cups cooked mashed potatoes
200g/7oz can tuna fish in soya oil, drained
115g/4oz/¼ cup canned or frozen corn
30ml/2 tbsp chopped fresh parsley
50g/2oz/1 cup fresh white or brown breadcrumbs
salt and ground black pepper
lemon wedges and steamed vegetables, to serve

1 Place the mashed potato in a bowl and stir in the tuna fish, corn and chopped parsley.

2 Season to taste with salt and pepper, then form into eight patty shapes with your hands.

3 Spread out the breadcrumbs on a plate and press the fishcakes into the breadcrumbs to coat lightly, then place on a baking sheet.

4 Cook the fishcakes under a medium hot grill (broiler) until crisp and golden, turning once. Serve hot with the lemon wedges, vegetables and parsley.

> **COOK'S TIP**
>
> For simple variations which are just as nutritious, try using canned sardines, red or pink salmon, or smoked mackerel in place of the tuna.

NUTRITION NOTES	
Per portion:	
Energy	203kcals/852kJ
Fat	4.62g
Saturated fat	0.81g
Cholesterol	21.25mg
Fibre	1.82g

FISH AND VEGETABLE KEBABS

Serves 4

275g/10oz cod fillets, or any other
*   firm, white fish fillets*
45ml/3 tbsp lemon juice
5ml/1 tsp grated fresh root ginger
2 green chillies, very finely
*   chopped*
15ml/1 tbsp very finely chopped
*   fresh coriander (cilantro)*
15ml/1 tbsp very finely chopped
*   fresh mint*
5ml/1 tsp ground coriander
5ml/1 tsp salt
1 red (bell) pepper
1 green (bell) pepper
½ cauliflower
8 button (white) mushrooms
8 cherry tomatoes
15ml/1 tbsp soya oil
1 lime, quartered, to garnish

COOK'S TIP
Try using different vegetables to
the ones suggested. Try baby corn
instead of mushrooms and broccoli
in place of the cauliflower.

1 Cut the fish fillets into large chunks
using a sharp knife.

2 In a large mixing bowl, blend
together the lemon juice, ginger,
chopped green chillies, fresh coriander,
mint, ground coriander and salt. Add
the fish chunks, toss to coat and leave
to marinate for about 30 minutes.

3 Cut the red and green peppers
into large squares and divide the
cauliflower into individual florets.

4 Preheat the grill (broiler) to hot.
Arrange the vegetables with the
fish pieces on four skewers.

5 Baste the kebabs with the oil and
any remaining marinade. Transfer
to a flameproof dish and grill (broil)
for about 7–10 minutes or until the
fish is cooked right through. Garnish
with the lime quarters, and serve the
kebabs either on their own or with
saffron rice.

NUTRITION NOTES	
Per portion:	
Energy	130kcals/546kJ
Fat	4.34g
Saturated fat	0.51g
Cholesterol	32.54mg

GLAZED GARLIC PRAWNS

A fairly simple and quick dish to prepare, it is best to peel the prawns as this helps them to absorb maximum flavour. Serve as a main course with a variety of accompaniments, or with a salad as an appetizer.

INGREDIENTS

Serves 4

15ml/1 tbsp sunflower oil
3 garlic cloves, roughly chopped
3 tomatoes, chopped
2.5ml/½ tsp salt
5ml/1 tsp crushed dried red chillies
5ml/1 tsp lemon juice
15ml/1 tbsp mango chutney
1 green chilli, chopped
15 cooked king prawns (jumbo shrimp), peeled
fresh coriander (cilantro) leaves and 2 chopped spring onions (scallions), to garnish

NUTRITION NOTES

Per portion:
Energy	90kcals/380kJ
Fat	3.83g
Saturated fat	0.54g
Cholesterol	30.37mg

1 Heat the oil in a medium pan, and add the chopped garlic.

2 Lower the heat. Add the chopped tomatoes with the salt, crushed chillies, lemon juice, mango chutney and chopped fresh chilli.

3 Finally add the prawns, turn up the heat and stir-fry quickly until they are heated through.

4 Transfer to a serving dish. Serve immediately, garnished with fresh coriander leaves and chopped spring onions.

COD CREOLE

INGREDIENTS

Serves 4

450g/1lb cod fillets, skinned
15ml/1 tbsp lime or lemon juice
10ml/2 tsp olive oil
1 medium onion, finely chopped
1 green (bell) pepper, seeded and sliced
2.5ml/½ tsp cayenne pepper
2.5ml/½ tsp garlic salt
400g/14oz can chopped tomatoes
boiled rice or potatoes, to serve

NUTRITION NOTES

Per portion:

Energy	130kcals/546kJ
Fat	2.61g
Saturated fat	0.38g
Cholesterol	51.75mg
Fibre	1.61g

1 Cut the cod fillets into bitesize chunks and sprinkle with the lime or lemon juice.

2 In a large, non-stick pan, heat the olive oil and fry the onion and pepper gently until softened. Add the cayenne pepper and garlic salt.

3 Stir in the cod with the chopped tomatoes. Bring to the boil, then cover and simmer for about 5 minutes, or until the fish flakes easily. Serve with boiled rice or potatoes.

FIVE-SPICE FISH

Chinese mixtures of spicy, sweet-and-sour flavours are particularly successful with fish, and dinner is ready in minutes.

INGREDIENTS

Serves 4

4 white fish fillets, such as cod, haddock
* or hoki, about 175g/6oz each*
5ml/1 tsp Chinese five-spice powder
20ml/4 tsp cornflour (cornstarch)
15ml/1 tbsp sesame or sunflower oil
3 spring onions (scallions), shredded
5ml/1 tsp finely chopped fresh
* root ginger*
150g/5oz button (white) mushrooms, sliced
115g/4oz baby corn, sliced
30ml/2 tbsp soy sauce
45ml/3 tbsp dry sherry or apple juice
5ml/1 tsp sugar
salt and ground black pepper

1 Toss the fish in the five-spice powder and cornflour to coat.

2 Heat the oil in a frying pan or wok and stir-fry the spring onions, ginger, mushrooms and corn for about 1 minute. Add the fish and cook for 2–3 minutes, turning once.

3 Mix together the soy sauce, sherry or apple juice and sugar, then pour over the fish. Simmer for 2 minutes, adjust the seasoning, then serve with noodles and stir-fried vegetables.

NUTRITION NOTES

Per portion:

Energy	213kcals/893kJ
Fat	4.41g
Saturated fat	0.67g
Cholesterol	80.5mg
Fibre	1.08g

GRILLED SNAPPER WITH MANGO SALSA

INGREDIENTS

Serves 4

350g/12oz new potatoes
3 eggs
115g/4oz green beans, trimmed
and halved
4 red snapper, about 350g/12oz each,
scaled and gutted
30ml/2 tbsp olive oil
45ml/3 tbsp chopped fresh
coriander (cilantro)
1 ripe mango, peeled, stoned (pitted)
and diced
½ red chilli, seeded and chopped
2.5cm/1in fresh root ginger, peeled
and grated
juice of 2 limes
generous pinch of celery salt
175g/6oz mixed lettuce leaves
10 cherry tomatoes
salt and ground black pepper

NUTRITION NOTES

Per portion:

Energy	405kcals/1702kJ
Fat	15.59g
Saturated fat	2.06g
Cholesterol	163.62mg
Fibre	2.03g

1 Place the potatoes in a large pan and cover with cold salted water. Bring to the boil and simmer for 15–20 minutes, until tender. Drain and set aside.

2 Bring a second large pan of salted water to the boil. Put in the eggs and boil for 4 minutes.

3 Add the beans and cook for a further 6 minutes, so that the eggs have had a total of 10 minutes. Remove the eggs from the pan, cool, peel and cut into quarters. Drain the beans and set aside. Preheat the grill (broiler) to medium.

4 Slash each snapper three times on either side, moisten with oil and cook for about 12 minutes, turning once, until tender.

5 For the salsa, place the coriander in a food processor or blender. Add the mango, chilli, ginger, lime juice and celery salt, and process until smooth.

6 Moisten the lettuce leaves with the olive oil, and divide them among four large plates.

7 Arrange the snapper over the lettuce and season to taste. Halve the new potatoes and tomatoes, and distribute them with the beans and quartered hard-boiled eggs over the salad. Serve with the salsa dressing.

SALMON RISOTTO WITH CUCUMBER

Any rice can be used for risotto, although the creamiest ones are made with short grain arborio and carnaroli rice. Fresh tarragon and cucumber combine well to bring out the flavour of the salmon.

INGREDIENTS

Serves 4

25g/1oz/2 tbsp sunflower margarine
1 small bunch spring onions (scallions), white part only, chopped
½ cucumber, peeled, seeded and chopped
400g/14oz/2 cups short grain risotto rice
900ml/1½ pints/3¾ cups chicken or fish stock
150ml/¼ pint/⅔ cup dry white wine
450g/1lb salmon fillet, skinned and diced
45ml/3 tbsp chopped fresh tarragon

> **COOK'S TIP**
> Long grain rice can also be used for this recipe. Reduce the stock to 750ml/1¼ pints/3¾ cups.

1 Heat the margarine in a large pan, and add the spring onions and cucumber. Cook for about 2–3 minutes without colouring.

2 Add the rice, stock and wine and bring to the boil.

NUTRITION NOTES

Per portion:

Energy	653kcals/2742kJ
Fat	19.88g
Saturated fat	6.99g
Cholesterol	70.63mg
Fibre	0.91g

3 Simmer the wine and stock mixture for 10 minutes, stirring occasionally. Stir in the diced salmon and tarragon. Continue cooking for a further 5 minutes, then remove from the heat. Cover and leave to stand for 5 minutes before serving.

JAMAICAN COD STEAKS WITH RAGOUT

Spicy hot from Kingston town,
this is a fast fish dish.

INGREDIENTS

Serves 4
finely grated rind of ½ orange
30ml/2 tbsp black peppercorns
15ml/1 tbsp allspice berries or
*   Jamaican pepper*
2.5ml/½ tsp salt
4 cod fillet steaks, about 175g/6oz each
groundnut (peanut) oil, for brushing
45ml/3 tbsp chopped fresh parsley,
*   to garnish*
new potatoes, to serve (optional)

For the ragoût
30ml/2 tbsp groundnut (peanut) oil
1 medium onion, chopped
2.5cm/1in piece fresh root ginger,
*   peeled and grated*
450g/1lb fresh pumpkin, peeled,
*   deseeded and chopped*
3–4 shakes of Tabasco sauce
30ml/2 tbsp soft light brown sugar
15ml/1 tbsp vinegar

1 For the ragoût, heat the oil in a
heavy pan and add the onion
and ginger. Cook gently, stirring,
for 3–4 minutes until soft.

2 Add the chopped pumpkin, Tabasco
sauce, brown sugar and vinegar,
cover and cook over a low heat for
about 10–12 minutes until softened.

3 Combine the orange rind,
pepper- corns, allspice or
Jamaican pepper and salt, then crush
coarsely using a mortar and pestle.
(Alternatively, coarsely grind the
peppercorns in a pepper mill and
combine with the orange rind and salt.)

4 Sprinkle the spice mixture over both
sides of the fish and brush with a
little oil.

5 Heat a large frying pan and dry-fry
the cod steaks for about 12 minutes,
turning once, until cooked through.

6 Serve the cod steaks with a spoonful
of pumpkin ragoût and new potatoes,
if required, and garnish the ragoût
with chopped fresh parsley.

NUTRITION NOTES

Per portion:

Energy	324kcals/1360kJ
Fat	14.9g
Saturated fat	2.75g
Cholesterol	80.5mg
Fibre	1.92g

COOK'S TIP

This recipe can be adapted using
any type of firm pink or white
fish that is available, such as
haddock, whiting, monkfish,
halibut or tuna.

TUNA FISH AND FLAGEOLET BEAN SALAD

Two cans of tuna fish form
the basis of this delicious
and easy-to-make salad.

INGREDIENTS

Serves 4
*90ml/6 tbsp reduced-calorie
    mayonnaise*
5ml/1 tsp mustard
30ml/2 tbsp capers
45ml/3 tbsp chopped fresh parsley
pinch of celery salt
*2 × 200g/7oz cans tuna fish in
    brine, drained*
3 Little Gem (Bibb) lettuces
400g/14oz can flageolet beans, drained
12 cherry tomatoes, halved
*400g/14oz can baby artichoke
    hearts, halved*
toasted sesame bread or sticks, to serve

NUTRITION NOTES

Per portion:
Energy	299kcals/1255kJ
Fat	13.91g
Saturated fat	2.12g
Cholesterol	33mg
Fibre	6.36g

1 Combine the mayonnaise, mustard,
capers and parsley in a mixing
bowl. Season to taste with celery salt.

2 Flake the tuna into the dressing and
toss gently.

3 Arrange the lettuce leaves on four
plates, then spoon the tuna mixture
on to the leaves.

COOK'S TIP
If flageolet beans are not
available, use cannellini beans.

4 Spoon the flageolet beans to one
side, followed by the tomatoes
and artichoke hearts.

5 Serve with slices of toasted sesame
bread or sticks.

VEGETABLES AND VEGETARIAN DISHES

Vegetarian food provides a tasty and nutritious choice at
mealtimes for everyone and is especially tempting when
it is low in fat too. Choose from delicious vegetable dishes
such as Roasted Mediterranean Vegetables, Devilled Onions
en Croûte and Courgettes in Citrus Sauce or wonderful
low fat vegetarian meals such as Winter Vegetable Stir-fry,
Ratatouille Pancakes, and Tofu and Green Bean Curry.

HERBY BAKED TOMATOES

INGREDIENTS

Serves 4–6

675g/1½ lb large red and yellow
  tomatoes
10ml/2 tsp red wine vinegar
2.5ml/½ tsp wholegrain mustard
1 garlic clove, crushed
10ml/2 tsp chopped fresh parsley
10ml/2 tsp chopped fresh chives
25g/1oz/½ cup fresh fine white
  breadcrumbs, for topping
salt and black pepper

NUTRITION NOTES

Per portion:	
Energy	37Kcals/156kJ
Fat	0.49g
Saturated fat	0.16g
Cholesterol	0mg
Fibre	1.36g

1 Preheat the oven to 200°C/400°F/
Gas 6. Thickly slice the tomatoes
and arrange half of them in a 900ml/
1½ pint/3¾ cup ovenproof dish.

COOK'S TIP
Use wholemeal (whole-wheat)
breadcrumbs in place of white,
for added flavour and fibre. Use
5–10ml/1–2 tsp mixed dried
herbs, if fresh are not available.

2 Mix the vinegar, mustard, garlic
and seasoning together in a bowl.
Stir in 10ml/2 tsp cold water. Sprinkle
the tomatoes with half the parsley
and chives, then drizzle over half
the dressing.

3 Lay the remaining tomato slices on
top, overlapping them slightly.
Drizzle with the remaining dressing.

4 Sprinkle over the breadcrumbs.
Bake for 25 minutes or until the
topping is golden. Sprinkle with the
remaining parsley and chives. Serve
immediately, garnished with sprigs
of parsley.

POTATO GRATIN

The flavour of Parmesan is wonderfully strong, so a little goes a long way. Leave the cheese out altogether for an almost fat-free dish.

INGREDIENTS

Serves 4
1 garlic clove
5 large baking potatoes, peeled
*45ml/3tbsp freshly grated
   Parmesan cheese*
*600ml/1 pint/2½ cups vegetable or
   chicken stock*
pinch of grated nutmeg
salt and black pepper

1 Preheat the oven to 200°C/400°F/ Gas 6. Halve the garlic clove and rub over the base and sides of a large shallow gratin dish.

2 Slice the potatoes very thinly and arrange a third of them in the dish. Sprinkle with a little grated Parmesan cheese, and season with salt and pepper. Pour over some of the stock to prevent the potatoes from discolouring.

3 Continue layering the potatoes and cheese as before, then pour over the rest of the stock. Sprinkle with the grated nutmeg.

COOK'S TIP
For a potato and onion gratin, thinly slice one medium onion and layer with the potato.

4 Bake in the preheated oven for about 1¼–1½ hours or until the potatoes are tender and the tops are well browned.

NUTRITION NOTES

Per portion:
Energy	178Kcals/749kJ
Protein	9.42g
Fat	1.57g
Saturated fat	0.30g
Fibre	1.82g

DEVILLED ONIONS EN CROUTE

Fill crisp bread cups with tender button onions tossed in a mustardy glaze. Try other low fat mixtures of vegetables, such as ratatouille, for a delicious change.

INGREDIENTS

Serves 4
*12 thin slices of white or wholemeal
 (whole-wheat) bread
225g/8oz button (pearl) onions or shallots
150ml/¼ pint/⅔ cup vegetable stock
15ml/1 tbsp dry white wine or
 dry sherry
2 turkey rashers (strips), sliced thinly
10ml/2 tsp Worcestershire sauce
5ml/1 tsp tomato purée (paste)
1.5ml/¼ tsp English (hot) mustard
salt and black pepper
sprigs of flat leaf parsley, to garnish*

1 Preheat the oven to 200°C/400°F/ Gas 6. Stamp out the bread into rounds with a 7.5cm/3in fluted cookie cutter and use to line a 12–cup patty tin.

2 Cover each bread case with non-stick baking paper and fill with baking beans. Bake blind for 5 minutes. Remove the paper and beans and bake for a further 5 minutes, until lightly browned and crisp.

3 Meanwhile, put the button onions or shallots in a bowl and cover with boiling water. Leave for 3 minutes, then drain and rinse under cold water. Trim off their top and root ends and slip them out of their skins.

4 Simmer the onions and stock in a covered pan for 5 minutes. Uncover and cook, stirring occasionally until the stock has reduced entirely. Add all the remaining ingredients, except the flat leaf parsley, and cook for 2–3 minutes.

5 Fill the toast cups with the devilled onions. Serve hot, garnished with sprigs of flat leaf parsley.

NUTRITION NOTES	
Per portion:	
Energy	178Kcals/749kJ
Protein	9.42g
Fat	1.57g
Saturated fat	0.30g
Fibre	1.82g

KOHLRABI STUFFED WITH PEPPERS

If you haven't sampled kohlrabi, or have only eaten it in stews where its flavour is lost, this dish is recommended. The slightly sharp flavour of the peppers are an excellent foil to the more earthy flavour of the kohlrabi.

INGREDIENTS

Serves 4

*4 small kohlrabies, about 175g–225g/
6–8oz each*
*about 400ml/14fl oz/²⁄₃ cup hot
vegetable stock*
15ml/1 tbsp sunflower oil
1 onion, chopped
*1 small red and 1 small green (bell)
pepper, seeded and sliced*
salt and black pepper
flat leaf parsley, to garnish (optional)

NUTRITION NOTES

Per portion:

Energy	112Kcals/470kJ
Fat	4.63g
Saturated fat	0.55g
Cholesterol	0mg
Fibre	5.8g

1 Preheat the oven to 180°C/350°F/ Gas 4. Trim and top and tail the kohlrabies and arrange in the base of a medium-sized ovenproof dish.

2 Pour over the stock to come about halfway up the vegetables. Cover and braise in the oven for about 30 minutes, until tender. Transfer to a plate and allow to cool, reserving the stock.

3 Heat the oil in a frying pan and fry the onion for 3–4 minutes over a gentle heat, stirring occasionally. Add the peppers and cook for a further 2–3 minutes, until the onion is lightly browned.

4 Add the reserved vegetable stock and a little seasoning and simmer, uncovered, over a moderate heat until the stock has almost evaporated.

5 Scoop out the insides of the kohl- rabies and chop roughly. Stir into the onion and pepper mixture, taste and adjust the seasoning. Arrange the shells in a shallow ovenproof dish.

6 Spoon the filling into the kohlrabi shells. Put in the oven for 5–10 minutes to heat through and then serve, garnished with a sprig of flat leaf parsley, if you like.

COURGETTES IN CITRUS SAUCE

If baby courgettes are unavailable, you can use larger ones, but they should be cooked whole so that they don't absorb too much water. After cooking, halve them lengthways and cut into 10cm/4in lengths. These tender, baby courgettes served in a very low fat sauce make this a tasty and low fat accompaniment to grilled fish fillets.

INGREDIENTS

Serves 4
350g/12oz baby courgettes (zucchini)
4 spring onions (scallions), finely sliced
2.5cm/1in fresh root ginger, grated
30ml/2 tbsp cider vinegar
15ml/1 tbsp light soy sauce
5ml/1 tsp soft light brown sugar
45ml/3 tbsp vegetable stock
finely grated rind and juice of ½ lemon
   and ½ orange
5ml/1 tsp cornflour (cornstarch)

NUTRITION NOTES	
Per portion:	
Energy	33Kcals/138kJ
Protein	2.18g
Fat	0.42g
Saturated fat	0.09g
Fibre	0.92g

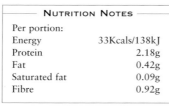

1 Cook the courgettes in lightly salted boiling water for 3–4 minutes, or until just tender. Drain well.

2 Meanwhile, put all the remaining ingredients, except the cornflour, into a small pan and bring to the boil. Simmer for 3 minutes.

3 Blend the cornflour with 10ml/2 tsp cold water and add to the sauce. Bring to the boil, stirring continuously, until the sauce has thickened.

4 Pour the sauce over the courgettes and heat gently, shaking the pan to coat them evenly. Transfer to a warmed serving dish and serve.

COOK'S TIP
Use baby corn or small aubergines (eggplants) in place of the courgettes (zucchini) for a change.

COURGETTE AND ASPARAGUS PARCELS

To appreciate the aroma, these
paper parcels should be broken
open at the table.

INGREDIENTS

Serves 4
2 medium courgettes (zucchini)
1 medium leek
225g/8oz young asparagus, trimmed
4 tarragon sprigs
4 whole garlic cloves, unpeeled
1 egg, beaten, to glaze
salt and black pepper

NUTRITION NOTES

Per portion:	
Energy	110 Kcals/460kJ
Protein	6.22g
Fat	2.29g
Saturated fat	0.49g
Fibre	6.73g

1 Preheat the oven to 200°C/400°F/
Gas 6. Using a potato peeler,
carefully slice the courgettes lengthways
into thin strips.

2 Cut the leek into very fine julienne
strips and cut the asparagus evenly
into 5cm/2in lengths.

3 Cut out four sheets of baking
parchment measuring 30 x 38cm/
12 x 15in and fold in half. Draw a
large curve to make a heart shape when
unfolded. Cut along the inside of the
line and open out.

4 Divide the courgettes, asparagus
and leek evenly between each paper
heart, positioning the filling on one side
of the fold line, and topping each with
a sprig of tarragon and an unpeeled
garlic clove. Season to taste.

5 Brush the edges lightly with the
beaten egg and fold over.

6 Twist the edges together so that
each parcel is completely sealed.
Lay the parcels on a baking sheet and
cook for 10 minutes. Serve immediately.

COOK'S TIP
Experiment with other vegetable
combinations, if you like.

VEGETABLES A LA GRECQUE

This simple side salad is made with winter vegetables, but you can vary it according to the season. This combination of vegetables makes an ideal, low fat side salad to serve with grilled (broiled) meat or poultry, or with thick slices of fresh, crusty bread.

INGREDIENTS

Serves 4

175ml/6fl oz/³⁄4 cup white wine
5ml/1 tsp olive oil
30ml/2 tbsp lemon juice
2 bay leaves
sprig of fresh thyme
4 juniper berries
450g/1lb leeks, trimmed and cut into
   2.5cm/1in lengths
1 small cauliflower, broken into florets
4 celery sticks, sliced on the diagonal
30ml/2 tbsp chopped fresh parsley
salt and black pepper

1 Put the wine, oil, lemon juice, bay leaves, thyme and juniper berries into a large, heavy pan and bring to the boil. Cover and let simmer for 20 minutes.

NUTRITION NOTES

Per portion:

Energy	88Kcals/368kJ
Protein	4.53g
Fat	2.05g
Saturated fat	0.11g
Fibre	4.42g

2 Add the leeks, cauliflower and celery. Simmer very gently for 5–6 minutes or until just tender.

3 Remove the vegetables with a slotted spoon and transfer them to a serving dish. Briskly boil the cooking liquid for 15–20 minutes, or until reduced by half. Strain.

4 Stir the parsley into the liquid and season with salt and pepper to taste. Pour over the vegetables and leave to cool. Chill in the refrigerator for at least 1 hour before serving.

COOK'S TIP
Choose a dry or medium-dry white wine for best results.

ROASTED MEDITERRANEAN VEGETABLES

For a really colourful dish, try these vegetables roasted in olive oil with garlic and rosemary. The flavour is wonderfully intense.

INGREDIENTS

Serves 6

1 each red and yellow (bell) pepper
2 Spanish (Bermuda) onions
2 large courgettes (zucchini)
1 large or 4 baby aubergines
  (egglants), trimmed
1 fennel bulb, thickly sliced
2 beef tomatoes
8 fat garlic cloves
30ml/2 tbsp olive oil
fresh rosemary sprigs
black pepper
lemon wedges and black olives
  (optional), to garnish

1 Halve and seed the peppers, then cut them into large chunks. Peel the onions and cut into thick wedges.

NUTRITION NOTES

Per portion:

Energy	120Kcals/504kJ
Fat	5.2g
Saturated fat	0.68g
Cholesterol	0

2 Cut the courgettes and aubergines into large chunks.

3 Preheat the oven to 220°C/425°F/ Gas 7. Spread the peppers, onions, courgettes, aubergines and fennel in a lightly oiled, shallow ovenproof dish or roasting pan, or, if you like, arrange in rows to make a colourful design.

4 Cut each tomato in half and place, cut-side up, with the vegetables.

5 Tuck the garlic cloves among the vegetables, then brush them with the olive oil. Place some sprigs of rosemary among the vegetables and grind over some black pepper, particularly on the tomatoes.

6 Roast for 20–25 minutes, turning the vegetables halfway through the cooking time. Serve from the dish or on a flat platter, garnished with lemon wedges. Sprinkle some black olives over the top, if you like.

RATATOUILLE PANCAKES

These pancakes are made slightly thicker than usual to hold the juicy vegetable filling. By using cooking spray, you can control the amount of fat you are using and keep it to a minimum.

INGREDIENTS

Serves 4
75g/3oz/²⁄₃ cup plain (all-purpose) flour
pinch of salt
25g/1oz/¹⁄₄ cup medium oatmeal
1 egg
300ml/¹⁄₂ pint/1¹⁄₄ cups skimmed milk
non-stick cooking spray
mixed salad, to serve

For the filling
1 large aubergine (egglant), cut into 2.5cm/1in cubes
1 garlic clove, crushed
2 medium courgettes (zucchini), sliced
1 green (bell) pepper, seeded and sliced
1 red (bell) pepper, seeded and sliced
75ml/5 tbsp vegetable stock
200g/7oz can chopped tomatoes
5ml/1 tsp cornflour (cornstarch)
salt and black pepper

NUTRITION NOTES

Per portion:
Energy	182Kcals/767kJ
Protein	9.36g
Fat	3.07g
Saturated fat	0.62g
Fibre	4.73g

COOK'S TIP
Adding oatmeal to the batter mixture adds flavour, colour and texture to the cooked pancakes. If you like, wholemeal (whole-wheat) flour may be used in place of white flour to add extra fibre and flavour too.

1 Sift the flour and a pinch of salt into a bowl. Stir in the oatmeal. Make a well in the centre, add the egg and half the milk and mix to a smooth batter. Gradually beat in the remaining milk. Cover the bowl and leave to stand for 30 minutes.

2 Spray an 18cm/7in heavy-based frying pan with cooking spray. Heat the pan, then pour in just enough batter to cover the base of the pan thinly. Cook for 2–3 minutes, until the underside is golden brown. Flip over and cook for a further 1–2 minutes.

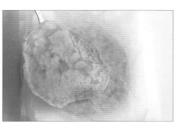

3 Slide the pancake out on to a plate lined with non-stick baking paper. Stack the other pancakes on top as they are made, interleaving each with non-stick baking paper. Keep warm.

4 For the filling, put the aubergine in a colander and sprinkle well with salt. Leave to stand on a plate for 30 minutes. Rinse thoroughly and drain well.

5 Put the garlic clove, courgettes, peppers, stock and tomatoes into a large saucepan. Simmer uncovered, stirring occasionally, for 10 minutes. Add the aubergine and cook for a further 15 minutes. Blend the cornflour with 10ml/2 tsp water and stir into the saucepan. Simmer for 2 minutes. Season to taste.

6 Spoon some of the ratatouille mixture into the middle of each pancake. Fold each one in half, then in half again to make a cone shape. Serve hot with a mixed salad.

CONCERTINA GARLIC POTATOES

With a low fat topping these would make a superb meal in themselves or could be enjoyed as a nutritious accompaniment to grilled fish or meat.

INGREDIENTS

Serves 4
4 baking potatoes
2 garlic cloves, cut into slivers
60ml/4 tbsp low fat fromage frais
60ml/4 tbsp low fat natural (plain) yogurt
30ml/2 tbsp chopped chives
6–8 watercress sprigs, finely chopped (optional)

NUTRITION NOTES

Per portion:
Energy	195Kcals/815kJ
Fat	3.5g
Saturated fat	2g
Cholesterol	10mg

1 Preheat the oven to 200°C/400°F/ Gas 6. Slice each potato at about 5mm/¹/₄in intervals, cutting not quite to the base, so that they retain their shape. Slip the slivers of the garlic between the cuts in the potatoes.

COOK'S TIP
The most suitable potatoes for baking are of the floury variety. Some of the best include Estima, Cara and Kerr's Pink.

2 Place the garlic-filled potatoes in a roasting pan and bake for 1–1¹/₄ hours or until soft when tested with a knife. Meanwhile, mix the low fat fromage frais and yogurt in a bowl, then stir in the chopped chives, along with the watercress, if using.

3 Serve the baked potatoes on individual plates, with a dollop of the yogurt and fromage frais mixture on top of each.

POTATO, LEEK AND TOMATO BAKE

INGREDIENTS

Serves 4
675g/1¹/₂lb potatoes
2 leeks, sliced
3 large tomatoes, sliced
a few fresh rosemary sprigs, crushed
1 garlic clove, crushed
300ml/¹/₂ pint/1¹/₄ cups vegetable stock
15ml/1 tbsp olive oil
salt and black pepper

NUTRITION NOTES

Per portion:
Energy	180Kcals/740kJ
Fat	3.5g
Saturated fat	0.5g
Cholesterol	0

1 Preheat the oven to 180°C/350°F/ Gas 4 and grease a 1.2 litre/ 2 pint/5 cup shallow ovenproof dish. Scrub and thinly slice the potatoes. Layer them with the leeks and tomatoes in the dish, sprinkling some rosemary between the layers and ending with a layer of potatoes.

2 Add the garlic to the stock, stir in salt if needed and pepper to taste, then pour over the vegetables. Brush the top layer of potatoes with olive oil.

3 Bake for 1¹/₄–1¹/₂ hours until the potatoes are tender and the topping is golden and slightly crisp.

MUSHROOM AND OKRA CURRY

This simple but delicious curry with its fresh gingery mango relish is best served with rice.

INGREDIENTS

Serves 4

4 garlic cloves, roughly chopped
2.5cm/1in piece fresh root ginger, peeled and roughly chopped
1–2 red chillies, seeded and chopped
175ml/6fl oz/³⁄₄ cup water
15ml/1 tbsp sunflower oil
5ml/1 tsp coriander seeds
5ml/1 tsp cumin seeds
5ml/1 tsp ground cumin
2 cardamom pods, seeds removed and crushed
pinch of ground turmeric
400g/14oz can chopped tomatoes
450g/1lb mushrooms, quartered if large
225g/8oz okra, trimmed and cut into 1cm/¹⁄₂in slices
30ml/2 tbsp chopped fresh coriander (cilantro)
basmati rice, to serve

For the mango relish
1 large ripe mango, about 500g/1¹⁄₄lb
1 small garlic clove, crushed
1 onion, finely chopped
10ml/2 tsp grated fresh root ginger
1 fresh red chilli, seeded and finely chopped
pinch of salt and sugar

1 For the mango relish, peel the mango and then cut off the fruit from the stone (pit). Put the mango into a bowl and mash with a fork, or use a food processor.

2 Add the rest of the relish ingredients to the mango, mix well and set aside.

3 Place the garlic, ginger, chillies and 45ml/3 tbsp of the water into a blender and blend until smooth. Heat the oil in a large pan. Add the coriander and cumin seeds and allow them to sizzle for a few seconds, then add the ground cumin, cardamom seeds and turmeric and cook for 1 minute more.

4 Add the paste from the blender, the tomatoes, remaining water, mushrooms and okra. Stir and bring to the boil. Reduce the heat, cover and simmer for 5 minutes. Uncover, turn up the heat slightly and cook for another 5–10 minutes until the okra is tender. Stir in the fresh coriander and serve with rice and the mango relish.

NUTRITION NOTES

Per portion:	
Energy	139Kcals/586kJ
Fat	4.6g
Saturated fat	0.63g
Cholesterol	0mg
Fibre	6.96g

TOFU AND GREEN BEAN CURRY

This exotic curry is simple and quick to make. This recipe uses beans and mushrooms, but you can use almost any kind of vegetable such as aubergines, bamboo shoots or broccoli.

INGREDIENTS

Serves 4
350ml/12fl oz/1½ cups coconut milk
15ml/1 tbsp red curry paste
45ml/3 tbsp fish sauce
10ml/2 tsp sugar
225g/8oz button (white) mushrooms
115g/4oz French (green) beans, trimmed
175g/6oz tofu, rinsed and cut into
2cm/¾in cubes
4 kaffir lime leaves, torn
2 red chillies, seeded and sliced
coriander leaves, to garnish

NUTRITION NOTES

Per portion:
Energy	100Kcals/420kJ
Fat	3.36g
Saturated fat	0.48g
Cholesterol	0mg
Fibre	1.35g

1 Put about one third of the coconut milk in a wok or pan. Cook until it starts to separate and an oily sheen appears on the surface.

2 Add the red curry paste, fish sauce and sugar to the coconut milk. Mix together thoroughly.

3 Add the mushrooms. Stir and cook for 1 minute.

4 Stir in the rest of the coconut milk and bring back to the boil.

COOK'S TIP
Use 5–10ml/1–2 tsp hot chilli powder, if fresh red chillies aren't available. When preparing fresh chillies, wear rubber gloves and wash hands, work surfaces and utensils afterwards. Chillies contain volatile oils which can irritate sensitive areas, especially eyes.

5 Add the French beans and cubes of tofu and simmer gently for another 4–5 minutes.

6 Stir in the kaffir lime leaves and chillies. Serve garnished with the coriander leaves.

VEGETARIAN CASSOULET

Every town in south-west France has its own version of this popular classic. Warm French bread is all that you need to accompany this hearty low fat vegetable version.

INGREDIENTS

Serves 4–6

400g/14oz/2 cups dried haricot
  (navy) beans
1 bay leaf
2 onions
3 whole cloves
2 garlic cloves, crushed
5ml/1 tsp olive oil
2 leeks, thickly sliced
12 baby carrots
115g/4oz button (white) mushrooms
400g/14oz can chopped tomatoes
15ml/1 tbsp tomato purée (paste)
5ml/1 tsp paprika
15ml/1 tbsp chopped fresh thyme
30ml/2 tbsp chopped fresh parsley
115g/4oz/2 cups fresh white
  breadcrumbs
salt and black pepper

NUTRITION NOTES

Per portion:

Energy	325Kcals/1378kJ
Fat	3.08g
Saturated fat	0.46g
Cholesterol	0mg
Fibre	15.68g

COOK'S TIP
If you're short of time, use canned haricot beans – you'll need two 400g/14oz cans. Drain, reserving the bean juices and make up to 400ml/14fl oz/1²/₃ cups with vegetable stock.

1 Soak the beans overnight in plenty of cold water. Drain and rinse them under cold running water. Put them in a pan with 1.75 litres/3 pints/7½ cups of cold water and the bay leaf. Bring to the boil and cook rapidly for 10 minutes.

2 Peel one of the onions and spike with the cloves. Add to the beans, then reduce the heat. Cover and simmer gently for 1 hour, until the beans are almost tender. Drain, reserving the stock but discarding the bay leaf and onion.

3 Chop the remaining onion and put it into a large flameproof casserole together with the crushed garlic and olive oil. Cook gently for 5 minutes, or until softened.

4 Preheat the oven to 160°C/325°F/ Gas 3. Add the leeks, carrots, mushrooms, chopped tomatoes, tomato purée, paprika and thyme to the casserole, then pour in about 400ml/14fl oz/1²/₃ cups of the reserved stock.

5 Bring to the boil, cover and simmer gently for 10 minutes. Stir in the cooked beans and parsley. Season to taste with salt and pepper.

6 Sprinkle the breadcrumbs over the top and bake uncovered for 35 minutes or until the topping is golden brown and crisp.

VEGETABLE RIBBONS

This may just tempt a few fussy eaters to eat up their vegetables!

INGREDIENTS

Serves 4
3 medium carrots
3 medium courgettes (zucchini)
120ml/4fl oz/½ cup chicken stock
30ml/2 tbsp chopped fresh parsley
salt and ground black pepper

1 Using a vegetable peeler or sharp knife, cut the carrots and courgettes into thin ribbons.

2 Bring the stock to the boil in a large pan and add the carrots. Return the stock to the boil, then add the courgettes. Boil rapidly for about 2–3 minutes, until the vegetable ribbons are just tender.

3 Stir in the parsley, season lightly and serve hot.

NUTRITION NOTES	
Per portion:	
Energy	35kcals/144kJ
Fat	0.53g
Saturated fat	0.09g
Cholesterol	0mg
Fibre	2.19g

VEGGIE BURGERS

INGREDIENTS

Serves 4
115g/4oz/2 cups mushrooms, chopped
1 small onion, chopped
1 small courgette (zucchini), chopped
1 carrot, chopped
25g/1oz/¼ cup unsalted peanuts or cashew nuts
115g/4oz/2 cups fresh breadcrumbs
30ml/2 tbsp chopped fresh parsley
5ml/1 tsp yeast extract
fine oatmeal or flour, for shaping
oil, for frying
salt and ground black pepper

1 Cook the mushrooms in a non-stick pan without oil, stirring, for 8–10 minutes to drive off all the moisture.

2 Process the onion, courgette, carrot and nuts in a food processor until beginning to bind together.

3 Stir in the mushrooms, breadcrumbs, parsley, yeast extract and seasoning to taste. With the oatmeal or flour, shape into four burgers. Chill.

4 Cook the burgers in a non-stick frying pan with very little oil or under a hot grill (broiler) for 8–10 minutes, turning once, until the burgers are cooked and golden brown. Serve hot with a crisp salad.

NUTRITION NOTES	
Per portion:	
Energy	126kcals/530kJ
Fat	3.8g
Saturated fat	0.73g
Cholesterol	0mg
Fibre	2.21g

CRACKED WHEAT AND FENNEL

This salad incorporates both sweet and savoury flavours. It can be served either as a side dish or as an appetizer with warm pitta bread.

INGREDIENTS

Serves 4
115g/4oz/¼ cup cracked wheat
1 large fennel bulb, finely chopped
115g/4oz green beans, chopped and blanched
1 small orange
1 garlic clove, crushed
30ml/2 tbsp sunflower oil
15ml/1 tbsp white wine vinegar
salt and ground black pepper
½ red or orange (bell) pepper, seeded and finely chopped, to garnish

NUTRITION NOTES	
Per portion:	
Energy	180kcals/755kJ
Fat	6.32 g
Saturated fat	0.8g
Cholesterol	0mg
Fibre	2.31g

1 Place the wheat in a bowl and cover with boiling water. Leave for about 10–15 minutes, until tender. Drain well and squeeze out any excess water.

2 While still slightly warm, stir in the chopped fennel and green beans. Finely grate the orange rind into a bowl. Peel and segment the orange and stir into the salad.

3 Add the crushed garlic to the orange rind, then add the sunflower oil, white wine vinegar, and seasoning to taste, and mix thoroughly. Pour the dressing over the salad and mix well. Chill the salad for 1–2 hours.

4 Serve the salad sprinkled with the chopped red or orange pepper.

> **COOK'S TIP**
> When buying green beans, choose young, crisp ones.

PROVENCAL PAN BAGNA

A wholemeal French baguette, filled with salad and sardines, provides protein, fibre, vitamins and minerals and gives a completely new meaning to the term "packed lunch".

INGREDIENTS

Serves 4

1 wholemeal (whole-wheat) baguette
   or 3 large wholemeal rolls
2 garlic cloves, crushed
45ml/3 tbsp olive oil
1 small onion, thinly sliced
2 tomatoes, sliced
7.5cm/3in length of cucumber, sliced
115g/4oz canned sardines in
   tomato sauce
30ml/2 tbsp chopped fresh parsley
ground black pepper

1 Cut the baguette into three equal pieces, then slice each piece in half lengthways. If using rolls, split them in half. Squash down the crumb on the inside of the bread to make a shallow hollow for the filling. Mix the garlic with the oil, then brush over the inside of the bread.

2 Lay slices of onion, tomato and cucumber on one half of the bread. Top with the sardines in tomato sauce. If you are concerned about the bones in the fish, you could slice open the sardines and remove the larger pieces, but it makes sound nutritional sense to leave them, as they are edible and are an excellent source of calcium.

3 Sprinkle the parsley over the fish and season with pepper. Sandwich the bread halves back together and wrap tightly in foil or clear film (plastic wrap). Chill for at least 30 minutes before eating.

NUTRITION NOTES

Per portion:

Energy	320Kcals/1340KJ
Fat	17.5g
Saturated fat	3.5g
Cholesterol	30.5mg

RED CABBAGE IN PORT AND RED WINE

A sweet and sour, spicy red cabbage dish, with the added crunch of walnuts.

INGREDIENTS

Serves 6
15ml/1 tbsp walnut oil
1 onion, sliced
2 whole star anise
5ml/1 tsp ground cinnamon
pinch of ground cloves
450g/1lb/4 cups, finely shredded red cabbage
30ml/2 tbsp soft dark brown sugar
45ml/3 tbsp red wine vinegar
300ml/½ pint/1¼ cups red wine
150ml/¼ pint/⅔ cup port
2 pears, cut into 1cm/½in cubes
115g/4oz/⅔ cup raisins
115g/4oz/1 cup walnut halves
salt and ground black pepper

<table>
<tr><td colspan="2" align="center">NUTRITION NOTES</td></tr>
<tr><td colspan="2">Per portion:</td></tr>
<tr><td>Energy</td><td>336kcals/1409kJ</td></tr>
<tr><td>Fat</td><td>15.41g</td></tr>
<tr><td>Saturated fat</td><td>1.58g</td></tr>
<tr><td>Cholesterol</td><td>0</td></tr>
<tr><td>Fibre</td><td>4.31g</td></tr>
</table>

1 Heat the walnut oil in a large flameproof casserole. Add the onion and cook gently for about 5 minutes until softened.

2 Add the star anise, cinnamon, cloves and cabbage, and cook for a further 3 minutes.

3 Stir in the sugar, vinegar, red wine and port. Cover the pan and simmer gently for a further 10 minutes, stirring occasionally.

4 Stir in the cubed pears and raisins, and cook for a further 10 minutes or until the cabbage is tender. Season to taste. Mix in the walnut halves and serve immediately.

COOK'S TIP
If you can't find walnut oil, use olive or any other vegetable oil.

CRUSTY LEEK AND CARROT GRATIN

Tender leeks are mixed with a creamy caraway sauce and given a crunchy carrot topping.

INGREDIENTS

Serves 4–6

675g/1½lb leeks, cut into 5cm/2in pieces
150ml/¼ pint/⅔ cup vegetable stock
  or water
45ml/3 tbsp dry white wine
5ml/1 tsp caraway seeds
pinch of salt
300ml/½ pint/1¼ cups skimmed milk,
  or as required
25g/1oz/2 tbsp sunflower margarine
25g/1oz/¼ cup plain (all-purpose) flour

For the topping
115g/4oz/2 cups fresh wholemeal
  (whole-wheat) breadcrumbs
115g/4oz/scant 1 cup grated carrot
30ml/2 tbsp chopped fresh parsley
75g/3oz/¾ cup coarsely grated
  Edam cheese
30ml/2 tbsp flaked (sliced) almonds

NUTRITION NOTES

Per portion:

Energy	314kcals/1320kJ
Fat	15.42g
Saturated fat	6.75g
Cholesterol	30.75mg
Fibre	6.98g

1 Place the leeks in a large pan and add the stock or water, wine, caraway seeds and salt. Bring to a simmer, cover and cook for 5–7 minutes until the leeks are just tender.

2 With a slotted spoon, transfer the leeks to an ovenproof dish. Boil the remaining liquid to half the original volume, then make up to 350ml/12fl oz/1½ cups with skimmed milk.

3 Preheat the oven to 180°C/350°F/Gas 4. Melt the sunflower margarine in a flameproof casserole, stir in the flour and cook without allowing it to colour for about 1–2 minutes. Over a low heat, gradually add the stock and milk, stirring constantly, until you have a smooth sauce.

4 Simmer the sauce for about 5–6 minutes, stirring constantly, until thickened and smooth, then pour the sauce over the leeks in the dish.

5 For the topping, mix all the ingredients together in a bowl and sprinkle over the leeks. Bake for about 20–25 minutes until golden.

SPICY BAKED POTATOES

INGREDIENTS

Serves 2–4

2 large baking potatoes
5ml/1 tsp sunflower oil
1 small onion, finely chopped
2.5cm/1in piece fresh root ginger,
    peeled and grated
5ml/1 tsp ground cumin
5ml/1 tsp ground coriander
2.5ml/½ tsp ground turmeric
garlic salt
natural (plain) yogurt and fresh
    coriander (cilantro) sprigs, to serve

1 Preheat the oven to 190°C/375°F/
Gas 5. Prick the potatoes with a fork.
Bake for 40 minutes, or until soft.

2 Cut the potatoes in half and scoop
out the flesh. Heat the oil in a non-
stick pan and fry the onion for a few
minutes to soften. Stir in the ginger,
cumin, coriander and turmeric.

3 Stir over a low heat for about
2 minutes, then add the potato
flesh, and garlic salt, to taste.

4 Cook the mixture for a further
2 minutes, stirring occasionally.
Spoon the mixture back into the potato
shells and top each with a spoonful of
natural yogurt and a sprig or two of
fresh coriander. Serve hot.

NUTRITION NOTES

Per portion:

Energy	212kcals/890kJ
Fat	2.54g
Saturated fat	0.31g
Cholesterol	0.4mg
Fibre	3.35g

TWO BEANS PROVENCAL

INGREDIENTS

Serves 4

5ml/1 tsp olive oil
1 small onion, finely chopped
1 garlic clove, crushed
225g/8oz French (green) beans
225g/8oz runner beans
2 tomatoes, skinned and chopped
salt and ground black pepper

NUTRITION NOTES

Per portion:

Energy	68kcals/286kJ
Fat	1.76g
Saturated fat	0.13g
Cholesterol	0mg
Fibre	5.39g

1 Heat the oil in a heavy, or
non-stick, pan and sauté the
chopped onion over a medium heat
until softened but not browned.

2 Add the garlic, the beans and the
tomatoes, then season well and
cover tightly.

3 Cook over a fairly low heat, shaking
the pan occasionally, for about
30 minutes, or until the beans are
tender. Serve hot.

SPRING VEGETABLE STIR-FRY

This is a colourful, dazzling medley of fresh, delicious and sweet young vegetables.

INGREDIENTS

Serves 4

15ml/1 tbsp groundnut (peanut) oil
1 garlic clove, sliced
2.5cm/1in piece fresh root ginger, finely chopped
115g/4oz baby carrots
115g/4oz patty-pan squash
115g/4oz/1¼ cups baby corn
115g/4oz green beans, trimmed
115g/4oz/1¼ cups sugar-snap peas, trimmed
115g/4oz young asparagus, cut into 7.5cm/3in pieces
8 spring onions (scallions), trimmed and cut into 5cm/2in pieces
115g/4oz cherry tomatoes

For the dressing
juice of 2 limes
15ml/1 tbsp clear honey
15ml/1 tbsp soy sauce
5ml/1 tsp sesame oil

NUTRITION NOTES

Per portion:

Energy	106kcals/444kJ
Fat	4.38g
Saturated fat	0.63g
Cholesterol	0mg
Fibre	3.86g

1 Heat the groundnut oil in a wok or large frying pan. Add the garlic and ginger and stir-fry for about 1 minute.

2 Add the carrots, patty-pan squash, baby corn and beans, and stir-fry for a further 3–4 minutes.

3 Add the sugar-snap peas, asparagus, spring onions and cherry tomatoes, and stir-fry for a further 1–2 minutes.

4 Mix all the dressing ingredients together and add to the pan.

5 Stir well, then cover the pan. Cook for 2–3 minutes more until the vegetables are just tender but still crisp.

BEETROOT AND CELERIAC GRATIN

Serves 6

350g/12oz raw beetroot (beets)
350g/12oz celeriac
4 thyme sprigs
6 juniper berries, crushed
120ml/4fl oz/½ cup fresh orange juice
120ml/4fl oz/½ cup vegetable stock
salt and ground black pepper

NUTRITION NOTES

Per portion:

Energy	37Kcals/157kJ
Fat	0.31g
Saturated fat	0g
Cholesterol	0mg
Fibre	3.28g

1 Preheat the oven to 190°C/375°F/ Gas 5. Peel and slice the beetroot very finely. Quarter and peel the celeriac and slice very finely.

2 Fill a 25cm/10in diameter cast iron or ovenproof frying pan with layers of beetroot and celeriac slices, sprinkling with the thyme, juniper and seasoning between each layer.

3 Mix the orange juice and stock together and pour over the gratin. Place over a medium heat and bring to the boil. Boil for about 2 minutes.

4 Cover with foil and place in the oven for 15 minutes. Remove the foil and raise the oven temperature to 200°C/400°F/Gas 6. Cook for a further 10 minutes or until tender. Serve garnished with a few extra crushed juniper berries and a sprig of thyme, if you like.

BROCCOLI CAULIFLOWER GRATIN

Broccoli and cauliflower make an attractive combination, and this dish is much lighter than a classic cauliflower cheese.

INGREDIENTS

Serves 4

1 small cauliflower (about 250g/9oz)
1 small head broccoli (about 250g/9oz)
150g/5oz/²⁄₃ cup low-fat natural (plain) yogurt
75g/3oz/¹⁄₄ cup grated reduced-fat Cheddar cheese
5ml/1 tsp wholegrain mustard
30ml/2 tbsp wholemeal (whole-wheat) breadcrumbs
salt and ground black pepper

1 Break the cauliflower and broccoli into florets and cook in lightly salted, boiling water for 8–10 minutes, until just tender. Drain well and transfer to a flameproof dish.

2 Mix together the yogurt, grated cheese and mustard, then season the mixture with pepper and spoon over the cauliflower and broccoli.

3 Sprinkle the breadcrumbs over the top and place under a medium heat grill until golden brown. Serve hot.

COOK'S TIP

When preparing the cauliflower and broccoli, discard the tougher part of the stalk, then break the florets into even-sized pieces, so they cook evenly.

NUTRITION NOTES

Per portion:

Energy	144kcals/601kJ
Fat	6.5g
Saturated fat	3.25g
Cholesterol	16.5mg
Fibre	3.25g

SUMMER VEGETABLE BRAISE

Tender, young vegetables are ideal for quick cooking in a minimum of liquid. Use any mixture of the family's favourite vegetables, as long as they are of similar size.

INGREDIENTS

Serves 4
175g/6oz/²⁄₃ cup baby carrots
175g/6oz/2 cups sugar-snap peas or
  mangetouts (snow peas)
115g/4oz/1¼ cups baby corn
90ml/6 tbsp vegetable stock
10ml/2 tsp lime juice
15ml/1 tbsp chopped fresh parsley
15ml/1 tbsp chopped fresh chives
salt and ground black pepper

1 Place the carrots, peas and baby corn in a large, heavy pan with the vegetable stock and lime juice. Bring to the boil.

2 Cover the pan and reduce the heat, then simmer for 6–8 minutes, shaking the pan occasionally, until the vegetables are just tender.

3 Season the vegetables to taste with salt and pepper, then stir in the chopped fresh parsley and chives. Cook the vegetables for a few seconds more, stirring them once or twice until the herbs are well mixed, then serve immediately with grilled (broiled) lamb chops or roast chicken.

COOK'S TIP
You can make this dish in the winter too, but cut larger, tougher vegetables into chunks and cook for slightly longer.

NUTRITION NOTES

Per portion:
Energy	36kcals/152kJ
Fat	0.45g
Saturated fat	0g
Cholesterol	0mg
Fibre	2.35g

NEW POTATO PARCELS

These delicious potatoes may be cooked in individual portions.

INGREDIENTS

Serves 4

16–20 very small potatoes in their skins
45ml/3 tbsp olive oil
1–2 sprigs each of fresh thyme, tarragon and oregano, or 15ml/1 tbsp mixed dried herbs
salt and ground black pepper

NUTRITION NOTES	
Per portion:	
Energy	206kcals/866kJ
Fat	11.49g
Saturated fat	1.54g
Cholesterol	0mg
Fibre	1.5g

1 Preheat the oven to 200°C/400°F/ Gas 6. Grease one large sheet or four small sheets of foil.

2 Put the potatoes in a large bowl and add the rest of the ingredients and seasoning. Mix well so the potatoes are thoroughly coated.

3 Put the potatoes on the foil and seal up the parcel(s). Place on a baking sheet and bake for 40–50 minutes. The potatoes will stay warm for quite some time if left wrapped up.

COOK'S TIP
This dish can also be cooked on a barbecue, if you like.

STIR-FRIED FLORETS WITH HAZELNUTS

INGREDIENTS

Serves 4

175g/6oz cauliflower florets
175g/6oz broccoli florets
15ml/1 tbsp sunflower oil
25g/1oz/¼ cup hazelnuts, finely chopped
¼ red chilli, finely chopped, or 5ml/ 1 tsp chilli powder (optional)
60ml/4 tbsp very low-fat crème fraîche or fromage frais
salt and ground black pepper
a little paprika, to garnish

NUTRITION NOTES	
Per portion:	
Energy	146kcals/614kJ
Fat	11.53g
Saturated fat	0.94g
Cholesterol	0.15mg
Fibre	2.84g

1 Make sure the cauliflower and broccoli florets are all of an even size. Heat the oil in a pan or wok and toss the florets over a high heat for 1 minute.

2 Reduce the heat and continue stir-frying for another 5 minutes, then add the hazelnuts, chilli, if using, and seasoning to taste.

3 Fry the cauliflower and broccoli florets until crisp and nearly tender, then stir in the crème fraîche or fromage frais and just heat through. Serve immediately, sprinkled with the paprika.

COOK'S TIP
The crisper these florets are the better, so cook them just long enough to heat them, and give them time to absorb the flavours.

ROSEMARY ROASTIES

These unusual roast potatoes use far less fat than traditional roast potatoes, and because they still have their skins they not only absorb less oil but have more flavour too.

INGREDIENTS

Serves 4

1kg/2¼lb small red potatoes
10ml/2 tsp walnut or sunflower oil
30ml/2 tbsp fresh rosemary leaves
salt and paprika

1 Preheat the oven to 240°C/475°F/ Gas 9. Leave the potatoes whole with the peel on, or if large, cut in half. Place the potatoes in a large pan of cold water and bring to the boil. Drain well.

2 Drizzle the walnut or sunflower oil over the potatoes and shake the pan to coat them evenly.

3 Turn the potatoes into a shallow roasting pan. Sprinkle with rosemary, salt and paprika. Roast for 30 minutes or until crisp. Serve hot.

NUTRITION NOTES

Per portion:

Energy	205kcals/865kJ
Fat	2.22g
Saturated fat	0.19g
Cholesterol	0mg
Fibre	3.25g

BAKED COURGETTES IN PASSATA

INGREDIENTS

Serves 4

5ml/1 tsp olive oil
3 large courgettes (zucchini), sliced
½ small red onion, finely chopped
300ml/½ pint/1¼ cups passata (bottled strained tomatoes)
30ml/2 tbsp chopped fresh thyme
garlic salt and ground black pepper
fresh thyme sprigs, to garnish

1 Preheat the oven to 190°C/375°F/ Gas 5. Arrange half the courgettes and onion in an oiled ovenproof dish.

2 Spoon half the passata over the vegetables and sprinkle with some of the fresh thyme, then season to taste with garlic salt and pepper.

3 Arrange the remaining courgettes and onion in the dish on top of the passata, then season to taste with more garlic salt and pepper. Spoon over the remaining passata and spread evenly.

4 Cover the dish with foil, then bake for 40–45 minutes, or until the courgettes are tender. Garnish with sprigs of thyme and serve hot.

NUTRITION NOTES

Per portion:

Energy	49kcals/205kJ
Fat	1.43g
Saturated fat	0.22g
Cholesterol	0mg
Fibre	1.73g

CHINESE SPROUTS

If you are bored with plain boiled Brussels sprouts, try pepping them up with this unusual stir-fried method, which uses the minimum of oil.

INGREDIENTS

Serves 4
450g/1lb Brussels sprouts
5ml/1 tsp sesame or sunflower oil
2 spring onions (scallions), sliced
2.5ml/½ tsp Chinese five-spice powder
15ml/1 tbsp light soy sauce

1 Trim the Brussels sprouts, then shred them finely using a large sharp knife or in a food processor.

2 Heat the oil and add the sprouts and spring onions, then stir-fry for about 2 minutes, without browning.

3 Stir in the five-spice powder and soy sauce, then cook, stirring, for a further 2–3 minutes, until just tender.

4 Serve hot, with grilled meats or fish, or Chinese dishes.

COOK'S TIP
Brussels sprouts are rich in Vitamin C, and this is a good way to cook them to preserve the vitamins. Larger sprouts cook particularly well by this method, and cabbage can also be cooked this way.

NUTRITION NOTES	
Per portion:	
Energy	58kcals/243kJ
Fat	2.38g
Saturated fat	0.26g
Cholesterol	0mg
Fibre	4.67g

LEMONY VEGETABLE PARCELS

INGREDIENTS

Serves 4

2 medium carrots
1 small swede (rutabaga)
1 large parsnip
1 leek, sliced
finely grated rind of ½ lemon
15ml/1 tbsp lemon juice
15ml/1 tbsp wholegrain mustard
5ml/1 tsp walnut or sunflower oil
salt and ground black pepper

1 Preheat the oven to 190°C/375°F/ Gas 5. Peel the root vegetables and cut into 1cm/½in cubes. Place in a large bowl, then add the sliced leek.

2 Stir the lemon rind and juice and the mustard into the vegetables and mix well, then season to taste.

3 Cut four 30cm/12in squares of baking parchment and brush lightly with the oil.

4 Divide the vegetables among them. Roll up the paper from one side, then twist the ends firmly to seal.

5 Place the parcels on a baking sheet and bake for 50–55 minutes, or until the vegetables are just tender. Serve hot with roast or grilled meats.

NUTRITION NOTES

Per portion:
Energy	78kcals/326kJ
Fat	2.06g
Saturated fat	0.08g
Cholesterol	0mg
Fibre	5.15g

ROOT VEGETABLE CASSEROLE

Potatoes, carrots and parsnips are all complex carbohydrates and make a hearty, sustaining vegetable dish, high in fibre and vitamin C. The carrots are also an excellent source of beta-carotene, which is converted to vitamin A in the body.

INGREDIENTS

Serves 4

225g/8oz carrots
225g/8oz parsnips
15ml/1 tbsp sunflower oil
knob of butter
15ml/1 tbsp demerara (raw) sugar
450g/1lb baby new potatoes, scrubbed
225g/8oz small onions, peeled
400ml/14fl oz/1⅔ cup vegetable stock
15ml/1 tbsp Worcestershire sauce
15ml/1 tbsp tomato purée (paste)
5ml/1 tsp wholegrain mustard
2 bay leaves
salt and ground black pepper
chopped parsley, to garnish

COOK'S TIP
Other vegetables could be added, such as leeks, mushrooms, sweet potato or celery. When they are in season, shelled chestnuts make a delicious addition.

1 Peel the carrots and parsnips and cut into large chunks.

2 Heat the oil, butter and sugar in a pan. Stir until the sugar dissolves.

3 Add the potatoes, onions, carrots and parsnips. Sauté for 10 minutes until the vegetables look glazed.

NUTRITION NOTES	
Per portion:	
Energy	215Kcals/895KJ
Fat	5.5g
Saturated fat	1g
Cholesterol	3mg

4 Mix the vegetable stock, Worcestershire sauce, tomato purée and mustard in a jug (pitcher). Stir well, then pour over the vegetables. Add the bay leaves. Bring to the boil, then lower the heat, cover and cook gently for about 30 minutes until the vegetables are tender.

5 Remove the bay leaves, add salt and pepper to taste and serve, sprinkled with the parsley.

WINTER VEGETABLE STIR-FRY

Brussels sprouts are not always popular with everyone, but they taste absolutely delicious when steamed and swiftly stir-fried. As a bonus, more of their vitamin B and C content is preserved when they are cooked this way.

INGREDIENTS

Serves 4
350g/12oz Brussels sprouts
2 courgettes
15ml/1 tbsp sunflower or nut oil
12 shallots, peeled
1 garlic clove, crushed
small piece of fresh root ginger,
*   peeled and finely chopped*
25g/1oz/¹/₄ cup walnut pieces

1 If necessary, trim the sprouts and remove any dirty outside leaves.

2 Cut the courgettes into even-size diagonal slices.

3 Steam the Brussels sprouts for about 7–10 minutes, or until they are just tender. Drain, if necessary, and set aside.

4 Heat the oil in a frying pan or wok. Add the shallots and courgettes and stir-fry for 2–3 minutes.

5 Add the sprouts, garlic and ginger and stir-fry for 2 minutes more. Scatter over the walnut pieces, toss them with the vegetable mixture and serve immediately.

NUTRITION NOTES	
Per portion:	
Energy	125Kcals/530KJ
Fat	8.5g
Saturated Fat	1g
Cholesterol	0

COOK'S TIP
Choose small, tight Brussels sprouts which don't need to be trimmed or have their outside leaves removed, as these are rich in vitamins and minerals. Shredded cabbage could be used instead of Brussels sprouts, and chestnuts in place of walnuts. Vacuum-packed ones are ready to use.

MUSHROOM, LEEK AND CASHEW RISOTTO

INGREDIENTS

Serves 4

225g/8oz/1⅓ cups brown rice
900ml/1½ pints/3¾ cups vegetable
    stock or a mixture of stock and dry
    white wine in the ratio 5:1
15ml/1 tbsp walnut or hazelnut oil
2 leeks, sliced
225g/8oz/2 cups mixed wild or
    cultivated mushrooms, trimmed
    and sliced
50g/2oz/½ cup cashew nuts
grated rind of 1 lemon
30ml/2 tbsp chopped fresh thyme
25g/1oz/scant ¼ cup pumpkin seeds
salt and ground black pepper
fresh thyme leaves and lemon wedges,
    to garnish

1 Place the brown rice in a large pan, pour in the vegetable stock (or stock and wine), and bring to the boil. Lower the heat and cook gently for about 30 minutes, until all the stock has been absorbed and the rice grains are tender.

2 About 6 minutes before the rice is cooked, heat the oil in a large frying pan, add the leeks and mushrooms and fry over a gentle heat for 3–4 minutes.

3 Add the cashew nuts, lemon rind and chopped thyme to the vegetables and cook for 1–2 minutes more. Season with salt and pepper.

4 Drain off any excess stock from the cooked rice and stir in the vegetable mixture. Turn into a serving dish. Sprinkle the pumpkin seeds over the top and garnish with the fresh thyme sprigs and lemon wedges. Serve immediately.

NUTRITION NOTES

Per portion:

Energy	395Kcals/1645KJ
Fat	14g
Saturated Fat	2.5g
Cholesterol	0

MUSHROOM AND MIXED NUT ROAST

INGREDIENTS

Serves 4

45ml/3 tbsp sunflower seeds
45ml/3 tbsp sesame seeds
30ml/2 tbsp sunflower oil, plus extra
  for greasing
1 onion, roughly chopped
2 celery sticks, roughly chopped
1 green (bell) pepper, seeded and chopped
225g/8oz/2 cups mixed mushrooms,
  chopped
1 garlic clove, crushed
115g/4oz/2 cups fresh wholemeal
  (whole-wheat) breadcrumbs
115g/4oz/1 cup chopped mixed nuts
50g/2oz/^{1}/$_3$ cup sultanas (golden raisins)
small piece of fresh root ginger, peeled
  and finely chopped
10ml/2 tsp coriander seeds, crushed
30ml/2 tbsp light soy sauce
1 egg, beaten
salt and ground black pepper
celery and coriander (cilantro) leaves,
  to garnish

For the tomato sauce

400g/14oz can chopped tomatoes
3 spring onions (scallions), chopped
30ml/2 tbsp chopped fresh coriander

NUTRITION NOTES

Per portion:

Energy	460Kcals/1925KJ
Fat	37.5g
Saturated fat	4.5g
Cholesterol	53mg

2 Preheat the oven to 190°C/375°F/
Gas 5. Heat the oil in a frying
pan, add the onion, celery, pepper,
mushrooms and garlic and cook over
a gentle heat for about 5 minutes until
the onion has softened.

3 Mix the breadcrumbs and nuts in a
large bowl. Tip in the contents of
the frying pan, then stir in the sultanas,
ginger, coriander seeds and soy sauce.
Bind with the egg, then season.

4 Press the mixture evenly into the
tin and bake for 45 minutes. Make
the sauce. Heat the tomatoes in
a small pan, add the spring onions and
fresh coriander and season to taste.

5 When the loaf is cooked, loosen it
with a knife, then allow to cool for
a few minutes. Turn out on to a serving
dish and garnish with the celery and
coriander leaves. Serve with the warm
tomato sauce.

1 Grease and line a 675g/1½lb loaf
tin. Sprinkle the sunflower and
sesame seeds on the base.

SALADS

Salads are healthy and refreshing and can be served either as accompaniments to other dishes or as perfect low fat meals in themselves. Presented here is a wonderful selection of recipes: vegetarian delights include Marinated Cucumber Salad and a fresh, fast and filling Fruit and Fibre Salad; there are fish and shellfish dishes, such as Prawn Noodle Salad and a tasty Thai-style Shellfish Salad with Fragrant Herbs; and healthy salads made with grains and rice, such as Bulgur Wheat Salad with Oranges and Brown Rice Salad with Fruit, which are hearty enough to serve as a meal on their own.

MARINATED CUCUMBER SALAD

Sprinkling cucumbers with salt draws out some of the water and makes them softer and sweeter.

INGREDIENTS

Serves 6
2 medium cucumbers
15ml/1 tbsp salt
90g/3½oz/½ cup sugar
175ml/6fl oz/¾ cup dry cider
15ml/1 tbsp cider vinegar
45ml/3 tbsp chopped fresh dill
pinch of pepper

NUTRITION NOTES

Per portion:
Energy	111Kcals/465kJ
Fat	0.14g
Saturated fat	0.01g
Fibre	0.62g

1 Slice the cucumbers thinly and place them in a colander, sprinkling salt between each layer. Put the colander over a bowl and leave to drain for 1 hour.

COOK'S TIP
As a shortcut, leave out the method for salting cucumber described in step 1.

2 Thoroughly rinse the cucumber under cold running water to remove excess salt, then pat dry on absorbent kitchen paper.

3 Gently heat the sugar, cider and vinegar in a pan, until the sugar has dissolved. Remove from the heat and leave to cool. Put the cucumber slices in a bowl, pour over the cider mixture and leave to marinate for about 2 hours.

4 Drain the cucumber and sprinkle with the dill and pepper to taste. Mix well and transfer to a serving dish. Chill until ready to serve.

TURNIP SALAD WITH HORSERADISH

The robust-flavoured turnip partners well with the taste of horseradish and caraway seeds. This salad is delicious with cold roast beef or smoked trout.

INGREDIENTS

Serves 4
350g/12oz medium turnips
2 spring onions (scallions), white part only, chopped
15ml/1 tbsp caster (superfine) sugar
salt
30ml/2 tbsp horseradish cream
10ml/2 tsp caraway seeds

NUTRITION NOTES

Per portion:	
Energy	48.25Kcals/204kJ
Fat	1.26g
Saturated fat	0.09g
Cholesterol	1mg
Fibre	2.37g

1 Peel, slice and shred the turnips – or grate them if you wish.

COOK'S TIP
If turnips are not available, giant white radish (mooli or daikon) can be used as a substitute. For extra sweetness, try red onion instead of spring onions.

2 Add the spring onions, sugar and salt, then rub together with your hands to soften the turnip.

3 Fold in the horseradish cream and caraway seeds and serve.

FRUIT AND FIBRE SALAD

Fresh, fast and filling, this salad makes a great supper or snack.

INGREDIENTS

Serves 6
225g/8oz red or white cabbage,
  or a mixture of both
3 medium carrots
1 pear
1 red-skinned eating apple
200g/7oz can green flageolet or
  cannellini beans, drained
50g/2oz/¼ cup chopped dates

For the dressing
2.5ml/½ tsp English (hot) mustard
10ml/2 tsp clear honey
30ml/2 tbsp orange juice
5ml/1 tsp white wine vinegar
2.5ml/½ tsp paprika
salt and black pepper

1 Shred the cabbage very finely, discarding the core and tough ribs.

2 Cut the carrots into very thin strips, about 5cm/2in long.

3 Quarter, core and slice the pear and the apple, leaving the peel on.

4 Put the fruit and vegetables in a bowl with the beans and dates. Mix well.

5 To make the dressing, blend the mustard with the honey until smooth. Add the orange juice, vinegar, paprika and seasoning and mix well.

6 Pour the dressing over the salad and toss to coat. Chill in the refrigerator for 30 minutes before serving.

NUTRITION NOTES

Per portion:
Energy	137Kcals/574kJ
Fat	0.87g
Saturated fat	0.03g
Fibre	6.28g

COOK'S TIP
Use other canned beans, such as red kidney beans or chickpeas, in place of the flageolet beans. Add 2.5ml/½ tsp ground spice, such as chilli powder, cumin or coriander, for extra flavour. Add 5ml/1 tsp finely grated orange or lemon rind to the dressing, for extra flavour.

AUBERGINE SALAD

An appetizing and unusual salad that you will find yourself making over and over again.

INGREDIENTS

Serves 6
2 aubergines (eggplants)
15ml/1 tbsp oil
30ml/2 tbsp dried shrimps, soaked
  and drained
15ml/1 tbsp coarsely chopped garlic
30ml/2 tbsp freshly squeezed lime juice
5ml/1 tsp palm sugar
30ml/2 tbsp fish sauce
1 hard-boiled egg, chopped
4 shallots, thinly sliced into rings
coriander (cilantro) leaves, to garnish
2 red chillies, seeded and sliced,
  to garnish

COOK'S TIP
For an interesting variation, try using salted duck's or quail's eggs, cut in half, instead of chopped hen's eggs.

1 Grill (broil) or roast the aubergines until charred and tender.

2 When cool enough to handle, peel away the skin and slice the aubergine into thick pieces.

3 Heat the oil in a small frying pan, add the drained shrimps and the garlic and fry until golden. Remove from the pan and set aside.

4 To make the dressing, put the lime juice, palm sugar and fish sauce in a small bowl and whisk together.

5 To serve, arrange the aubergine on a serving dish. Top with the chopped egg, shallot rings and dried shrimp mixture. Drizzle over the dressing and garnish with coriander and red chillies.

NUTRITION NOTES

Per portion:
Energy	70.5Kcals/295kJ
Fat	3.76g
Saturated fat	0.68g
Cholesterol	57mg
Fibre	1.20g

BAMBOO SHOOT SALAD

This salad, which has a hot and sharp flavour, originated in north-east Thailand. Use fresh young bamboo shoots if you can find them, otherwise substitute canned bamboo shoots.

INGREDIENTS

Serves 4
400g/14oz can whole bamboo shoots
25g/1oz glutinous rice
30ml/2 tbsp chopped shallots
15ml/1 tbsp chopped garlic
45ml/3 tbsp chopped spring onions
  (scallions)
30ml/2 tbsp fish sauce
30ml/2 tbsp lime juice
5ml/1 tsp sugar
2.5ml/¹/₂ tsp dried flaked chillies
20–25 small mint leaves
15ml/1 tbsp toasted sesame seeds

1 Rinse and drain the bamboo shoots, then slice and set aside.

2 Dry roast the rice in a frying pan until it is golden brown. Remove and grind to fine crumbs with a pestle and mortar.

3 Tip the rice into a bowl, add the shallots, garlic, spring onions, fish sauce, lime juice, sugar, chillies and half the mint leaves.

4 Mix thoroughly, then pour over the bamboo shoots and toss together. Serve sprinkled with sesame seeds and the remaining mint leaves.

COOK'S TIP
Omit the sesame seeds to reduce calories and fat. Use ready-minced (ground) or "lazy" garlic instead of crushing your own.

NUTRITION NOTES	
Per portion:	
Energy	73.5Kcals/308kJ
Fat	2.8g
Saturated fat	0.41g
Cholesterol	0
Fibre	2.45g

BULGUR WHEAT SALAD WITH ORANGES

Bulgur wheat makes an excellent alternative to rice or pasta.

Serves 6

1 small green (bell) pepper
150g/5oz/1 cup bulgur wheat
600ml/1 pint/2½ cups water
½ cucumber, diced
15g/½oz/½ cup chopped fresh mint
40g/1½oz/⅓ cup sliced almonds, toasted
grated rind and juice of 1 lemon
2 seedless oranges
salt and black pepper
mint sprigs, to garnish

1 Using a sharp vegetable knife, carefully halve and seed the green pepper. Cut it on a board into small cubes and put to one side.

2 Place the bulgur wheat in a pan and add the water. Bring to the boil, lower the heat, cover and simmer for 10–15 minutes until tender. Alternatively, place the bulgur wheat in a heatproof bowl, pour over boiling water and leave to soak for 30 minutes. Most, if not all, of the water should be absorbed; drain off any excess.

3 Toss the bulgur wheat with the cucumber, green pepper, mint and toasted almonds in a serving bowl. Add the grated lemon rind and juice.

4 Cut the rind from the oranges, then working over the bowl to catch the juice, cut the oranges into neat segments. Add to the bulgur mixture, then season and toss lightly. Garnish with the mint sprigs.

NUTRITION NOTES	
Per portion:	
Energy	160Kcals/672kJ
Fat	4.3g
Saturated fat	0.33g
Cholesterol	0mg

BROWN RICE SALAD WITH FRUIT

An Oriental-style dressing gives this colourful rice salad extra piquancy. Whole grains like brown rice are unrefined, so they retain their natural fibre, vitamins and minerals.

INGREDIENTS

Serves 4–6

115g/4oz/²⁄₃ cup brown rice
1 small red (bell) pepper, seeded, diced
200g/7oz can corn niblets, drained
45ml/3 tbsp sultanas (golden raisins)
225g/8oz can pineapple pieces in
   fruit juice
15ml/1 tbsp light soy sauce
5ml/1 tsp sunflower oil
10ml/2 tsp hazelnut oil
1 garlic clove, crushed
5ml/1 tsp finely chopped fresh
   root ginger
ground black pepper
4 spring onions (scallions), sliced,
   to garnish

COOK'S TIP
Hazelnut oil, which contains mainly monounsaturated fats, adds a wonderful flavour.

1 Cook the brown rice in a large pan of lightly salted boiling water for about 30 minutes, or until it is tender. Drain thoroughly and cool. Meanwhile, prepare the garnish by slicing the spring onions at an angle and setting aside.

2 Tip the rice into a bowl and add the red pepper, corn and sultanas. Drain the pineapple pieces, reserving the juice, add them to the rice mixture and toss lightly.

3 Pour the reserved pineapple juice into a clean screw-top jar. Add the soy sauce, sunflower and hazelnut oils, garlic and root ginger. Add some salt and pepper, then close the jar tightly and shake well to combine.

4 Pour the dressing over the salad and toss well. Sprinkle the spring onions over the top.

NUTRITION NOTES

Per portion:

Energy	245Kcals/1029kJ
Fat	4.25g
Saturated fat	0.6g
Cholesterol	0mg

SHELLFISH SALAD WITH FRAGRANT HERBS

Serves 6

250ml/8fl oz/1 cup fish stock or water
250g/12oz squid, cleaned, cut into rings
12 uncooked king prawns (jumbo
 shrimp), shelled
12 scallops
50g/2oz bean thread noodles, soaked in
 warm water for 30 minutes
½ cucumber, cut into thin sticks
1 lemon grass stalk, finely chopped
2 kaffir lime leaves, finely shredded
2 shallots, finely sliced
juice of 1–2 limes
30ml/2 tbsp fish sauce
30ml/2 tbsp chopped spring
 onions (scallions)
30ml/2 tbsp chopped fresh coriander
 (cilantro) leaves
12–15 mint leaves, roughly torn
4 red chillies, seeded and sliced
coriander (cilantro) sprigs, to garnish

1 Pour the stock or water into a medium pan, set over a high heat and bring to the boil.

2 Cook each type of shellfish separately in the stock. Don't over-cook – it takes only a few minutes for each shellfish. Remove and set aside.

3 Drain the bean thread noodles and cut them into short lengths, about 5cm/2in long. Combine the noodles with the cooked shellfish.

4 Add all the remaining ingredients, mix together well and serve garnished with coriander sprigs.

NUTRITION NOTES	
Per portion:	
Energy	78Kcals/332kJ
Fat	1.12g
Saturated fat	0.26g
Cholesterol	123mg
Fibre	0.37g

COOK'S TIP
Use other prepared shellfish, such as mussels, cockles and clams, in place of the prawns or scallops. If fresh chillies are not available, use 10–15ml/2–3 tsp of hot chilli powder or, alternatively, use ready-chopped chillies.

GREEN PAPAYA SALAD

There are many variations of this salad in south-east Asia. As green papaya is not easy to get hold of, shredded carrots, cucumber or green apple may be substituted. Serve this salad with raw white cabbage and rice.

INGREDIENTS

Serves 4
1 medium green papaya
4 garlic cloves
15ml/1 tbsp chopped shallots
3–4 red chillies, seeded and sliced
2.5ml/½ tsp salt
2–3 French or runner beans, cut into
    2cm/¾in lengths
2 tomatoes, cut into wedges
45ml/3 tbsp fish sauce
15ml/1 tbsp caster (superfine) sugar
juice of 1 lime
30ml/2 tbsp crushed roasted peanuts
sliced red chillies, to garnish

1 Peel the papaya and cut in half lengthways, scrape out the seeds with a spoon and finely shred the flesh.

2 Grind the garlic, shallots, chillies and salt together in a large mortar with a pestle.

3 Add the shredded papaya a little at a time and pound until it becomes slightly limp and soft.

4 Add the sliced beans and tomatoes and lightly crush. Season with fish sauce, sugar and lime juice.

5 Transfer the salad to a serving dish, sprinkle with crushed peanuts and garnish with chillies.

COOK'S TIP
If you do not have a large pestle and mortar, use a bowl and crush the shredded papaya with a wooden meat tenderizer or the end of a rolling pin.

NUTRITION NOTES	
Per portion:	
Energy	96Kcals/402kJ
Fat	4.2g
Saturated fat	0.77g
Cholesterol	0mg

THAI-STYLE CHICKEN SALAD

This salad comes from Chiang Mai, a city in the north-east of Thailand. It's hot and spicy, and wonderfully aromatic. Choose strong-flavoured leaves, such as curly endive or rocket (arugula), for the salad.

INGREDIENTS

Serves 6

450g/1lb minced (ground) chicken
1 lemon grass stalk, finely chopped
3 kaffir lime leaves, finely chopped
4 red chillies, seeded and chopped
60ml/4 tbsp lime juice
30ml/2 tbsp fish sauce
15ml/1 tbsp roasted ground rice
2 spring onions (scallions), chopped
30ml/2 tbsp coriander (cilantro) leaves
mixed salad leaves, cucumber and
*   tomato slices, to serve*
mint sprigs, to garnish

1 Heat a large non-stick frying pan. Add the minced chicken and cook in a little water.

2 Stir constantly until cooked, which will take about 7–10 minutes.

COOK'S TIP
Use sticky (glutinous) rice to make roasted ground rice. Put the rice in a frying pan and dry roast until golden brown. Remove and grind to a powder with a pestle and mortar or in a food processor. Keep in a glass jar in a cool dry place and use as required.

3 Transfer the cooked chicken to a large bowl and add the rest of the ingredients. Mix thoroughly.

4 Serve on a bed of mixed salad leaves, cucumber and tomato slices, garnished with mint sprigs.

NUTRITION NOTES	
Per portion:	
Energy	106Kcals/446kJ
Fat	1.13g
Saturated fat	0.28g
Cholesterol	52.5mg
Fibre	0.7g

FRUITY PASTA AND PRAWN SALAD

Orange cantaloupe or Charentais melon look spectacular in this salad. Or try a mixture of ogen, cantaloupe and water melon.

INGREDIENTS

Serves 6

175g/6oz pasta shapes
225g/8oz/2 cups frozen prawns
   (shrimp), thawed and drained
1 large or 2 small melons
30ml/2 tbsp olive oil
15ml/1 tbsp tarragon vinegar
30ml/2 tbsp chopped fresh chives
   or chopped parsley
herb sprigs, to garnish
shredded Chinese leaves (Chinese
   cabbage), to serve

NUTRITION NOTES

Per portion:	
Energy	167Kcals/705kJ
Fat	4.72g
Saturated fat	0.68g
Cholesterol	105mg
Fibre	2.08g

1 Cook the pasta in boiling salted water according to the instructions on the packet. Drain well and allow to cool.

COOK'S TIP
Use whole-wheat pasta in place of white pasta, and mussels or scallops in place of prawns (shrimp).

2 Peel the prawns and discard the shells.

3 Halve the melon(s) and remove the seeds with a teaspoon. Scoop the flesh into balls with a melon baller and mix with the prawns and pasta.

4 Whisk the oil, vinegar and chopped herbs together. Pour on to the prawn mixture and turn to coat. Cover and chill for at least 30 minutes.

5 Meanwhile, shred the Chinese leaves and use to line a shallow bowl or the empty melon shells. Pile the prawn mixture on to the Chinese leaves and garnish with herb sprigs.

PRAWN NOODLE SALAD

A light, refreshing salad with all the tangy flavour of the sea. Instead of prawns (shrimp), try squid, scallops, mussels or crab.

INGREDIENTS

Serves 4

115g/4oz cellophane noodles, soaked
  in hot water until soft
16 cooked prawns (shrimp), peeled
1 small red (bell) pepper, seeded and
  cut into strips
½ cucumber, cut into strips
1 tomato, cut into strips
2 shallots, finely sliced
salt and black pepper
coriander (cilantro) leaves, to garnish

For the dressing

15ml/1 tbsp rice vinegar
30ml/2 tbsp fish sauce
30ml/2 tbsp fresh lime juice
pinch of salt
2.5ml/½ tsp grated fresh root ginger
1 lemon grass stalk, finely chopped
1 red chilli, seeded and finely sliced
30ml/2 tbsp roughly chopped mint
a few sprigs of tarragon, roughly chopped
15ml/1 tbsp chopped chives

1 Make the dressing by combining all the ingredients in a small bowl or jug; whisk well.

2 Drain the noodles, then plunge them in a pan of boiling water for 1 minute. Drain, rinse under cold running water and drain again well.

3 In a large bowl, combine the noodles with the prawns, red pepper, cucumber, tomato and shallots. Lightly season with salt and pepper, then toss with the dressing.

4 Spoon the noodles on to individual plates. Garnish with a few coriander leaves and serve immediately.

NUTRITION NOTES	
Per portion:	
Energy	164.5Kcals/697kJ
Fat	2.9g
Saturated fat	0.79g
Cholesterol	121mg
Fibre	1.86g

COOK'S TIP
Prawns (shrimp) are available ready-cooked and often shelled. To cook prawns, boil them for 5 minutes. Leave them to cool in the cooking liquid, then gently pull off the tail shell and twist off the head.

CACHUMBAR

Cachumbar is a salad relish most served with Indian curries. There are many versions; this one will leave your mouth feeling cool and fresh after a spicy meal.

INGREDIENTS

Serves 4

3 ripe tomatoes
2 chopped spring onions (scallions)
1.5ml/¼ tsp caster (superfine) sugar
salt
45ml/3 tbsp chopped fresh coriander
   (cilantro)

NUTRITION NOTES

Per portion:	
Energy	9.5Kcals/73.5kJ
Fat	0.23g
Saturated fat	0.07g
Cholesterol	0mg
Fibre	0.87g

1 Remove the tough cores from the bottom of the tomatoes using a small, sharp knife.

COOK'S TIP
Cachumbar also makes a fine accompaniment to fresh crab, lobster and shellfish.

2 Halve the tomatoes, remove the seeds and dice the flesh.

3 Combine the tomatoes with the spring onions, sugar, salt and chopped coriander. Serve at room temperature.

WARM CHICKEN LIVER SALAD

Although warm salads may seem over-fussy or trendy, there are times when they are just right. Serve this delicious combination as either an appetizer or a light meal, with hunks of bread.

INGREDIENTS

Serves 4

115g/4oz each fresh young spinach leaves, rocket (arugula) and lollo rosso lettuce
2 pink grapefruit
90ml/6 tbsp sunflower oil
10ml/2 tsp sesame oil
10ml/2 tsp soy sauce
225g/8oz chicken livers, chopped
salt and black pepper

1 Wash, dry and tear up all the leaves. Mix them together well in a large salad bowl.

2 Carefully cut away all the peel and white pith from the grapefruit, then neatly segment them catching all the juices in a bowl. Add the grapefruit segments to the leaves in the bowl.

3 To make the dressing, mix together 60ml/4 tbsp of the sunflower oil with the sesame oil, soy sauce, seasoning and grapefruit juice to taste.

4 Heat the rest of the sunflower oil in a small pan and cook the liver, stirring gently, until firm and lightly browned.

5 Tip the chicken livers and dressing over the salad and serve at once.

NUTRITION NOTES	
Per portion:	
Energy	266Kcals/1107kJ
Fat	20.10g
Saturated fat	2.74g
Cholesterol	213.75mg

WATERCRESS POTATO SALAD BOWL

New potatoes are equally good hot or cold, and this colourful, nutritious salad is an ideal way of making the most of them.

INGREDIENTS

Serves 4

450g/1lb small new potatoes, unpeeled
1 bunch watercress
200g/7oz cherry tomatoes, halved
30ml/2 tbsp pumpkin seeds
45ml/3 tbsp low-fat fromage frais or crème fraîche
15ml/1 tbsp cider vinegar
5ml/1 tsp soft light brown sugar
salt and paprika

1 Cook the potatoes in lightly salted, boiling water until just tender, then drain and leave to cool.

2 Toss together the potatoes, watercress, tomatoes and pumpkin seeds.

3 Place the fromage frais, vinegar, sugar, salt and paprika in a screw-topped jar and shake well to mix. Pour over the salad just before serving.

NUTRITION NOTES

Per portion:

Energy	150kcals/630kJ
Fat	4.15g
Saturated fat	0.81g
Cholesterol	0.11mg
Fibre	2.55g

COOK'S TIP

If you can't find watercress, use rocket (arugula) or any other strongly flavoured salad leaves.

FENNEL AND HERB COLESLAW

Serve this delicious vegetarian salad as an accompaniment, or turn it into a main meal with the addition of some low fat cottage cheese and thick slices of crisp red-skinned apples.

INGREDIENTS

Serves 4

175g/6oz fennel
2 spring onions (scallions)
175g/6oz white cabbage
115g/4oz celery
175g/6oz carrots
50g/2oz sultanas (golden raisins)
2.5ml/½ tsp caraway seeds (optional)
15ml/1 tbsp chopped fresh parsley
45ml/3 tbsp fat-free French dressing
5ml/1 tsp lemon juice
salt and ground black pepper
shreds of spring onion, to garnish

VARIATION
Use reduced fat mayonnaise in place of the French dressing.

2 Slice the cabbage and celery finely and cut the carrots into fine strips. Place in a large serving bowl with the other vegetables. Add the sultanas and caraway seeds, if using, and toss lightly to mix.

3 Stir in the chopped parsley, French dressing and lemon juice and mix well, then season with salt and pepper. Cover and chill for 3 hours to allow the flavours to mingle, then serve, garnished with spring onion shreds.

1 Using a sharp knife, cut the fennel and spring onions into thin slices.

NUTRITION NOTES

Per portion:
Energy	74Kcals/315KJ
Fat	0.5g
Saturated fat	0.05g
Cholesterol	0mg

SWEET POTATO AND CARROT SALAD

INGREDIENTS

Serves 4

1 sweet potato, peeled and
roughly diced
2 carrots, cut into thick diagonal slices
3 tomatoes
8–10 iceberg lettuce leaves
75g/3oz/¾ cup canned
chickpeas, drained

For the dressing
15ml/1 tbsp clear honey
90ml/6 tbsp low-fat natural (plain) yogurt
2.5ml/½ tsp salt
5ml/1 tsp coarsely ground black pepper

For the garnish
15ml/1 tbsp walnuts
15ml/1 tbsp sultanas (golden raisins)
1 small onion, cut into rings

NUTRITION NOTES

Per portion:
Energy	176kcals/741kJ
Fat	4.85g
Saturated fat	0.58g
Cholesterol	0.85mg

1 Place the sweet potato in a large pan and cover with water. Bring to the boil and cook until soft but not mushy, cover the pan and set aside. Meanwhile, boil the carrots for a few minutes, making sure they remain crunchy. Add to the sweet potatoes.

2 Drain the water from the sweet potatoes and carrots, and place together in a bowl.

3 Slice the tops off the tomatoes, then scoop out and discard the seeds. Roughly chop the flesh.

4 Line a glass bowl with the lettuce leaves. Mix together the sweet potatoes, carrots, chickpeas and tomatoes, and place in the bowl.

5 For the dressing, blend together all the ingredients and beat together with a fork.

6 Spoon the dressing over the salad or serve it in a separate bowl, if desired. Garnish the salad with the walnuts, sultanas and onion rings.

BEETROOT, CHICORY AND ORANGE SALAD

A refreshing salad which goes well with grilled meats or fish. Alternatively, arrange it prettily on individual plates and serve as a summer appetizer.

INGREDIENTS

Serves 4
2 medium cooked beetroot
 (beets), diced
2 heads chicory (Belgian endive), sliced
1 large orange
60ml/4 tbsp low-fat natural (plain)
 yogurt
10ml/2 tsp wholegrain mustard
salt and ground black pepper

1 Mix together the diced, cooked beetroot and sliced chicory in a large serving bowl.

2 Finely grate the rind from the orange. With a sharp knife, remove all the peel and white pith. Cut out the segments, catching the juice in a bowl. Add the segments to the salad.

3 Add the orange rind, yogurt, mustard and seasoning to the orange juice, mix thoroughly, then spoon over the salad.

COOK'S TIP
Fresh baby spinach leaves or rocket (arugula) could be used in place of the chicory, if you prefer.

NUTRITION NOTES	
Per portion:	
Energy	41kcals/172kJ
Fat	0.60g
Saturated fat	0.08g
Cholesterol	0.60mg
Fibre	1.42g

ROASTED PEPPER SALAD

This colourful salad is very easy and can be made up to a day in advance, as the sharp-sweet dressing mingles with the mild pepper flavours.

INGREDIENTS

Serves 4
3 large red, green and yellow (bell)
 peppers, halved and seeded
115g/4oz feta cheese, diced
 or crumbled
15ml/1 tbsp sherry vinegar or red
 wine vinegar
15ml/1 tbsp clear honey
salt and ground black pepper

1 Arrange the pepper halves in a single layer, skin side upwards, on a baking sheet. Place the peppers under a hot grill (broiler) until the skin is blackened and beginning to blister.

2 Lift the peppers into a plastic bag and close the end. Leave until cool, then peel off and discard the skin.

3 Arrange the peppers on a platter and sprinkle the cheese over them. Mix together the vinegar, honey and seasonings, then sprinkle over the salad. Chill until ready to serve.

NUTRITION NOTES	
Per portion:	
Energy	110kcals/462kJ
Fat	6.15g
Saturated fat	3.65g
Cholesterol	20.13mg
Fibre	1.84g

CABBAGE SLAW WITH DATE AND APPLE

Three types of cabbage are shredded together for serving raw, so that the maximum amount of vitamin C is retained in this cheerful salad.

INGREDIENTS

Serves 6–8
1/4 *small white cabbage, shredded*
1/4 *small red cabbage, shredded*
1/4 *small Savoy cabbage, shredded*
175g/6oz/1 cup dried pitted dates
3 eating apples
juice of 1 lemon
10ml/2 tsp caraway seeds

For the dressing
60ml/4 tbsp olive oil
15ml/1 tbsp cider vinegar
5ml/1 tsp clear honey
salt and ground black pepper

1 Finely shred all the cabbages and place them in a large salad bowl.

2 Chop the dates and add them to the cabbage.

3 Core the eating apples and slice them thinly into a mixing bowl. Add the lemon juice and toss together to prevent discoloration before adding to the salad bowl.

4 Make the dressing. Combine the oil, vinegar and honey in a screw-top jar. Add salt and pepper, then close the jar tightly and shake well. Pour the dressing over the salad, toss lightly, then sprinkle with the caraway seeds and toss again.

> **COOK'S TIP**
> Support local orchards by looking for different home-grown apples.

NUTRITION NOTES	
Per portion:	
Energy	200Kcals/835KJ
Fat	8g
Saturated fat	1g
Cholesterol	0mg

SPROUTED SEED SALAD

If you sprout beans, lentils and whole grains it increases their nutritional value, and they make a deliciously crunchy salad.

INGREDIENTS

Serves 4
2 eating apples
115g/4oz alfalfa sprouts
115g/4oz beansprouts
115g/4oz aduki beansprouts
1/4 *cucumber, sliced*
1 bunch watercress, trimmed
1 carton mustard and cress, trimmed

For the dressing
150ml/1/4 pint/2/3 cup low fat natural (plain) yogurt
juice of 1/2 lemon
bunch of chives, chopped
30ml/2 tbsp chopped fresh herbs
ground black pepper

1 Core and slice the apples and mix with the other salad ingredients.

2 Mix the dressing ingredients in a jug. Drizzle over the salad and toss together just before serving.

NUTRITION NOTES	
Per portion:	
Energy	85Kcals/355KJ
Fat	1.5g
Saturated fat	0.5g
Cholesterol	1.5mg

FATTOUSH

This Middle Eastern mixed salad is traditionally topped with pieces of unleavened bread to soak up the dressing. It provides the perfect solution of what to do with slightly stale pitta breads.

INGREDIENTS

Serves 4
2 wholemeal (whole-wheat)
    pitta breads
1 iceberg, cos or romaine lettuce,
    torn into pieces
1 green (bell) pepper, seeded
10cm/4in length of cucumber
4 tomatoes
4 spring onions (scallions)
a few black olives, to garnish

For the dressing
60ml/4 tbsp olive oil
45ml/3 tbsp freshly squeezed
    lemon juice
2 garlic cloves, crushed
45ml/3 tbsp finely chopped
    fresh parsley
30ml/2 tbsp finely chopped
    fresh mint
few drops of harissa or chilli sauce
    (optional)
salt and ground black pepper

1 Toast the pitta breads on both sides until crisp and golden. Cut into rough squares and set aside.

2 Place the lettuce in a large bowl. Chop the green pepper, cucumber, tomatoes and spring onions roughly, making sure they are all about the same size. Add them to the lettuce and toss together well.

3 Make the dressing by shaking all the ingredients together in a screw-top jar.

4 Just before serving the dish, pour the dressing from the jar over the salad and toss well to combine together. Scatter pieces of pitta bread over the salad and garnish with the black olives.

NUTRITION NOTES	
Per portion:	
Energy	225Kcals/935KJ
Fat	13g
Saturated fat	2g
Cholesterol	0

COOK'S TIP
Any salad leaves can be used instead of lettuce. Try young spinach or Swiss chard.

GREEN GREEN SALAD

You could make this lovely dish at any time of the year using imported or frozen vegetables and still get a pretty, healthy – and unusual – salad.

INGREDIENTS

Serves 4

175g/6oz shelled broad (fava) beans
115g/4oz French (green) or flat beans,
  cut into quarters
115g/4oz mangetouts (snow peas)
8–10 small fresh mint leaves
3 spring onions (scallions), chopped
60ml/4 tbsp green olive oil
15ml/1 tbsp cider vinegar
15ml/1 tbsp chopped fresh mint,
  or 5ml/1 tsp dried
1 garlic clove, crushed
salt and black pepper

1 Plunge the broad beans into a saucepan of boiling water and bring back to the boil. Remove from the heat immediately and plunge into cold water. Drain. Repeat with the French or flat beans.

2 Mix together the blanched beans, the raw mangetouts, mint leaves and spring onions.

3 Mix together the olive oil, vinegar, chopped mint, garlic and seasoning thoroughly, then pour over the salad and toss well. Chill until ready to serve.

NUTRITION NOTES

Per portion:	
Energy	153Kcals/635kJ
Fat	11.5g
Saturated fat	1.65g
Cholesterol	0mg

MANGO, PRAWN AND TOMATO SALAD

INGREDIENTS

Serves 4
1 large mango
225g/8oz extra large cooked tiger
  prawns (shrimp), peeled and deveined
16 cherry tomatoes, halved
fresh mint, to garnish

For the dressing
15ml/1 tbsp white wine vinegar
2.5ml/½ tsp clear honey
15ml/1 tbsp mango or apricot chutney
15ml/1 tbsp chopped fresh mint
15ml/1 tbsp chopped fresh lemon balm
45ml/3 tbsp olive oil
salt and ground black pepper

NUTRITION NOTES	
Per portion:	
Energy	230Kcals/960KJ
Fat	10g
Saturated fat	1.5g
Cholesterol	45.5mg

1 Using a sharp knife, peel, stone and dice the mango carefully. Mix with the tiger prawns and cherry tomatoes in a bowl. Toss lightly to mix, then cover and chill.

2 Make the salad dressing by mixing the vinegar, clear honey, chutney and fresh herbs in a bowl. Gradually whisk in the oil, then add salt and pepper to taste.

3 Spoon the prawn mixture into the dressing and toss lightly, then divide among serving dishes. Garnish with the fresh mint sprigs and serve.

COOK'S TIP
If you use frozen prawns, thaw them in a colander, then drain thoroughly on kitchen paper before use or the water will dilute the salad dressing and spoil the flavour.

CHICKEN AND CRANBERRY SALAD

INGREDIENTS

Serves 4
4 boned chicken breast portions, total
  weight about 675g/1½lb
300ml/½ pint/1¼ cups stock or a
  mixture of stock and white wine
fresh herb sprigs
200g/7oz mixed salad leaves
50g/2oz/½ cup chopped walnuts
  or hazelnuts

For the dressing
30ml/2 tbsp olive oil
15ml/1 tbsp walnut or hazelnut oil
15ml/1 tbsp raspberry or red
  wine vinegar
30ml/2 tbsp cranberry relish
salt and ground black pepper

1 Skin the chicken. Pour the stock (or stock and wine mixture) into a large shallow pan. Add the herbs and bring the liquid to simmering point. Poach the chicken for about 15 minutes until cooked through. Alternatively, leave the skin on the chicken and grill (broil) or roast until tender, then remove the skin.

2 Arrange the salad leaves on four plates. Slice each chicken portion neatly, keeping the slices together, then place each portion on top of a portion of salad, fanning the slices out slightly.

3 Make the dressing by shaking all the ingredients together in a screw-top jar. Spoon a little dressing over each salad and sprinkle with the walnuts or hazelnuts.

NUTRITION NOTES	
Per portion:	
Energy	365Kcals/1530KJ
Fat	22g
Saturated fat	3.5g
Cholesterol	64.5mg

TWO PEAR SALAD

Serves 4
2 courgettes (zucchini), grated
2 avocados
2 ripe eating pears
1 large carrot

For the dressing
250ml/8fl oz/1 cup low fat natural
* (plain) yogurt*
60ml/4 tbsp reduced-calorie
* mayonnaise*
grated rind of 1 lemon
8–10 chives, chopped
30ml/2 tbsp chopped fresh mint
ground black pepper
4 mint sprigs, to garnish

1 Pile the grated courgettes on to four individual serving plates.

2 Cut the avocados in half, remove the stones (pits) and peel. Slice each half lengthways. Core and slice the pears. Arrange avocado and pear slices on top of each courgette salad.

3 Peel the carrot, then use the peeler to peel off fine ribbons.

4 Make the dressing. Mix the yogurt and mayonnaise together in a bowl, then stir in the lemon rind, chives and chopped mint. Season with pepper. Drizzle some of the dressing over each salad and garnish with a mint sprig. Serve immediately.

> COOK'S TIP
> If the salad is not to be served straight away, sprinkle the avocado with lemon juice or the flesh will discolour.

NUTRITION NOTES	
Per portion:	
Energy	260Kcals/1090KJ
Fat	19.5g
Saturated fat	3g
Cholesterol	2.5g

FOUR SEASONS SALAD PLATTER

Fresh vegetable salads are packed with vitamin C. Include some protein foods and serve with a hunk of crusty bread for a well-balanced snack or simple lunch.

INGREDIENTS

Serves 4
4 chicory (Belgian endive) leaves
115g/4oz French (green) beans,
  lightly cooked
7.5cm/3in length of cucumber,
  cut into sticks
6 cherry tomatoes
1 hard-boiled egg, halved

Carrot and Radish Salad
2 carrots
2 radishes
15ml/1 tbsp chopped mixed nuts

Beetroot and Onion Salad
2–3 cooked beetroot (beets), sliced
15ml/1 tbsp balsamic or wine vinegar
2–3 spring onions (scallions),
  finely chopped
30ml/2 tbsp chopped fresh parsley

Mushroom and Thyme Salad
75g/3oz/³⁄4 cup button (white)
  mushrooms, sliced
30ml/2 tbsp lemon juice
15ml/1 tbsp chopped fresh thyme

Tuna and Haricot Bean Salad
90g/3¹⁄2oz can tuna in oil
200g/7oz can haricot (navy) beans
¹⁄2 red onion, thinly sliced
30ml/2 tbsp chopped fresh parsley

NUTRITION NOTES

Per portion:
Energy	405Kcals/1690KJ
Fat	13.5g
Saturated fat	2.5g
Cholesterol	122.5mg

1 Grate the carrots and radishes. Mix together with the nuts in a bowl.

2 Sprinkle the beetroot with vinegar, add the spring onions and parsley and toss lightly.

3 Mix the mushrooms with the lemon juice and thyme.

4 Drain the tuna and beans, tip them both into a bowl and toss with the onion and parsley.

5 Divide the chicory leaves between two large salad plates. Add a portion of each salad, arranging them attractively with the French beans, cucumber sticks, tomatoes and egg halves. Serve with crusty bread.

CITRUS GREEN SALAD WITH CROUTONS

Wholemeal croûtons add a delicious crunch to leaf salads. The kumquats or orange segments provide a colour contrast as well as a good helping of vitamin C.

INGREDIENTS

Serves 4–6
4 kumquats or 2 seedless oranges
200g/7oz mixed green salad leaves
4 slices of wholemeal (whole-wheat) bread, crusts removed
30–45ml/2–3 tbsp pine nuts, lightly toasted

For the dressing
grated rind of 1 lemon and 15ml/1tbsp juice
45ml/3 tbsp olive oil
5ml/1 tsp wholegrain mustard
1 garlic clove, crushed

1 Thinly slice the kumquat, or peel and segment the oranges.

NUTRITION NOTES	
Per portion:	
Energy	250Kcals/1000KJ
Fat	15g
Saturated fat	2g
Cholesterol	0mg

2 Tear all the salad leaves into bite-size pieces and place together in a large salad bowl.

3 Toast the bread on both sides and cut into cubes. Add to the salad leaves with the sliced kumquats or orange segments.

4 Shake all the dressing ingredients together in a jar. Pour over the salad just before serving and scatter the toasted pine nuts over the top.

BEAN SALAD WITH TOMATO DRESSING

All beans are a good source of vegetable protein, and minerals.

INGREDIENTS

Serves 4
115g/4oz French (green) beans
425g/15oz can mixed beans, drained and rinsed
2 celery sticks, finely chopped
1 small onion, finely chopped
3 tomatoes, chopped
45ml/3 tbsp chopped fresh parsley, to garnish

For the dressing
45ml/3 tbsp olive oil
10ml/2 tsp red wine vinegar
1 garlic clove, crushed
15ml/1 tbsp tomato chutney
salt and ground black pepper

1 Remove the ends from the French beans, then cook the beans in boiling water for 5–6 minutes (or steam for 10 minutes) until tender. Drain, then refresh under cold running water and cut into thirds.

2 Place the French beans and mixed beans in a large bowl. Add the celery, onion and tomatoes and toss together lightly.

3 Shake the dressing ingredients together in a jar. Pour over the salad and sprinkle with the parsley.

COOK'S TIP
Cans of mixed beans and peas include several different types such as chickpeas, pinto, black-eye, red kidney, soya and aduki beans, and save the hassle of long soaking and cooking that dried beans require.

NUTRITION NOTES	
Per portion:	
Energy	175Kcals/740KJ
Fat	9.5g
Saturated fat	1.5g
Cholesterol	0mg

DESSERTS

When we talk of desserts and puddings we tend to imagine deliciously rich, creamy, calorie-laden treats which are well out of reach if you are following a low fat diet. However, it is very easy to create wonderful low fat desserts, full of flavour, colour and appeal that will satisfy a sweet tooth any day. We include a tasty selection of hot and cold desserts, including temptations such as Floating Islands in Hot Plum Sauce, Baked Apples in Honey and Lemon, Papaya Skewers with Passionfruit, Blushing Pears, and Fruit Fondue with Hazelnut Dip.

BAKED APPLES IN HONEY AND LEMON

A classic mix of flavours in a healthy, traditional family pudding. Serve warm, with skimmed-milk custard or low fat frozen yogurt.

INGREDIENTS

Serves 4
4 medium cooking apples
15ml/1 tbsp clear honey
grated rind and juice of 1 lemon
15ml/1 tbsp low fat spread
skimmed-milk custard, to serve

1 Preheat the oven to 180°C/350°F/ Gas 4. Remove the cores from the apples, leaving them whole.

NUTRITION NOTES

Per portion:
Energy	61Kcals/259.5kJ
Fat	1.62g
Saturated fat	0.42g
Cholesterol	0.25mg

2 With a cannelle or sharp knife, cut lines through the apple skin at intervals. Put the apples in an oven-proof dish.

3 Mix together the honey, lemon rind, juice and low fat spread.

4 Spoon the mixture into the apples and cover the dish with foil or a lid. Bake for 40–45 minutes, or until the apples are tender. Serve with skimmed-milk custard.

APPLE AND BLACKCURRANT PANCAKES

These pancakes are made with a wholewheat batter and are filled with a delicious fruit mixture.

INGREDIENTS

Makes 10
115g/4oz/1 cup wholemeal (whole-
  wheat) flour
300ml/½ pint/1¼ cups skimmed milk
1 egg, beaten
15ml/1 tbsp sunflower oil, plus extra
  for greasing
half fat crème fraîche, to serve (optional)
toasted nuts or sesame seeds, for
  sprinkling (optional)

For the filling
450g/1lb cooking apples
225g/8oz blackcurrants
30–45ml/2–3 tbsp water
30ml/2 tbsp demerara (raw) sugar

1 To make the pancake batter, put the flour in a mixing bowl and make a well in the centre.

2 Add a little of the milk with the egg and the oil. Beat the flour into the liquid, then gradually beat in the rest of the milk, keeping the batter smooth and free from lumps. Cover the batter and chill while you prepare the filling.

> COOK'S TIP
> If you wish, substitute other combinations of fruit for apples and blackcurrants.

3 Quarter, peel and core the apples. Slice them into a pan and add the blackcurrants and water. Cook over a gentle heat for 10–15 minutes until the fruit is soft. Stir in enough demerara sugar to sweeten.

NUTRITION NOTES

Per portion:	
Energy	120Kcals/505kJ
Fat	3g
Saturated fat	0.5g
Cholesterol	25mg

4 Lightly grease a non-stick pan with just a smear of oil. Heat the pan, pour in about 30ml/2 tbsp of the batter, swirl it around and cook for about 1 minute. Flip the pancake over and cook the other side. Put on a sheet of kitchen paper and keep hot while cooking the remaining pancakes.

5 Fill the pancakes with the apple and blackcurrant mixture and roll them up. Serve with a dollop of crème fraîche, if using, and sprinkle with nuts or sesame seeds, if you like.

FLOATING ISLANDS IN HOT PLUM SAUCE

An unusual pudding that is simpler to make than it looks. The plum sauce can be made in advance, and reheated just before you cook the meringues.

INGREDIENTS

Serves 4
450g/1lb red plums
300ml/½ pint/1¼ cups apple juice
2 egg whites
30ml/2 tbsp concentrated apple juice
freshly grated nutmeg, to sprinkle

NUTRITION NOTES

Per portion:

Energy	90kcals/380kJ
Fat	0.3g
Saturated fat	0g
Cholesterol	0mg
Fibre	1.69g

1 Halve the plums and remove the stones (pits). Place them in a wide pan, with the apple juice.

2 Bring to the boil, then cover and simmer gently until the plums have become tender.

3 Meanwhile, place the egg whites in a clean, dry bowl and whisk them until they hold soft peaks.

4 Gradually whisk in the concentrated apple juice, whisking until the meringue holds fairly firm peaks.

5 Using a tablespoon, scoop the meringue mixture into the gently simmering plum sauce. You may need to cook the "islands" in two batches.

6 Cover and simmer gently for about 2–3 minutes, until the meringues are set. Serve immediately, sprinkled with a little freshly grated nutmeg.

COOK'S TIP
A bottle of concentrated apple juice is a useful sweetener, but if you don't have any, use a little clear honey instead.

LATTICED PEACHES

Serves 6
For the pastry
115g/4oz/1 cup plain (all-purpose)
  flour
45ml/3 tbsp butter or margarine
45ml/3 tbsp low fat natural (plain) yogurt
30ml/2 tbsp orange juice
skimmed milk, for brushing

For the filling
3 ripe peaches or nectarines
45ml/3 tbsp ground almonds
30ml/2 tbsp low fat natural (plain) yogurt
finely grated rind of 1 small orange
1.25ml/¹/4 tsp almond extract

For the sauce
1 ripe peach or nectarine
45ml/3 tbsp orange juice

NUTRITION NOTES

Per portion:	
Energy	192Kcals/806kJ
Fat	9.6g
Saturated fat	4.07g
Cholesterol	15.92mg

1 Sift the flour into a bowl and use your fingers to rub in the butter or margarine. Stir in the yogurt and orange juice to make a firm dough.

2 Roll out half of the pastry and cut out rounds about 7.5cm /3in across. Place on a lightly greased baking sheet.

3 Skin and halve the peaches or nectarines. Mix together the almonds, yogurt, orange rind and almond extract. Spoon the mixture into the hollows of each fruit half.

4 Place each peach or nectarine half cut-side down on a pastry round. Cut thin pastry strips and arrange on top to form a lattice. Brush with milk to secure firmly. Chill for 30 minutes.

5 Heat the oven to 200°C/400°F/Gas 6. Brush the fruit with milk. Bake for 15 minutes, until golden brown.

6 For the sauce, skin a ripe peach or nectarine and halve it to remove the pit. Place the flesh in a food processor with the orange juice and purée it until smooth. Serve the latticed peaches or nectarines hot with the smooth sauce spooned around.

BLUEBERRY AND ORANGE CREPE BASKETS

Impress your guests with these pretty fruit-filled crêpes. When blueberries are out of season, replace them with other soft fruit, such as raspberries.

INGREDIENTS

Serves 6
150g/5oz/1¼ cups plain (all-purpose) flour
pinch of salt
2 egg whites
200ml/7fl oz/⅞ cup skimmed milk
150ml/¼ pint/⅔ cup orange juice
oil, for frying
yogurt or light crème fraîche, to serve

For the filling
4 medium oranges
225g/8oz/2 cups blueberries

1 Preheat the oven to 200°C/400°F/ Gas 6. To make the pancakes, sift the flour and salt into a bowl. Make a well in the centre and add the egg whites, milk and orange juice. Whisk hard, until all the liquid has been incorporated and the batter is smooth and bubbly.

2 Lightly grease a heavy or non-stick pancake pan and heat it until it is very hot. Pour in just enough batter to cover the base of the pan, swirling it to cover the pan evenly.

3 Cook until the pancake has set and is golden, then turn it to cook the other side. Remove the pancake to a sheet of kitchen paper. Cook the remaining batter in the same way to make 6–8 pancakes.

4 Place six small ovenproof bowls or moulds on a baking sheet and lay the pancakes over these. Bake them in the oven for about 10 minutes, until they are crisp and set into shape. Lift the 'baskets' off the moulds.

5 Pare a thin piece of orange rind from one orange and cut it into fine strips. Blanch the strips in boiling water for 30 seconds, rinse them in cold water and set them aside. Cut all the peel and white pith from the oranges.

6 Divide the oranges into segments, catching the juice, combine with the blueberries and warm them gently. Spoon the fruit into the baskets and scatter the rind over the top. Serve with yogurt or light crème fraîche.

COOK'S TIP
Don't fill the pancake baskets until you're ready to serve them, because they will absorb the fruit juice and begin to soften.

NUTRITION NOTES	
Per portion:	
Energy	157.3Kcals/668.3kJ
Fat	2.20g
Saturated fat	0.23g
Cholesterol	0.66mg
Fibre	2.87g

FILO CHIFFON PIE

Filo pastry is low in fat and is very easy to use. Keep a pack in the freezer, ready to make impressive desserts like this one.

INGREDIENTS

Serves 6
500g/1¼lb rhubarb
5ml/1 tsp mixed (apple pie) spice
finely grated rind and juice of 1 orange
15ml/1 tbsp sugar
15g/½oz/1 tbsp butter
3 filo pastry sheets

1 Preheat the oven to 200°C/400°F/ Gas 6. Chop the rhubarb into 2.5cm/1in pieces and put them in a bowl.

2 Add the mixed spice, orange rind and juice and sugar. Tip the rhubarb into a 1 litre/1¾ pint/4 cup pie dish.

NUTRITION NOTES

Per portion:
Energy	71Kcals/299kJ
Fat	2.5g
Saturated fat	1.41g
Cholesterol	5.74mg
Fibre	1.48g

3 Melt the butter and brush it over the pastry. Lift the pastry on to the pie dish, butter-side up, and crumple it up decoratively to cover the pie.

VARIATION
Other fruit can be used in this pie – just prepare depending on type.

4 Put the dish on a baking sheet and bake for 20 minutes, until golden brown. Reduce the heat to 180°C/350°F/ Gas 4 and bake for a further 10–15 minutes, until the rhubarb is tender.

BLUSHING PEARS

Pears poached in rosé wine and sweet spices absorb all the subtle flavours and turn a delightful soft pink colour.

INGREDIENTS

Serves 6
6 firm eating pears
300ml/1/2 pint/1¼ cups rosé wine
150ml/¼ pint/⅔ cup cranberry or
   clear apple juice
strip of thinly pared orange rind
1 cinnamon stick
4 whole cloves
1 bay leaf
75ml/5 tbsp caster (superfine) sugar
small bay leaves, to decorate

3 Heat gently, stirring all the time, until the sugar has dissolved. Add the pears and stand them upright in the pan. Pour in enough cold water to barely cover them. Cover and cook gently for 20–30 minutes, or until just tender, turning and basting occasionally.

6 Strain the syrup and pour over the pears. Serve hot or well-chilled, decorated with small bay leaves.

NUTRITION NOTES

Per portion:

Energy	148Kcals/620kJ
Fat	0.16g
Saturated fat	0g
Fibre	2.93g

1 Thinly peel the pears with a sharp knife or vegetable peeler, leaving the stalks attached.

4 Using a slotted spoon, gently lift the pears out of the syrup and transfer to a serving dish.

COOK'S TIP
Check the pears by piercing with a skewer or sharp knife towards the end of the poaching time, because some may cook more quickly than others. Serve straight away, or leave to cool in the syrup and then chill.

2 Pour the wine and cranberry or apple juice into a large heavy-based pan. Add the orange rind, cinnamon stick, cloves, bay leaf and sugar.

5 Bring the syrup to the boil and boil rapidly for 10–15 minutes, or until it has reduced by half.

SNOW-CAPPED APPLES

INGREDIENTS

Serves 4

4 small cooking apples
90ml/6 tbsp orange marmalade or jam
2 egg whites
50g/2oz/¼ cup caster (superfine) sugar

1 Preheat the oven to 180°C/350°F/
Gas 4. Core the apples and score
through the skins around the middle
with a sharp knife.

2 Place in a wide ovenproof dish and
spoon 15ml/1 tbsp marmalade or
jam into the centre of each. Cover and
bake for 35–40 minutes, or until tender.

3 Whisk the egg whites in a large
bowl until stiff enough to hold soft
peaks. Whisk in the sugar, then fold in
the remaining marmalade or jam.

4 Spoon the meringue over the
apples, then return to the oven for
10–15 minutes, until golden. Serve hot.

NUTRITION NOTES

Per portion:	
Energy	165kcals/394kJ
Fat	0.16g
Saturated fat	0g
Cholesterol	0mg
Fibre	1.9g

STRAWBERRY APPLE TART

INGREDIENTS

Serves 4–6

150g/5oz/1¼ cups self-raising
  (self-rising) flour
50g/2oz/⅔ cup rolled oats
50g/2oz/¼ cup sunflower margarine
2 medium cooking apples
200g/7oz/2 cups strawberries, halved
50g/2oz/¼ cup caster (superfine) sugar
15ml/1 tbsp cornflour (cornstarch)

1 Preheat the oven to 200°C/400°F/
Gas 6. Mix together the flour and
oats and rub in the margarine. Stir in
just enough cold water to bind the
mixture. Knead lightly until smooth.

2 Roll out the pastry and line a
23cm/ 9in loose-based flan tin
(pan) to make the pastry case (pie
shell). Trim the edges, prick the base
and line with baking parchment and
baking beans. Roll out the pastry
trimmings and stamp out heart shapes.

3 Bake the pastry case for 10 minutes,
remove paper and beans and bake
for 10–15 minutes or until golden
brown. Bake the hearts until golden.

4 Peel, core and slice the apples. Place
in a pan with the strawberries,
sugar and cornflour. Cover and cook
gently, stirring, until the fruit is just
tender. Spoon into the cooled pastry
case and decorate with pastry hearts.

NUTRITION NOTES

Per portion:	
Energy	382kcals/1602kJ
Fat	11.93g
Saturated fat	2.18g
Cholesterol	0.88mg
Fibre	4.37g

GOLDEN GINGER COMPOTE

Warm, spicy and full of sun-ripened ingredients – this is the perfect winter dessert.

INGREDIENTS

Serves 4
200g/7oz/2 cups kumquats
200g/7oz/scant 1 cup (ready-to-eat)
*   dried apricots*
30ml/2 tbsp sultanas (golden raisins)
400ml/14fl oz/1⅔ cups water
1 orange
2.5cm/1in piece fresh root ginger
4 cardamom pods
4 cloves
30ml/2 tbsp clear honey
15ml/1 tbsp flaked (sliced)
*   almonds, toasted*

NUTRITION NOTES

Per portion:
Energy	196kcals/825kJ
Fat	2.84g
Saturated fat	0.41g
Cholesterol	0mg
Fibre	6.82g

2 Pare the rind thinly from the orange, peel and grate the ginger, crush the cardamom pods and add to the pan, with the cloves.

1 Wash the kumquats and, if they are large, cut them in half. Place them in a pan with the apricots, sultanas and water. Bring to the boil.

3 Reduce the heat, cover the pan and simmer gently for about 30 minutes, or until the fruit is tender.

4 Squeeze the juice from the orange and add to the pan with honey to sweeten to taste, sprinkle with flaked almonds, and serve warm.

VARIATION
You can replace half or all of the apricots with other dried fruits, such as prunes, pears, apples, peaches or figs.

NECTARINES WITH SPICED RICOTTA

This easy dessert is good at any time of year – use canned peach halves if fresh nectarines are out of season.

INGREDIENTS

Serves 4

4 ripe nectarines or peaches
115g/4oz/½ cup ricotta cheese
15ml/1 tbsp soft light brown sugar
2.5ml/½ tsp ground star anise,
  to decorate

NUTRITION NOTES

Per portion:	
Energy	92kcals/388kJ
Fat	3.27g
Saturated fat	0g
Cholesterol	14.38mg
Fibre	1.65g

1 Using a sharp knife, cut the nectarines or peaches in half and remove the stones (pits). Preheat the grill (broiler) to medium.

2 Arrange the nectarines or peaches, cut side upwards, in a shallow flameproof dish or on a baking sheet.

3 Place the ricotta cheese in a small mixing bowl. Stir the light brown sugar into the ricotta cheese. Using a teaspoon, spoon equal amounts of the mixture into the hollow of each nectarine or peach half.

4 Sprinkle with the star anise. Cook under the grill for 6–8 minutes, or until the nectarines or peaches are hot. Serve warm.

> COOK'S TIP
> Star anise has a warm, rich flavour – if you can't get it, use ground cloves or ground allspice as an alternative.

COCONUT AND LEMON DUMPLINGS

Serves 4
For the dumplings
75g/3oz/⅓ cup cottage cheese
1 egg white
25g/1oz/2 tbsp low-fat spread
15ml/1 tbsp soft light brown sugar
30ml/2 tbsp self-raising (self-rising)
  wholemeal (whole-wheat) flour
finely grated rind of ½ lemon
30ml/2 tbsp desiccated (dry unsweetened
  shredded) coconut, toasted, plus
  extra, to decorate

For the sauce
225g/8oz can apricot halves in juice
15ml/1 tbsp lemon juice

─────── **NUTRITION NOTES** ───────

Per portion:

Energy	162kcals/681kJ
Fat	9.5g
Saturated fat	5.47g
Cholesterol	33.69mg
Fibre	2.21g

1 Half-fill a steamer with boiling water and put it on to boil, or place a heatproof dish over a pan of boiling water.

2 Beat together the cottage cheese, egg white and low-fat spread.

3 Stir in the sugar, flour, lemon rind and coconut, mixing evenly to form a fairly firm dough.

4 Place eight to 12 spoonfuls of the mixture in the steamer or on the dish, leaving space between them.

5 Cover the steamer or pan tightly with a lid or a plate and steam for about 10 minutes, until the dumplings have risen and are firm to the touch.

6 Meanwhile make the sauce: put the apricots and juice in a food processor or blender, and process until smooth. Stir in the lemon juice. Pour into a small pan and heat until boiling, then serve with the dumplings. Sprinkle with extra coconut to decorate.

WARM BAGELS WITH POACHED APRICOTS

Serves 4

a few strips of orange peel
225g/8oz/1⅓ cups ready-to-eat dried
 apricots
250ml/8fl oz/1 cup fresh orange juice
2.5ml/½ tsp orange flower water
2 cinnamon and raisin bagels
20ml/4 tsp reduced-sugar orange
 marmalade
60ml/4 tbsp half-fat crème fraîche or
 sour cream
15g/½oz/2 tbsp chopped pistachio nuts,
 to decorate

1 Cut the strips of orange peel into fine shreds. Place them in boiling water until softened, then drain and place in cold water.

2 Preheat the oven to 160°C/325°F/ Gas 3. Combine the apricots and orange juice in a small pan. Heat gently for about 10 minutes until the juice has reduced and looks syrupy. Allow to cool, then stir in the orange flower water. Meanwhile, place the bagels on a baking sheet and warm in the oven for 5–10 minutes.

3 Split the bagels in half horizontally. Lay one half, crumb uppermost, on each serving plate. Spread 5ml/1 tsp orange marmalade on each bagel.

―――― **NUTRITION NOTES** ――――

Per portion:	
Energy	260Kcals/1090KJ
Fat	9g
Saturated fat	4g
Cholesterol	51.5mg

4 Spoon 15ml/1 tbsp crème fraîche or sour cream into the centre of each bagel and place a quarter of the apricot compôte at the side. Sprinkle orange peel and pistachio nuts over the top to decorate. Serve immediately.

CRISPY PEACH BAKE

A golden, crisp-crusted, family dessert that's easy to make and always popular.

INGREDIENTS

Serves 4
400g/14oz can peach slices in juice
30ml/2 tbsp sultanas (golden raisins)
1 cinnamon stick
strip of fresh orange rind
25g/1oz/2 tbsp low-fat spread
50g/2oz/1½ cups cornflakes
15ml/1 tbsp sesame seeds

COOK'S TIP
If you don't have a cinnamon stick, sprinkle in about 2.5ml/½ tsp ground cinnamon instead.

NUTRITION NOTES	
Per portion:	
Energy	184kcals/772kJ
Fat	8.42g
Saturated fat	4.26g
Cholesterol	17.25mg

1 Drain the peaches, reserving the juice, and arrange the peach slices in a shallow ovenproof dish.

2 Preheat the oven to 200°C/400°F/ Gas 6. Place the peach juice, sultanas, cinnamon stick and orange rind in a pan and bring to the boil. Simmer, uncovered, for about 3–4 minutes, to reduce the liquid by about half. Remove the cinnamon stick and orange rind, and spoon the syrup over the peaches.

3 Melt the low-fat spread in a small pan and stir in the cornflakes and sesame seeds.

4 Spread the cornflake mixture over the fruit. Bake for approximately 15–20 minutes, or until the topping is crisp and golden. Serve hot.

BAKED BLACKBERRY CHEESECAKE

This light cheesecake is also
delicious made with other soft
fruits such as raspberries,
loganberries or pitted cherries.

INGREDIENTS

Serves 5
175g/6oz/¼ cup cottage cheese
150g/5oz/⅔ cup low-fat natural
(plain) yogurt
15ml/1 tbsp wholemeal
(whole-wheat) flour
30ml/2 tbsp golden caster
(superfine) sugar
1 egg
1 egg white
finely grated rind and juice of ½ lemon
200g/7oz/scant 2 cups blackberries

NUTRITION NOTES	
Per portion:	
Energy	94kcals/394kJ
Fat	1.67g
Saturated fat	1.03g
Cholesterol	5.75mg
Fibre	1.71g

1 Preheat the oven to 180°C/350°F/
Gas 4. Lightly grease and line the
base of an 18cm/7in cake tin (pan).

2 Whizz the cottage cheese in a food
processor or blender until smooth,
or rub it through a sieve (strainer).

3 Add the yogurt, flour, sugar, egg
and egg white, and mix. Add the
lemon rind and juice, and blackberries,
reserving a few for decoration.

4 Turn the mixture into the prepared
tin and bake it for about
30–35 minutes, or until just set. Turn
off the oven and leave for 30 minutes.

5 Run a knife around the edge of the
cheesecake, and then turn it out.

6 Remove the lining paper and place
the cheesecake on a warm serving
plate. Decorate with the reserved
blackberries and serve it warm.

COOK'S TIP
If you prefer to use canned
blackberries, choose those
preserved in natural juice and
drain the fruit well before adding
it to the cheesecake mixture.
The juice may be served with the
cheesecake, but this will increase
the total calories.

CHERRY PANCAKES

INGREDIENTS

Serves 4

50g/2oz/½ cup plain (all-purpose) flour
50g/2oz/½ cup wholemeal
  (whole-wheat) flour
pinch of salt
1 egg white
150ml/¼ pint/⅔ cup skimmed milk
150ml/¼ pint/⅔ cup water
15ml/1 tbsp sunflower oil, for frying
low-fat fromage frais, to serve

For the filling
425g/15oz can black cherries in juice
7.5ml/1½ tsp arrowroot

NUTRITION NOTES

Per portion:
Energy	173kcals/725kJ
Fat	3.33g
Saturated fat	0.44g
Cholesterol	0.75mg
Fibre	2.36g

1 Sift the flours and salt into a bowl, adding any bran left in the sieve (strainer) to the bowl at the end.

2 Make a well in the centre of the flour and add the egg white. Gradually beat in the milk and water, whisking hard until all the liquid is incorporated and the batter is smooth and frothy.

3 Heat a non-stick frying pan with a small amount of oil until the pan is very hot. Pour in just enough batter to cover the base of the pan, swirling the pan to cover the base evenly.

4 Cook until the pancake is set and golden, and then turn to cook the other side. Remove to a sheet of kitchen paper and then cook the remaining bat-ter, to make about eight pancakes.

5 For the filling, drain the cherries, reserving the juice. Blend about 30ml/2 tbsp of the juice from the can of cherries with the arrowroot in a pan. Stir in the rest of the juice. Heat gently, stirring, until boiling. Stir over a medium heat for about 2 minutes, until thickened and clear.

6 Add the cherries to the sauce and stir until thoroughly heated. Spoon the cherries into the pancakes and fold them into quarters.

COOK'S TIP
If fresh cherries are in season, cook them gently in enough apple juice just to cover them, and then thicken the juice with arrowroot as in Step 5. The unfilled pancakes will freeze successfully between layers of baking parchment.

SOUFFLEED RICE PUDDING

INGREDIENTS

Serves 4

65g/2½ oz/¼ cup short grain rice
45ml/3 tbsp clear honey
750ml/1¼ pints/3 cups skimmed milk
1 vanilla pod (bean) or 2.5ml/½ tsp
* vanilla extract*
2 egg whites
5ml/1 tsp freshly grated nutmeg

NUTRITION NOTES

Per portion:
Energy	163kcals/683kJ
Fat	0.62g
Saturated fat	0.16g
Cholesterol	3.75mg
Fibre	0.08g

1 Place the rice, honey and milk in a heavy or non-stick pan, and bring the milk to the boil. Add the vanilla pod, if using.

2 Reduce the heat and put the lid on the pan. Leave to simmer gently for about 1–1¼ hours, stirring occasionally to prevent sticking, until most of the liquid has been absorbed.

3 Remove the vanilla pod, or if using vanilla extract, add this to the rice mixture now. Preheat the oven to 220°C/425°F/Gas 7.

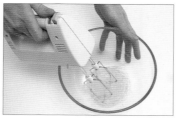

4 Place the egg whites in a clean, dry bowl and whisk them until they hold soft peaks.

5 Using either a large metal spoon or spatula, carefully fold the egg whites evenly into the rice and milk mixture and pour into a 1 litre/1¾ pint/4 cup ovenproof dish.

6 Sprinkle with grated nutmeg and bake for about 15–20 minutes, until the pudding is well risen and golden brown. Serve hot.

COOK'S TIP
Be very careful when simmering skimmed milk. With so little fat, it tends to boil over very easily. Use semi-skimmed if you wish.

CRUNCHY GOOSEBERRY CRUMBLE

A traditional favourite that is also good made with apples, plums or rhubarb.

INGREDIENTS

Serves 4

500g/1¼lb/5 cups gooseberries
50g/2oz/¼ cup caster (superfine) sugar
75g/3oz/scant 1 cup rolled oats
75g/3oz/⅔ cup wholemeal
  (whole-wheat) flour
60ml/4 tbsp sunflower oil
50g/2oz/¼ cup demerara (raw) sugar
30ml/2 tbsp chopped walnuts
natural (plain) yogurt or custard,
  to serve

1 Preheat the oven to 200°C/400°F/ Gas 6. Place the gooseberries in a pan with the caster sugar. Cover the pan and cook over a low heat for 10 minutes, until the gooseberries are just tender. Turn into an ovenproof dish.

2 To make the crumble, place the oats, flour and oil in a bowl and stir with a fork until evenly mixed.

3 Stir in the demerara sugar and walnuts, then spread evenly over the gooseberries. Bake for 25–30 minutes, or until golden and bubbling. Serve hot with yogurt, or custard made with skimmed milk.

> COOK'S TIP
> The best cooking gooseberries are the early, small, firm green ones.

NUTRITION NOTES

Per portion:

Energy	422kcals/1770kJ
Fat	18.5g
Saturated fat	2.32g
Cholesterol	0mg
Fibre	5.12g

GINGERBREAD UPSIDE DOWN PUDDING

A warming pudding goes down
well on a cold winter's day.

INGREDIENTS

Serves 4–6

For the topping
sunflower oil, for brushing
15ml/1 tbsp soft light brown sugar
4 medium peaches, halved and stoned
(pitted), or canned peach halves
8 walnut halves

For the base
130g/4½oz/generous 1 cup wholemeal
(whole-wheat) flour
2.5ml/½ tsp bicarbonate of soda
(baking soda)
7.5ml/1½ tsp ground ginger
5ml/1 tsp ground cinnamon
115g/4oz/½ cup muscovado
(molasses) sugar
1 egg
120ml/4fl oz/½ cup skimmed milk
50ml/2 fl oz/¼ cup sunflower oil

1 Preheat the oven to 175°C/350°F/
Gas 4. For the topping, brush the
base and sides of a 23cm/9in round
springform tin (pan) with oil. Sprinkle
the sugar over the base.

2 Arrange the peaches cut side down in
the tin with a walnut half in each.

3 For the base, sift together the flour,
bicarbonate of soda, ginger and
cinnamon, then stir in the sugar. Beat
together the egg, milk and oil, then mix
into the dry ingredients until smooth.

4 Pour the mixture evenly over
the peaches and bake for
35–40 minutes, until firm to the
touch. Turn out on to a serving plate.
Serve hot with yogurt or custard.

NUTRITION NOTES

Per portion:

Energy	432kcals/1812kJ
Fat	16.54g
Saturated fat	2.27g
Cholesterol	48.72mg
Fibre	4.79g

PLUM FILO POCKETS

INGREDIENTS

Serves 4

115g/4oz/½ cup skimmed milk soft cheese
15ml/1 tbsp light muscovado (brown) sugar
2.5ml/½ tsp ground cloves
8 large, firm plums, halved and
    stoned (pitted)
8 sheets filo pastry, thawed if frozen
sunflower oil, for brushing
icing (confectioners') sugar, to sprinkle

1 Preheat the oven to 220°C/425°F/
Gas 7. Mix together the cheese,
sugar and cloves.

2 Sandwich the plum halves back
together in twos with a spoonful
of the cheese mixture.

3 Spread out the pastry and cut into
16 pieces, about 23cm/9in square.
Brush one lightly with oil and place a
second at a diagonal on top. Repeat
with the remaining squares.

4 Place a plum on each pastry square,
and pinch corners together. Place on
baking sheet. Bake for 15–18 minutes,
until golden, then dust with icing sugar.

NUTRITION NOTES	
Per portion:	
Energy	188kcals/790kJ
Fat	1.87g
Saturated fat	0.27g
Cholesterol	0.29mg
Fibre	2.55g

APPLE COUSCOUS PUDDING

This unusual mixture makes a
delicious family pudding with a
rich fruity flavour, but virtually
no fat.

INGREDIENTS

Serves 4

600ml/1 pint/2½ cups apple juice
115g/4oz/⅔ cup couscous
40g/1½ oz/¼ cup sultanas (golden raisins)
2.5ml/½ tsp mixed (apple pie) spice
1 large cooking apple, peeled, cored
    and sliced
30ml/2 tbsp demerara (raw) sugar
low-fat natural (plain) yogurt, to serve

1 Preheat the oven to 200°C/400°F/
Gas 6. Place the apple juice, couscous, sultanas and spice in a pan and
bring to the boil, stirring. Cover and
simmer for 10–12 minutes, until all the
free liquid is absorbed.

2 Spoon half the couscous mixture
into a 1.2 litre/2 pint/5 cup ovenproof dish and top with half the apple
slices. Top with remaining couscous.

3 Arrange the remaining apple slices
overlapping over the top and
sprinkle with demerara sugar. Bake for
25–30 minutes or until golden brown.
Serve hot, with yogurt.

NUTRITION NOTES	
Per portion:	
Energy	194kcals/815kJ
Fat	0.58g
Saturated fat	0.09g
Cholesterol	0mg
Fibre	0.75g

FRUITY BREAD PUDDING

A delicious family favourite
from grandmother's day, with
a lighter, healthier touch.

INGREDIENTS

Serves 4

75g/3oz/½ cup mixed dried fruit
150ml/¼ pint/⅔ cup apple juice
115g/4oz stale bread, diced
5ml/1 tsp mixed (apple pie) spice
1 large banana, sliced
150ml/¼ pint/⅔ cup skimmed milk
15ml/1 tbsp demerara (raw) sugar
low-fat natural (plain) yogurt, to serve

1 Preheat the oven to 200°C/400°F/
Gas 6. Place the dried fruit in a
small pan with the apple juice and
bring to the boil.

2 Remove the pan from the heat and
stir in the bread, spice and banana.
Spoon the mixture into a shallow
1.2 litre/2 pint/5 cup ovenproof dish
and pour over the milk.

3 Sprinkle with demerara sugar and
bake for 25–30 minutes, until firm
and golden brown. Serve hot or cold
with natural yogurt.

COOK'S TIP
Different types of bread will
absorb varying amounts of liquid,
so you may need to adjust the
amount of milk to allow for this.

NUTRITION NOTES

Per portion:

Energy	190Kcals/800kJ
Fat	0.89g
Saturated fat	0.21g
Cholesterol	0.75mg
Fibre	1.8g

SPICED PEARS IN CIDER

Any variety of pear can be used for cooking, but it is best to choose firm pears for this recipe, or they will break up easily – Conference are a good choice.

INGREDIENTS

Serves 4

4 medium firm pears
250ml/8fl oz/1 cup dry (hard) cider
thinly pared strip of lemon rind
1 cinnamon stick
30ml/2 tbsp light muscovado
*   (brown) sugar*
5ml/1 tsp arrowroot
ground cinnamon, to sprinkle

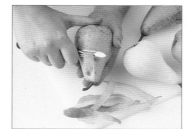

1 Peel the pears thinly, leaving them whole with the stems on. Place in a pan with the cider, lemon rind and cinnamon. Cover and simmer gently, turning the pears occasionally, for 15–20 minutes, or until tender.

2 Lift out the pears. Boil the syrup, uncovered, to reduce by about half. Remove the lemon rind and cinnamon stick, then stir in the sugar.

3 Mix the arrowroot with 15ml/ 1 tbsp cold water in a small bowl until smooth, then stir into the syrup. Bring to the boil and stir over the heat until thickened and clear.

4 Pour the sauce over the pears and sprinkle with ground cinnamon. Leave to cool slightly, then serve warm with low-fat fromage frais or yogurt.

COOK'S TIP

Whole pears look very impressive, but if you prefer, they can be halved and cored before cooking and this will reduce the cooking time slightly.

NUTRITION NOTES

Per portion:

Energy	102kcals/428kJ
Fat	0.18g
Saturated fat	0.01g
Cholesterol	0mg
Fibre	1.65g

MELON, GINGER AND GRAPEFRUIT

This pretty fruit combination is very light and refreshing for any summer meal.

INGREDIENTS

Serves 4
500g/1¼ lbs diced watermelon flesh
2 ruby or pink grapefruit
2 pieces stem ginger in syrup
30ml/2 tbsp stem ginger syrup

NUTRITION NOTES

Per portion:

Energy	76Kcals/324.5kJ
Fat	0.42g
Saturated fat	0.125g
Cholesterol	0mg
Fibre	0.77g

1 Remove any seeds from the watermelon and discard. Cut the fruit into bitesize chunks. Set aside.

2 Using a small sharp knife, cut away all the peel and white pith from the grapefruits and carefully lift out the segments, catching any juice in a bowl.

3 Finely chop the stem ginger and put in a serving bowl with the melon cubes and grapefruit segments, also adding the juice.

4 Spoon over the ginger syrup and toss the fruits lightly to mix evenly. Chill before serving.

> COOK'S TIP
> Take care to toss the fruits gently – grapefruit segments will break up easily and the appearance of the dish will be spoiled.

MANGO AND LIME SORBET IN LIME SHELLS

This richly flavoured sorbet looks pretty served in the lime shells, but is also good served in scoops for a more traditional presentation.

INGREDIENTS

Serves 4
4 large limes
1 medium-size ripe mango
7.5ml/½ tsp powdered gelatine
2 egg whites
15ml/1 tbsp sugar
lime rind strips, to decorate

1 Cut a thick slice from the top of each of the limes, and then cut a thin slice from the bottom end so that the limes will stand upright. Squeeze out the juice, then use a small knife to remove all the white membrane from the centre.

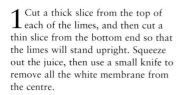

2 Halve, stone, peel and chop the mango, then purée the flesh in a blender or food processor with 30ml/2 tbsp of the lime juice. Dissolve the gelatine in 45ml/3 tbsp of lime juice and stir it into the mango mixture.

3 Whisk the egg whites until they hold soft peaks. Whisk in the sugar, then quickly fold the egg-white mixture into the mango mixture. Spoon the sorbet into the lime shells. (Any leftover sorbet that will not fit in can be frozen in small ramekins.)

COOK'S TIP
If you have any lime juice left over, it will freeze well for future use. Pour into a freezer container, seal and freeze for up to six months.

4 Wrap the shells in clear film (plastic wrap) and put in the freezer until the sorbet is firm. Before serving, allow the shells to stand at room temperature for about 10 minutes; decorate them with strips of lime rind.

NUTRITION NOTES

Per portion:

Energy	50.5Kcals/215kJ
Fat	0.09g
Saturated fat	0.3g
Cholesterol	0mg
Fibre	1g

GOOSEBERRY CHEESE COOLER

NUTRITION NOTES

Per portion:

Energy	123Kcals/525kJ
Fat	1.29g
Saturated fat	0.69g
Cholesterol	3.25mg
Fibre	3.64g

1 Top and tail the gooseberries and place them in a pan. Finely grate the rind from the orange and squeeze out the juice, then add them both to the pan. Cover the pan and cook gently, stirring occasionally, until the fruit is tender.

2 Remove from the heat and stir in the honey. Purée the gooseberries with their juice in a blender or food processor until almost smooth. Cool.

3 Press the cottage cheese through a sieve (strainer) until smooth. Stir half the cooled gooseberry purée into the cheese.

4 Spoon the cheese mixture into four serving glasses. Top each with gooseberry purée. Serve chilled.

COOK'S TIP
If fresh or frozen gooseberries are not available, canned ones are often packed in heavy syrup, so substitute a different fresh fruit.

ICED ORANGES

The ultimate fat-free treat –
these delectable orange sorbets
served in fruit shells were
originally sold in the beach
cafés in the south of France.

INGREDIENTS

Serves 8

150g/5oz/²/₃ cup sugar
juice of 1 lemon
14 medium oranges
8 fresh bay leaves, to decorate

NUTRITION NOTES

Per portion:

Energy	139Kcals/593kJ
Fat	0.17g
Saturated Fat	0g
Cholesterol	0mg
Fibre	3g

COOK'S TIP
Use crumpled kitchen paper to
keep the shells upright.

1 Put the sugar in a heavy pan.
Add half the lemon juice, then
add 120ml/4fl oz/½ cup water. Cook
over a low heat until the sugar has
dissolved. Bring to the boil and boil
for 2–3 minutes until the syrup is clear.

2 Slice the tops off eight of the
oranges to make "hats". Scoop out
the flesh of the oranges and reserve.
Freeze the empty orange shells and
"hats" until needed.

3 Grate the rind of the remaining
oranges and add to the syrup.
Squeeze the juice from the oranges, and
from the reserved flesh. There should
be 750ml/1¼ pints/3 cups. Squeeze
another orange or add bought orange
juice, if necessary.

4 Stir the orange juice and remaining
lemon juice, with 90ml/6 tbsp water
into the syrup. Taste, adding more
lemon juice or sugar as desired. Pour
the mixture into a shallow freezer
container and freeze for 3 hours.

5 Turn the orange sorbet mixture into
a bowl and whisk thoroughly to
break up the ice crystals. Freeze for
4 hours more, until firm, but not solid.

6 Pack the mixture into the hollowed-
out orange shells, mounding it up,
and set the "hats" on top. Freeze the
sorbet shells until ready to serve. Just
before serving, push a skewer into the
tops of the "hats" and push in a bay
leaf, to decorate.

APPLE AND BLACKBERRY TERRINE

Apples and blackberries are a classic autumn combination; they really complement each other. This pretty, three-layered terrine can be frozen, so you can enjoy it at any time of year.

INGREDIENTS

Serves 6
500g/1½lb cooking or eating apples
300ml/½ pint/1¼ cups sweet cider
15ml/1 tbsp clear honey
5ml/1 tsp vanilla extract
200g/7oz fresh or frozen and thawed
  blackberries
15ml/1 tbsp/1 sachet powdered gelatine
2 egg whites
apple slices and blackberries, to
  decorate

NUTRITION NOTES

Per portion:
Energy	72Kcals/306kJ
Fat	0.13g
Saturated fat	0g
Cholesterol	0mg
Fibre	2.1g

COOK'S TIP

For a quicker version, the mixture can be set without layering. Purée the apples and blackberries together, stir the dissolved gelatine and whisked egg whites into the mixture, turn the whole thing into the tin (pan) and leave the mixture to set.

1 Peel, core and chop the apples and place them in a pan, with half the cider. Bring the cider to the boil, and then cover the pan and let the apples simmer gently on a medium heat until tender.

2 Tip the apples into a blender or food processor and process them to a smooth purée. Stir in the honey and vanilla. Add half the blackberries to half the apple purée, and then process the mixture again until smooth. Strain.

3 Heat the remaining cider until it is almost boiling, then sprinkle the powdered gelatine over and stir until the gelatine has completely dissolved. Add half the gelatine and cider liquid to the apple purée and half to the blackberry purée.

4 Leave the purées to cool until almost set. Whisk the egg whites until they are stiff, then quickly fold them into the apple purée. Remove half the purée to another bowl. Stir the remaining whole blackberries into half the apple purée, and then turn this into a 1.75 litre/3 pint/7½ cup loaf tin (pan).

5 Top with the blackberry purée and spread it evenly. Finally, add a layer of the apple purée and smooth it evenly. To make sure the layers remain clearly separated, you can freeze each one until firm before adding the next.

6 Freeze until firm. To serve, allow to stand at room temperature for about 20 minutes to soften, then serve in thick slices, decorated with apples and blackberries.

CRUNCHY FRUIT LAYER

This simple dessert could also be served as a healthy breakfast.

NUTRITION NOTES

Per portion:
Energy	240Kcals/1005kJ
Fat	3g
Saturated fat	1g
Cholesterol	3mg

INGREDIENTS

Serves 2

1 peach or nectarine
75g/3oz/1 cup crunchy toasted
*   oat cereal*
150ml/¹/4 pint/²/3 cup low fat natural
*   (plain) yogurt*
15ml/1 tbsp jam
15ml/1 tbsp fruit juice

1 Remove the stone (pit) from the peach or nectarine and cut the fruit into bitesize pieces with a sharp knife.

2 Divide the chopped fruit between two tall glasses, reserving a few pieces for decoration.

3 Sprinkle the oat cereal over the fruit in an even layer, then top with the low fat yogurt.

4 Stir the jam and the fruit juice together in a jug (pitcher) with a spoon, then drizzle the mixture over the yogurt. Decorate with the reserved peach or nectarine pieces and serve the dessert immediately.

RASPBERRY-PASSION FRUIT CHINCHILLAS

Simple, yet delicious, beaten egg whites and sugar are baked in a dish, turned out and served with soft fruit and custard.

INGREDIENTS

Serves 4

25g/1oz/2 tbsp butter, softened
5 egg whites
150g/5oz/¾ cup caster
  (superfine) sugar
2 passion fruit
675g/1½lb/6 cups fresh raspberries
250ml/8fl oz/1 cup low-fat ready-made
  custard from a carton or can
skimmed milk, as required
icing (confectioners') sugar, for dusting

NUTRITION NOTES

Per portion:
Energy	309kcals/1296kJ
Fat	5.74g
Saturated fat	3.3g
Cholesterol	15.81mg
Fibre	4.47g

1 Preheat the oven to 180°C/350°F/ Gas 4. With a brush, paint four 300ml/½ pint/1¼ cup soufflé dishes with a visible layer of soft butter.

2 Whisk the egg whites in a mixing bowl until firm. (You can use an electric mixer.) Add the caster sugar, a little at a time, and whisk into a firm meringue.

3 Halve the passion fruit, take out the seeds with a spoon and fold them into the meringue.

4 Turn the meringue out into the four prepared dishes, stand them in a deep roasting pan, half-fill the pan with boiling water and bake for about 10 minutes, until set.

5 Turn the chinchillas out upside down on to individual plates.

6 Top the chinchillas with the fresh raspberries. Thin the custard with a little skimmed milk and pour around the edge. Dredge with icing sugar and serve warm or cold.

COOK'S TIP
If raspberries are out of season, use either fresh, bottled or canned soft berry fruit such as strawberries, blueberries or redcurrants.

YOGURT SUNDAES WITH PASSION FRUIT

Here is a sundae you can enjoy
every day! The frozen yogurt has
less fat and fewer calories than
traditional ice cream, and the
fruits provide vitamins A and C.

INGREDIENTS

Serves 4
350g/12oz strawberries, halved
2 passion fruit, halved
10ml/2 tsp icing (confectioners')
  sugar (optional)
2 ripe peaches, stoned (pitted)
  and chopped
8 scoops (about 350g/12oz) vanilla
  or strawberry frozen yogurt

COOK'S TIP
Choose reduced fat or virtually
fat free frozen yogurt or ice
cream, to cut the calories and fat.

1 Purée half the strawberries. Scoop
out the passion fruit pulp and add
it to the coulis. Sweeten, if necessary.

NUTRITION NOTES	
Per portion:	
Energy	135Kcals/560kJ
Fat	1g
Saturated fat	0.5g
Cholesterol	3.5mg

2 Spoon half the remaining
strawberries and half the chopped
peaches into four tall sundae glasses.
Top each dessert with a scoop of frozen
yogurt. Set aside a few choice pieces of
fruit for decoration, and use the rest to
make a further layer on the top of each
sundae. Top each sundae with a final
scoop of frozen yogurt.

3 Pour over the passion fruit coulis
and decorate the sundaes with the
remaining strawberries and pieces of
peach. Serve immediately.

FRUIT FONDUE WITH HAZELNUT DIP

INGREDIENTS

Serves 2
selection of fresh fruit for dipping,
  such as satsumas, kiwi fruit, grapes
  and physalis
50g/2oz/¹/2 cup reduced fat soft cheese
150ml/5fl oz/1¹/4 cup low fat
  hazelnut yogurt
5ml/1 tsp vanilla extract
5ml/1 tsp caster (superfine) sugar

NUTRITION NOTES	
Per portion (dip only):	
Energy	170Kcals/714kJ
Fat	4g
Saturated fat	2.5g
Cholesterol	6.5mg

1 First prepare the fruit. Peel and
segment the satsumas, removing
as much of the white pith as possible.
Quarter the kiwi fruits, wash the
grapes and peel back the papery casing
on the physalis.

2 Beat the soft cheese with the yogurt,
vanilla extract and sugar in a bowl.
Spoon the mixture into a glass serving
dish set on a platter or into small pots
on individual plates.

3 Arrange the prepared fruits around
the dip and serve immediately.

PINEAPPLE, ALLSPICE AND LIME

Fresh pineapple is easy to prepare and always looks very festive, so this dish is perfect for easy entertaining.

INGREDIENTS

Serves 4
1 ripe medium pineapple
1 lime
15ml/1 tbsp muscovado (molasses) sugar
5ml/1 tsp ground allspice

1 Cut the pineapple lengthways into quarters and remove the core.

NUTRITION NOTES

Per portion:
Energy	39Kcals/163kJ
Fat	0.12g
Saturated fat	0g
Cholesterol	0mg
Fibre	0.68g

2 Loosen the fruit by sliding a knife between it and the skin. Cut the pineapple flesh into thick slices.

3 Remove a few shreds of rind from the lime and set aside, then squeeze out the juice.

4 Sprinkle the pineapple with the lime juice and rind, muscovado sugar and allspice. Serve immediately, or chill for up to 1 hour.

PAPAYA SKEWERS WITH PASSION FRUIT

Tropical fruits, full of natural
sweetness, make a simple dessert.

INGREDIENTS

Serves 6
3 ripe papayas
10 small passion fruit or kiwi fruit
30ml/2 tbsp lime juice
30ml/2 tbsp icing (confectioners') sugar
30ml/2 tbsp white rum
lime slices, to decorate (optional)

NUTRITION NOTES

Per portion:
Energy	83Kcals/351kJ
Fat	0.27g
Saturated fat	0g
Cholesterol	0mg
Fibre	2.8g

1 Cut the papayas in half and scoop
out the seeds. Peel and cut the flesh
into even-size chunks. Thread the
chunks on to six bamboo skewers.

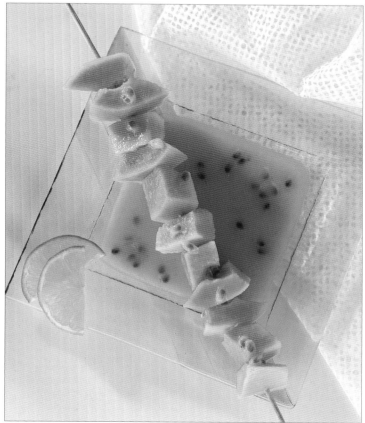

2 Halve eight of the passion fruit or
kiwi fruit and scoop out the insides.
Purée for a few seconds in a blender or
food processor.

3 Press the passion fruit or kiwi fruit
pulp through a sieve (strainer) and
discard the seeds. Add the lime juice,
icing sugar and white rum, then stir the
coulis well until the sugar has dissolved.

4 Spoon a little of the coulis on to six
serving plates. Place the skewers on
top. Scoop the flesh from the remaining
passion fruit or kiwi fruit and spoon it
over. Decorate with lime slices.

RASPBERRY VACHERIN

Meringue rounds filled with orange-flavoured low fat fromage frais and fresh raspberries make this a perfect dinner party dessert.

INGREDIENTS

Serves 6
3 egg whites
175g/6oz/³⁄4 cup caster (superfine) sugar
5ml/1 tsp chopped almonds
icing (confectioners') sugar, for dusting
raspberry leaves, to decorate (optional)

For the filling
175g/6oz/³⁄4 cup low fat soft cheese
15–30ml/1–2 tbsp clear honey
15–30ml/1–2 tbsp Cointreau
120ml/4fl oz/¹⁄2 cup low fat
   fromage frais
225g/8oz raspberries

NUTRITION NOTES

Per portion:	
Energy	197Kcals/837.5kJ
Fat	1.02g
Saturated fat	0.36g
Cholesterol	1.67mg
Fibre	1g

COOK'S TIP
When making the meringue, whisk the egg whites until they are so stiff that you can turn the bowl upside-down without them falling out.

1 Preheat the oven to 140°C/275°F/ Gas 1. Draw a 20cm/8in circle on two pieces of non-stick baking paper. Turn the paper over so the marking is on the underside and use it to line two heavy baking sheets.

2 Whisk the egg whites in a clean bowl until very stiff, then gradually whisk in the caster sugar to make a stiff meringue mixture.

3 Spoon the mixture on to the circles on the prepared baking sheets, spreading the meringue evenly to the edges. Sprinkle one meringue round with the chopped almonds.

4 Bake for 1¹⁄2–2 hours until crisp and dry, and then carefully lift the meringue rounds off the baking sheets. Peel away the paper and cool the meringues on a wire rack.

5 To make the filling, cream the soft cheese with the honey and liqueur in a bowl. Gradually fold in the fromage frais and the raspberries, reserving three berries for decoration.

6 Place the plain meringue round on a board, spread with the filling and top with the nut-covered round. Dust with the icing sugar, transfer to a serving plate and decorate with the reserved raspberries and a sprig of raspberry leaves, if you like.

STRAWBERRY ROSE-PETAL PASHKA

This lighter version of a Russian dessert is ideal for dinner parties – make it a day or two in advance for best results.

INGREDIENTS

Serves 4
350g/12oz/1½ cups cottage cheese
175g/6oz/¾ cup low fat natural (plain) yogurt
30ml/2 tbsp clear honey
2.5ml/½ tsp rose-water
275g/10oz strawberries
handful of scented pink rose petals, to decorate

NUTRITION NOTES

Per portion:
Energy	150.5Kcals/634kJ
Fat	3.83g
Saturated fat	2.32g
Cholesterol	0.13mg
Fibre	0.75g

COOK'S TIP
The flowerpot shape is traditional for pashka, but you could make it in any shape – the small porcelain heart-shaped moulds with draining holes usually reserved for *coeurs à la crème* make a pretty alternative.

1 Drain any free liquid from the cheese and tip the cheese into a sieve (strainer). Use a wooden spoon to rub it through the sieve into a bowl.

2 Stir the yogurt, honey and rose-water into the cheese.

3 Roughly chop about half the strawberries and stir them into the cheese mixture.

4 Line a new, clean flowerpot or a sieve with muslin and tip the cheese mixture in. Leave it to drain over a bowl for several hours, or overnight.

5 Invert the flowerpot or sieve on to a serving plate, turn out the pashka and remove the muslin.

6 Decorate with strawberries and petals. Serve chilled.

CREAMY MANGO CHEESECAKE

Cheesecakes are always a favourite but sadly they are often high in fat. This one is the exception.

INGREDIENTS

Serves 4

115g/4oz/generous 1 cup rolled oats
40g/1½oz/3 tbsp sunflower margarine
30ml/2 tbsp clear honey
1 large ripe mango
300g/10oz/1¼ cups low-fat soft cheese
150g/5oz/⅔ cup low-fat natural (plain) yogurt
finely grated rind of 1 small lime
45ml/3 tbsp apple juice
20ml/4 tsp powdered gelatine
fresh mango and lime slices, to decorate

1 Preheat the oven to 200°C/400°F/ Gas 6. Mix together the oats, margarine and honey. Press the mixture into the base of a 20cm/8in loose-based cake tin (pan). Bake for 12–15 minutes, until lightly browned. Cool.

2 Peel, stone (pit) and roughly chop the mango. Place the chopped mango, cheese, yogurt and lime rind in a food processor and process until smooth.

3 Heat the apple juice until boiling, sprinkle on the gelatine and stir to dissolve. Stir into the cheese mixture.

4 Pour the cheese mixture into the tin and chill until set, then turn out on to a serving plate. Decorate the top with mango and lime slices.

NUTRITION NOTES

Per portion:

Energy	422kcals/1774kJ
Fat	11.37g
Saturated fat	2.2g
Cholesterol	2.95mg
Fibre	7.15g

FRUDITES WITH HONEY DIP

INGREDIENTS

Serves 4

225g/8oz/1 cup Greek (US strained plain) yogurt
45ml/3 tbsp clear honey
selection of fresh fruit for dipping, such as apples, pears, tangerines, grapes, figs, cherries, strawberries and kiwi fruit

NUTRITION NOTES

Per portion:

Energy	161kcals/678kJ
Fat	5.43g
Saturated fat	3.21g
Cholesterol	7.31mg
Fibre	2.48g

1 Place the yogurt in a dish, beat until smooth, then stir in the honey, leaving a little marbled effect.

2 Cut the fruits into wedges or bite-size pieces or leave whole.

3 Arrange the fruits on a platter with the bowl of dip in the centre. Serve the dish chilled.

GRAPE CHEESE WHIP

INGREDIENTS

Serves 4

*150g/5oz/1 cup black or green seedless
  grapes, plus 4 sprigs*
2 egg whites
15ml/1 tbsp caster (superfine) sugar
finely grated rind and juice of ½ lemon
*225g/8oz/1 cup skimmed-milk
  soft cheese*
45ml/3 tbsp clear honey
30ml/2 tbsp brandy (optional)

NUTRITION NOTES

Per portion:
Energy	135Kcals/563kJ
Fat	0g
Saturated fat	0g
Cholesterol	0.56mg
Fibre	1.05g

1 Brush the sprigs of grapes lightly
with egg white and sprinkle with
sugar to coat. Leave to dry.

2 Mix the lemon rind and juice,
cheese, honey and brandy, if using.
Chop the remaining grapes and stir in.

3 Whisk the egg whites until stiff
enough to hold soft peaks. Fold
the whites into the grape mixture, then
spoon into serving glasses.

4 Top with sugar-frosted grapes and
serve chilled.

STRAWBERRIES IN SPICED GRAPE JELLY

INGREDIENTS

Serves 4

*450ml/¾ pint/scant 2 cups red
  grape juice*
1 cinnamon stick
1 small orange
15ml/1 tbsp/1 sachet powdered gelatine
*225g/8oz/2 cups strawberries, chopped
strawberries and orange rind, to decorate*

1 Place the grape juice in a pan with
the cinnamon. Thinly pare the rind
from the orange and add to the pan.
Warm over a very low heat for 10
minutes, then remove the flavourings.

2 Squeeze the juice from the orange
and sprinkle over the gelatine. Stir
into the grape juice to dissolve. Allow
to cool until just beginning to set.

3 Stir in the strawberries and quickly
turn into a 1 litre/1¾ pint/4 cup
mould or serving dish. Chill until set.

4 To turn out, dip the mould quickly
into hot water and invert on to
a serving plate. Decorate with fresh
strawberries and shreds of orange rind.

NUTRITION NOTES

Per portion:
Energy	85kcals/355kJ
Fat	0.2g
Saturated fat	0g
Cholesterol	0mg
Fibre	1.04g

FRESH CITRUS JELLY

Fresh fruit jellies make a stunning fat-free dessert and are also rich in vitamins.

INGREDIENTS

Serves 4

3 oranges
1 lemon
1 lime
300ml/½ pint/1¼ cups water
75g/3oz/6 tbsp golden caster (superfine) sugar
15ml/1 tbsp/1 sachet powdered gelatine
extra slices of fruit, to decorate

NUTRITION NOTES

Per portion:
Energy	136kcals/573kJ
Fat	0.21g
Saturated fat	0g
Cholesterol	0mg
Fibre	2.13g

1 With a sharp knife, cut all the peel and white pith from one orange and carefully remove the segments. Arrange all of the segments in the base of a 900ml/1½ pint/3¾ cup mould or dish.

2 Remove some shreds of citrus rind with a zester and reserve them for decoration. Grate the remaining rind from the lemon and lime and one orange. Place all the grated rind in a pan with the water and sugar.

3 Heat gently until the sugar has dissolved. Remove from the heat. Squeeze the juice from all the rest of the fruit and stir it into the pan.

4 Strain the liquid into a measuring jug (cup) to remove the rind (you should have about 600ml/1 pint/2½ cups: if necessary, make up the amount with water). Sprinkle the gelatine over the liquid and stir until dissolved.

5 Pour a little of the jelly over the orange segments and chill until it has set. Leave the remaining jelly at room temperature to cool, but do not allow it to set.

6 Pour the remaining cooled jelly into the dish and chill until set. To serve, turn out the jelly and decorate it with the reserved citrus rind shreds and slices of citrus fruit.

COOK'S TIP
To speed up the setting of the fruit segments in jelly, stand the dish in a bowl of ice.

AUTUMN PUDDING

Summer pudding is far too good to be reserved for the soft fruit season. Here is an autumn version, with apples, plums and blackberries, which makes a high-fibre dessert full of vitamins.

INGREDIENTS

Serves 6
450g/1lb eating apples
450g/1lb plums, halved and stoned
225g/8oz blackberries, hulled
60ml/4 tbsp apple juice
sugar or honey, to sweeten (optional)
8 slices of wholemeal (whole-wheat)
   bread, crusts removed
mint sprig and blackberry, to decorate
half-fat crème fraîche, to serve

1 Quarter the apples, remove the cores and peel, then slice them into a pan. Add the plums, blackberries and apple juice. Cover and cook gently for 10–15 minutes until tender. Sweeten, if necessary, with a little sugar or honey, although the fruit should be sweet enough.

2 Line the bottom and sides of a 1.2 litre/2 pint/5 cup pudding basin with 6–7 slices of bread, cut to fit. Press together tightly.

3 Spoon the fruit into the basin. Pour in just enough juice to moisten. Reserve any remaining juice.

4 Cover the fruit completely with the remaining bread. Fit a plate on top, so that it rests on the bread just below the rim. Stand the basin in a larger bowl to catch any juice. Place a weight on the plate and chill overnight.

5 Turn the pudding out on to a plate and pour the reserved juice over any areas which have not absorbed the juice. Decorate with the mint and blackberry and serve with crème fraîche.

NUTRITION NOTES	
Per portion:	
Energy	185Kcals/765KJ
Fat	1.5g
Saturated fat	0.5g
Cholesterol	0mg

PLUM AND PORT SORBET

Rather a grown-up sorbet, this one, but you could use fresh red grape juice in place of the port if you prefer.

INGREDIENTS

Serves 4–6

1kg/2¼lb ripe red plums, halved and stoned (pitted)
75g/3oz/6 tbsp caster (superfine) sugar
45ml/3 tbsp water
45ml/3 tbsp ruby port or red wine
crisp, sweet biscuits (cookies), to serve

1 Place the plums in a pan with the sugar and water. Stir over a gentle heat until the sugar is dissolved, then cover and simmer gently for about 5 minutes, until the fruit is soft.

2 Turn into a food processor and purée until smooth, then stir in the port or wine. Cool completely, then transfer to a freezer container and freeze until firm around the edges.

3 Spoon into the food processor and process until smooth. Return to the freezer and freeze until solid.

4 Allow the sorbet to soften slightly at room temperature for 15–20 minutes before serving in scoops, with sweet biscuits.

NUTRITION NOTES	
Per portion:	
Energy	166kcals/699kJ
Fat	0.25g
Saturated fat	0g
Cholesterol	0mg
Fibre	3.75g

TOFU BERRY BRULEE

This is a lighter variation of a classic dessert, usually forbidden on a low-fat diet, using tofu, which is low in fat and free from cholesterol. Use any soft fruits that are in season.

INGREDIENTS

Serves 4

300g/11oz packet silken tofu
45ml/3 tbsp icing (confectioners') sugar
225g/8oz/2 cups red berry fruits,
  such as raspberries, strawberries
  and redcurrants
about 75ml/5 tbsp demerara (raw) sugar

1 Place the tofu and icing sugar in a food processor or blender and process until smooth.

2 Stir in the fruits and spoon into a 900ml/1½ pint/3¾ cup flameproof dish. Sprinkle the top with enough demerara sugar to cover evenly.

3 Place under a very hot grill (broiler) until the sugar melts and caramelizes. Chill before serving.

COOK'S TIP
Choose silken tofu rather than firm tofu as it gives a smoother texture in this type of dish. Firm tofu is better for cooking in chunks.

NUTRITION NOTES	
Per portion:	
Energy	180kcals/760kJ
Fat	3.01g
Saturated fat	0.41g
Cholesterol	0mg
Fibre	1.31g

APRICOT MOUSSE

This light, fluffy dessert can be made with any dried fruits instead of apricots – try dried peaches, prunes or apples.

INGREDIENTS

Serves 4
300g/11oz/scant 1½ cups dried apricots
300ml/½ pint/1¼ cups fresh
   orange juice
200g/7oz/scant 1 cup low-fat fromage
   frais or crème fraîche
2 egg whites
mint sprigs, to decorate

1 Place the apricots in a pan with the orange juice and heat gently until boiling. Cover and simmer gently for 3 minutes.

2 Cool slightly. Place in a food processor or blender and process until smooth. Stir in the fromage frais.

3 Whisk the egg whites until stiff enough to hold soft peaks, then fold into the apricot mixture.

4 Spoon into four stemmed glasses or one large serving dish. Chill before serving, decorated with mint sprigs.

COOK'S TIP
To make a speedier fool-type dish, omit the egg whites and simply swirl together the apricot mixture and fromage frais.

NUTRITION NOTES	
Per portion:	
Energy	180kcals/757kJ
Fat	0.63g
Saturated fat	0.06g
Cholesterol	0.5mg
Fibre	4.8g

APPLE FOAM WITH BLACKBERRIES

Any seasonal soft fruit can be used for this if blackberries are not available.

INGREDIENTS

Serves 4
225g/8oz/2 cups blackberries
150ml/¼ pint/⅔ cup apple juice
5ml/1 tsp powdered gelatine
15ml/1 tbsp clear honey
2 egg whites

1 Place the blackberries in a pan with 60ml/4 tbsp of the apple juice and heat gently until the fruit is soft. Remove from the heat, cool and chill.

2 Sprinkle the gelatine over the remaining apple juice in a small pan and stir over a low heat until dissolved. Stir in the honey.

3 Whisk the egg whites until they hold stiff peaks. Continue whisking hard and pour in the hot gelatine mixture gradually, until well mixed.

4 Quickly spoon the foam into rough mounds on individual plates. Chill. Serve with the blackberries and juice spooned around.

COOK'S TIP
Make sure that you dissolve the gelatine over a very low heat. It must not boil, or it will lose its setting ability.

NUTRITION NOTES	
Per portion:	
Energy	49kcals/206kJ
Fat	0.15g
Saturated fat	0g
Cholesterol	0mg
Fibre	1.74g

CAKES AND BAKES

We tend to think of cakes and bakes being out of bounds for those following a low fat diet, but you will be pleased to learn that this is not the case at all. There are many ways of creating delicious cakes and bakes without the need for high fat mixtures, and all the ones in this chapter, both sweet and savoury, are low in fat. Choose from tempting recipes for such delights as Tia Maria Gâteau, Coffee Sponge Drops, Banana Ginger Parkin, Raspberry Muffins, Granary Baps, and Courgette and Walnut Loaf.

IRISH WHISKEY CAKE

This moist rich fruit cake is drizzled with whiskey as soon as it comes out of the oven.

INGREDIENTS

Serves 12

115g/4oz/⅔ cup glacé (candied) cherries
175g/6oz/1 cup muscovado (molasses) sugar
115g/4oz/⅔ cup sultanas (golden raisins)
115g/4oz/⅔ cup raisins
115g/4oz/½ cup currants
300ml/½ pint/1¼ cups cold tea
300g/10oz/2½ cups self-raising
  (self-raising) flour, sifted
1 egg
45ml/3 tbsp Irish whiskey

COOK'S TIP
If time is short, use hot tea and soak the fruit for just 2 hours.

1 Mix the cherries, sugar, dried fruit and tea in a large bowl. Leave to soak overnight until all the tea has been absorbed into the fruit.

NUTRITION NOTES

Per portion:

Energy	265Kcals/1115kJ
Fat	0.88g
Saturated fat	0.25g
Cholesterol	16mg
Fibre	1.48g

2 Preheat the oven to 180°C/350°F/ Gas 4. Grease and line a 1kg/2¼lb loaf tin (pan). Add the flour, then the egg to the fruit mixture and beat thoroughly until well mixed.

3 Pour the mixture into the prepared tin and bake for 1½ hours or until a skewer inserted into the centre of the cake comes out clean.

4 Prick the top of the cake with a skewer and drizzle over the whiskey while the cake is still hot. Allow to stand for about 5 minutes, then remove from the tin and cool on a wire rack.

ANGEL CAKE

A delicious light cake to serve as a dessert for a special occasion.

INGREDIENTS

Serves 10

40g/1½oz/⅓ cup cornflour (cornstarch)
40g/1½oz/⅓ cup plain (all-purpose) flour
8 egg whites
225g/8oz/1 cup caster (superfine) sugar, plus extra for sprinkling
5ml/1 tsp vanilla extract
90ml/6 tbsp orange-flavoured glacé icing, 4–6 physalis and a little icing (confectioners') sugar, to decorate

1 Preheat the oven to 180°C/350°F/ Gas 4. Sift both flours on to a sheet of baking parchment.

2 Whisk the egg whites in a large, clean, dry bowl until very stiff, then gradually add the sugar and vanilla extract, whisking until the mixture is thick and glossy.

3 Gently fold in the flour mixture with a large metal spoon. Spoon into an ungreased 25cm/10in angel cake tin (pan), smooth the surface and bake for about 45–50 minutes, until the cake springs back when lightly pressed.

COOK'S TIP
If you prefer, omit the glacé icing and physalis and simply dust the cake with a little icing sugar – it is delicious to serve as a coffee-time treat, and also makes the perfect accompaniment to vanilla yogurt ice cream for a dessert.

4 Sprinkle a piece of baking parchment with caster sugar and set an egg cup in the centre. Invert the cake tin over the paper, balancing it carefully on the egg cup. When cold, the cake will drop out of the tin (pan). Transfer it to a plate, spoon over the glacé icing, arrange the physalis on top and then dust with icing sugar and serve.

NUTRITION NOTES

Per portion:

Energy	139Kcals/582kJ
Fat	0.08g
Saturated fat	0.01g
Cholesterol	0mg
Fibre	0.13g

TIA MARIA GATEAU

A feather-light coffee sponge
with a creamy liqueur-flavoured
filling and a glossy icing.

INGREDIENTS

Serves 8
75g/3oz/³/4 cup plain (all-purpose) flour
30ml/2 tbsp instant coffee powder
3 eggs
115g/4oz/¹/2 cup caster (superfine) sugar
coffee beans, to decorate (optional)

For the filling
175g/6oz/³/4 cup low fat soft cheese
15ml/1 tbsp clear honey
15ml/1 tbsp Tia Maria liqueur
50g/2oz/¹/4 cup stem ginger,
  roughly chopped

For the icing
225g/8oz/1³/4 cups icing (confectioners')
  sugar, sifted
10ml/2 tsp coffee essence
15ml/1 tbsp water
5ml/1 tsp reduced fat cocoa powder

NUTRITION NOTES	
Per portion:	
Energy	226Kcals/951kJ
Fat	3.14g
Saturated fat	1.17g
Cholesterol	75.03mg
Fibre	0.64g

COOK'S TIP
When folding in the flour mixture
in step 3, be careful not to remove
the air, as it helps the cake to rise.

1 Preheat the oven to 190°C/375°F/
Gas 5. Grease and line a 20cm/8in
deep round cake tin (pan). Sift the flour
and coffee powder together on to a
sheet of baking parchment.

2 Whisk the eggs and sugar in a bowl
with a hand-held electric whisk
until thick and mousse-like. (When
the whisk is lifted, a trail should
remain on the surface of the mixture
for at least 15 seconds.)

3 Gently fold in the flour mixture
with a metal spoon. Turn the
mixture into the prepared tin. Bake the
sponge for 30–35 minutes or until it
springs back when lightly pressed. Turn
on to a wire rack to cool completely.

4 To make the filling, mix the soft
cheese with the honey in a bowl.
Beat until smooth, then stir in the
Tia Maria and chopped stem ginger.

5 Split the cake in half horizontally
and sandwich the two halves
together with the Tia Maria filling.

6 Make the icing. In a bowl, mix the
icing sugar and coffee essence with
enough water to make a consistency
that coats the back of a wooden spoon.

7 Pour three-quarters of the icing over
the cake, spreading it evenly to the
edges. Stir the cocoa into the remaining
icing until smooth. Spoon into a piping
bag fitted with a writing nozzle and pipe
the mocha icing over the coffee icing.
Decorate with coffee beans, if you like.

SNOWBALLS

These light and airy little mouthfuls make an excellent accompaniment to low fat yogurt ice cream.

INGREDIENTS

Makes about 20
2 egg whites
115g/4oz/¹/₂ cup caster (superfine) sugar
15ml/1 tbsp cornflour (cornstarch), sifted
5ml/1 tsp white wine vinegar
1.5ml/¹/₄ tsp vanilla extract

1 Preheat the oven to 150C°/300°F/ Gas 2. Line two baking sheets with non-stick baking paper. Whisk the egg whites in a large grease-free bowl until very stiff, using an electric whisk.

2 Add the sugar, whisking until the meringue is very stiff. Whisk in the cornflour, vinegar and vanilla extract.

3 Drop teaspoonfuls of the mixture on to the baking sheets, shaping them into mounds, and bake for 30 minutes until crisp.

4 Remove from the oven and leave to cool on the baking sheet. When the snowballs are cold, remove them from the baking paper with a palette knife.

NUTRITION NOTES	
Per portion:	
Energy	29Kcals/24kJ
Fat	0.01g
Saturated fat	0g
Cholesterol	0mg

APRICOT SPONGE BARS

These fingers are delicious at tea time – the apricots keep them moist for several days.

INGREDIENTS

Makes 18
225g/8oz/2 cups self-raising (self-raising) flour
115g/4oz/¹/₂ cup soft light brown sugar
50g/2oz/¹/₂ cup semolina
175g/6oz/1 cup ready-to-eat dried apricots, chopped
30ml/2 tbsp clear honey
30ml/2 tbsp malt extract
2 eggs
60ml/4 tbsp skimmed milk
60ml/4 tbsp sunflower oil
a few drops of almond extract
30ml/2 tbsp flaked (sliced) almonds

1 Preheat the oven to 160°C/325°F/ Gas 3. Lightly grease and then line an 18 x 28cm/7 x 11in baking tin (pan).

2 Sift the flour into a bowl and mix in the sugar, semolina and apricots. Make a well in the centre and add the honey, malt extract, eggs, milk, oil and almond essence. Mix the ingredients together thoroughly until smooth.

3 Spoon the mixture into the tin, spreading it to the edges, then sprinkle over the flaked almonds.

4 Bake for 30–35 minutes, or until the centre springs back when lightly pressed. Remove from the tin and turn on to a wire rack to cool. Cut into 18 slices using a sharp knife.

COOK'S TIP
If you can't find pre-soaked apricots, just chop ordinary dried apricots, soak them in boiling water for 1 hour, then drain and add to the mixture.

NUTRITION NOTES	
Per portion:	
Energy	153Kcals/641kJ
Fat	4.56g
Saturated fat	0.61g
Cholesterol	21.5mg
Fibre	1.27g

COFFEE SPONGE DROPS

These are delicious on their own, but taste even better with a filling made by mixing low fat soft cheese with drained and chopped stem ginger.

INGREDIENTS

Makes 12

50g/2oz/½ cup plain (all-purpose) flour
15ml/1 tbsp instant coffee powder
2 eggs
75g/3oz/6 tbsp caster (superfine) sugar

For the filling
115g/4oz/½ cup low fat soft cheese
40g/1½oz/¼ cup chopped
  stem ginger

COOK'S TIP
As an alternative to stem ginger in the filling, try walnuts.

1 Preheat the oven to 190°C/375°F/ Gas 5. Line two baking sheets with baking parchment. Make the filling by beating together the soft cheese and stem ginger. Chill until required. Sift the flour and instant coffee powder together.

NUTRITION NOTES

Per portion:
Energy	69Kcals/290kJ
Fat	1.36g
Saturated fat	0.50g
Cholesterol	33.33mg
Fibre	0.29g

2 Combine the eggs and caster sugar in a bowl. Beat with a hand-held electric whisk until thick and mousse-like. (When the whisk is lifted, a trail should remain on the surface of the mixture for at least 15 seconds.)

3 Carefully add the sifted flour and coffee mixture and gently fold in with a metal spoon, being careful not to knock out any air.

4 Spoon the mixture into a piping bag fitted with a 1cm/½in plain nozzle. Pipe 4cm/1½in rounds on the baking sheets. Bake for 12 minutes. Cool on a wire rack, then sandwich together with the filling.

CHOCOLATE AND BANANA BROWNIES

Nuts traditionally give brownies their chewy texture. Here oat bran is used instead, creating a low fat, moist, moreish, yet healthy alternative.

INGREDIENTS

Serves 9

75ml/5 tbsp reduced fat cocoa powder
15ml/1 tbsp caster (superfine) sugar
75ml/5 tbsp skimmed milk
3 large bananas, mashed
215g/7½oz/1 cup soft light brown sugar
5ml/1 tsp vanilla extract
5 egg whites
75g/3oz/¾ cup self-raising (self-rising) flour
75g/3oz/¾ cup oat bran
15ml/1 tbsp icing (confectioners') sugar, for dusting

NUTRITION NOTES

Per portion:	
Energy	230Kcals/968kJ
Fat	2.15g
Saturated fat	0.91g
Fibre	1.89g

COOK'S TIPS
Store these brownies in an airtight tin for a day before eating – they improve with keeping.

You'll find reduced fat cocoa powder in health food stores. If you can't find it, ordinary cocoa powder will work just as well, but, of course, the fat content will be much higher!

1 Preheat the oven to 180°C/350°F/ Gas 4. Line a 20cm/8in square tin (pan) with baking parchment.

2 Blend the reduced fat cocoa powder and caster sugar with the skimmed milk. Add the bananas, soft light brown sugar and vanilla extract.

3 Lightly beat the egg whites with a fork. Add the chocolate mixture and continue to beat well. Sift the flour over the mixture and fold in with the oat bran. Pour into the prepared tin.

4 Cook in the preheated oven for 40 minutes or until firm. Cool in the tin for 10 minutes, then turn out on to a wire rack. Cut into squares and lightly dust with icing sugar before serving.

LEMON CHIFFON CAKE

Lemon mousse provides a tangy filling for this light sponge.

Serves 8
2 eggs
75g/3oz/6 tbsp caster (superfine) sugar
grated rind of 1 lemon
50g/2oz/½ cup sifted plain
   (all-purpose) flour
lemon shreds, to decorate

For the filling
2 eggs, separated
75g/3oz/6 tbsp caster (superfine) sugar
grated rind and juice of 1 lemon
30ml/2 tbsp water
15ml/1 tbsp gelatine
125ml/4fl oz/½ cup low fat fromage
   frais or ricotta cheese

For the icing
15ml/1 tbsp lemon juice
115g/4oz/scant 1 cup icing
   (confectioners') sugar, sifted

1 Preheat the oven to 180°C/350°F/ Gas 4. Grease and line a 20cm/8in loose-bottomed cake tin (pan). Whisk the eggs, sugar and lemon rind together with a hand-held electric whisk until thick and mousse-like. Gently fold in the flour, then turn the mixture into the prepared tin.

2 Bake for 20–25 minutes until the cake springs back when lightly pressed in the centre. Turn on to a wire rack to cool. Once cold, split the cake in half horizontally and return the lower half to the clean cake tin.

3 Make the filling. Put the egg yolks, sugar, lemon rind and juice in a bowl. Beat with a hand-held electric whisk until thick, pale and creamy.

4 Pour the water into a heatproof bowl and sprinkle the gelatine on top. Leave until spongy, then stir over simmering water until dissolved. Cool, then whisk into the yolk mixture. Fold in the fromage frais or ricotta cheese. When the mixture begins to set, whisk the egg whites to soft peaks. Fold the egg whites into the mousse mixture.

5 Pour the lemon mousse over the sponge in the cake tin, spreading it to the edges. Set the second layer of sponge on top and chill until set.

6 Slide a palette knife or spatula dipped in hot water between the tin and the cake to loosen it, then carefully transfer the cake to a serving plate. Make the icing by adding enough lemon juice to the icing sugar to make a mixture thick enough to coat the back of a wooden spoon. Pour over the cake and spread evenly to the edges. Decorate with the lemon shreds.

NUTRITION NOTES	
Per portion:	
Energy	202Kcals/849kJ
Fat	2.81g
Saturated fat	0.79g
Cholesterol	96.41mg
Fibre	0.20g

COOK'S TIP
The mousse should be just setting when the egg whites are added. Speed up this process by placing the bowl of mousse in iced water.

BANANA AND GINGERBREAD SLICES

Very quick to make and
deliciously moist due to the
addition of bananas.

INGREDIENTS

Makes 20

275g/10oz/2 cups plain (all-purpose) flour
20ml/4 tsp ground ginger
10ml/2 tsp mixed (apple pie) spice
5ml/1 tsp bicarbonate of soda
  (baking soda)
115g/4oz/¹/2 cup soft light brown sugar
60ml/4 tbsp sunflower oil
30ml/2 tbsp molasses or black treacle
30ml/2 tbsp malt extract
2 eggs
60ml/4 tbsp orange juice
3 bananas
115g/4oz/²/3 cup raisins

NUTRITION NOTES

Per portion:	
Energy	148Kcals/621kJ
Fat	3.07g
Saturated fat	0.53g
Cholesterol	19.30mg
Fibre	0.79g

VARIATION
To make Spiced Honey and
Banana Cake: omit the ground
ginger and add another 5ml/1 tsp
mixed spice; omit the malt extract
and the molasses or treacle and
add 60ml/4 tbsp strong-flavoured
clear honey instead; and replace
the raisins with either sultanas
(golden raisins) or coarsely
chopped ready-to-eat dried
apricots, or semi-dried pineapple.
If you choose to use pineapple,
then you could also replace
the orange juice with fresh
pineapple juice.

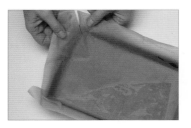

1 Preheat the oven to 180°C/350°F/
Gas 4. Lightly grease and line an
18 x 28cm/7 x 11in baking tin (pan).

2 Sift the flour into a bowl with the
spices and bicarbonate of soda. Mix
in the sugar with some of the flour and
sift it all into the bowl.

3 Make a well in the centre, add the
oil, molasses or black treacle, malt
extract, eggs and orange juice and mix
together thoroughly.

4 Mash the bananas, add them to
the bowl with the raisins and mix
well together.

5 Pour the mixture into the prepared
tin and bake for 35–40 minutes,
until the centre springs back when
lightly pressed.

6 Leave the cake in the tin to cool for
5 minutes, then turn out on to a
wire rack and leave to cool completely.
Cut into 20 slices.

COOK'S TIP
The flavour of this cake develops
as it keeps, so if you can, store it
for a few days before eating.

GREEK HONEY AND LEMON CAKE

INGREDIENTS

Makes 16 slices

40g/1½oz/3 tbsp sunflower margarine
60ml/4 tbsp clear honey
finely grated rind and juice of 1 lemon
150ml/¼ pint/⅔ cup skimmed milk
150g/5oz/1¼ cups plain (all-purpose) flour
7.5ml/1½ tsp baking powder
2.5ml/½ tsp freshly grated nutmeg
50g/2oz/⅓ cup semolina
2 egg whites
10ml/2 tsp sesame seeds

1 Preheat the oven to 200°C/400°F/ Gas 6. Lightly oil a 19cm/7½in square deep cake tin (pan) and line the base with baking parchment.

2 Place the margarine and 45ml/ 3 tbsp of the honey in a pan and heat gently until melted. Reserve 15ml/1 tbsp lemon juice, then stir in the rest with the lemon rind and milk.

3 Sift together the flour, baking powder and nutmeg, then beat in the honey mixture with the semolina. Whisk the egg whites until they form soft peaks, then fold evenly into the mixture.

4 Spoon into the tin and sprinkle with sesame seeds. Bake for 25–30 minutes, until golden brown. Mix the reserved honey and lemon juice and drizzle over the cake while warm. Cool in the tin, then cut into fingers to serve.

NUTRITION NOTES

Per portion:
Energy	82kcals/342kJ
Fat	2.62g
Saturated fat	0.46g
Cholesterol	0.36mg
Fibre	0.41g

STRAWBERRY ROULADE

INGREDIENTS

Serves 6

4 egg whites
115g/4oz/generous ½ cup golden caster (superfine) sugar
75g/3oz/⅔ cup plain (all-purpose) flour
30ml/2 tbsp orange juice
caster (superfine) sugar, for sprinkling
115g/4oz/1 cup strawberries, chopped
150g/5oz/¼ cup low-fat fromage frais or mascarpone
strawberries, to decorate

1 Preheat the oven to 200°C/400°F/ Gas 6. Oil a 23 × 33cm/9 × 13in Swiss roll tin (jelly roll pan) and line with baking parchment.

2 Whisk the egg whites until they form soft peaks. Gradually whisk in the sugar. Fold in half of the flour, then fold in the rest with the orange juice.

3 Spoon the mixture into the prepared tin, spreading evenly. Bake for 15–18 minutes, or until golden brown and firm to the touch.

4 Meanwhile, spread out a sheet of baking parchment and sprinkle with caster sugar. Turn out the cake on to this and remove the lining paper. Roll up the sponge loosely from one short side, with the paper inside. Cool.

5 Unroll and remove the paper. Stir the strawberries into the fromage frais or mascarpone and spread over the sponge. Re-roll and serve decorated with strawberries.

NUTRITION NOTES

Per portion:
Energy	154kcals/646kJ
Fat	0.24g
Saturated fat	0.05g
Cholesterol	0.25mg
Fibre	0.6g

BANANA GINGER PARKIN

INGREDIENTS

Makes 1 cake
*200g/7oz/1¼ cups plain
  (all-purpose) flour*
*10ml/2 tsp bicarbonate of soda
  (baking soda)*
10ml/2 tsp ground ginger
150g/5oz/1¼ cups medium oatmeal
60ml/4 tbsp muscovado (molasses) sugar
75g/3oz/6 tbsp sunflower margarine
*150g/5oz/generous ⅓ cup golden
  (light corn) syrup*
1 egg, beaten
3 ripe bananas, mashed
*75g/3oz/¼ cup icing
  (confectioners') sugar*
stem ginger, to decorate (optional)

1 Preheat the oven to 160°C/325°F/
Gas 3. Grease and line an 18 ×
28cm/7 × 11in cake tin (pan).

2 Sift together the flour, bicarbonate
of soda and ginger, then stir in the
oatmeal. Melt the sugar, margarine
and syrup in a pan, then stir into the
flour mixture. Beat in the egg and
mashed bananas.

3 Spoon into the tin and bake for
about 1 hour, or until firm to the
touch. Allow to cool in the tin, then
turn out and cut into squares.

4 Sift the icing sugar into a bowl and
stir in just enough water to make a
smooth, runny icing. Drizzle the icing
over each square and top with a piece
of stem ginger, if you like.

COOK'S TIP
This is a nutritious, energy-giving
cake that is a really good choice
for packed luches. It improves with
keeping – store it in an airtight
container for up to two months.

NUTRITION NOTES

Per cake:
Energy	3320Kcals/13946kJ
Fat	83.65g
Saturated fat	16.34g
Cholesterol	24mg
Fibre	20.69g

SPICED DATE AND WALNUT CAKE

Rich in flavour, this spiced cake
is low in fat and high in fibre.

INGREDIENTS

Makes 1 cake

300g/11oz/2²/₃ cups wholemeal self-
raising (whole-wheat self-rising) flour
10ml/2 tsp mixed (apple pie) spice
150g/5oz/³/₄ cup chopped dates
50g/2oz/¹/₂ cup chopped walnuts
60ml/4 tbsp sunflower oil
115g/4oz/¹/₂ cup muscovado
(molasses) sugar
300ml/¹/₂ pint/1¹/₄ cups skimmed milk
walnut halves, to decorate

1 Preheat the oven to 180°C/350°F/
Gas 4. Grease and line a 900g/2lb
loaf tin (pan) with baking parchment.

2 Sift together the flour and spice,
adding back any bran from the
sieve. Stir in the dates and walnuts.

3 Mix the oil, sugar and milk, then
stir evenly into the dry ingredients.
Spoon into the prepared tin and
arrange the walnut halves on top.

4 Bake the cake in the oven for about
45–50 minutes, or until golden
brown and firm. Turn out the cake,
remove the lining paper and leave to
cool on a wire rack.

NUTRITION NOTES

Per cake:

Energy	2654kcals/11146kJ
Fat	92.78g
Saturated fat	11.44g
Cholesterol	6mg
Fibre	35.1g

COOK'S TIP

Pecan nuts can be used in place of
the walnuts in this cake.

EGGLESS CHRISTMAS CAKE

INGREDIENTS

Makes 1 × 18cm/7in square cake
75g/3oz/½ cup sultanas (golden raisins)
75g/3oz/generous ½ cup raisins
75g/3oz/⅓ cup currants
75g/3oz/⅓ cup glacé (candied)
    cherries, halved
50g/2oz/⅓ cup cut mixed (candied) peel
250ml/8fl oz/1 cup apple juice
25g/1oz/¼ cup toasted hazelnuts
30ml/2 tbsp pumpkin seeds
2 pieces preserved stem ginger, chopped
finely grated rind of 1 lemon
120ml/4fl oz/½ cup skimmed milk
50ml/2fl oz/¼ cup sunflower oil
225g/8oz/2 cups wholemeal self-raising
    (whole-wheat self-rising) flour
10ml/2 tsp mixed (apple pie) spice
45ml/3 tbsp brandy or dark rum
apricot jam, for brushing
glacé (candied) fruits, to decorate

1 Place the first five ingredients and peel in a bowl and stir in the apple juice. Cover and leave overnight.

2 Preheat the oven to 150°C/300°F/ Gas 2. Grease and line an 18cm/7in square cake tin (pan).

3 Add the hazelnuts, pumpkin seeds, ginger and lemon rind to the soaked fruit. Stir in the milk and oil. Sift the flour and spice and stir into the mixture with the brandy or rum.

4 Spoon into the prepared tin (pan) and bake for about 1½ hours, or until the cake is golden brown and firm to the touch.

5 Turn out and cool on a wire rack. Brush with sieved (strained) apricot jam and decorate with glacé fruits.

NUTRITION NOTES

Per cake:
Energy	2702kcals/11352kJ
Fat	73.61g
Saturated fat	10.69g
Cholesterol	2.4mg
Fibre	29.46g

CRANBERRY AND APPLE RING

Tangy cranberries add an unusual flavour to this low fat cake. It is best eaten very fresh.

INGREDIENTS

Makes 1 ring cake
225g/8oz/2 cups self-raising
   (self-rising) flour
5ml/1 tsp ground cinnamon
75g/3oz/⅓ cup light muscovado
   (brown) sugar
1 crisp eating apple, cored and diced
75g/3oz/¼ cup cranberries
60ml/4 tbsp sunflower oil
150ml/¼ pint/⅔ cup apple juice
cranberry jelly and apple slices,
   to decorate

1 Preheat the oven to 180°C/350°F/ Gas 4. Lightly grease a 1 litre/ 1¾ pint/4 cup ring tin (pan) with oil.

2 Sift together the flour and ground cinnamon, then stir in the sugar.

3 Toss together the diced apple and cranberries. Stir into the dry ingredients, then add the oil and apple juice and beat well.

4 Spoon the mixture into the prepared ring tin and bake for about 35–40 minutes, or until the cake is firm to the touch. Turn out and leave to cool completely on a wire rack.

5 To serve, drizzle warmed cranberry jelly over the cake and decorate with apple slices.

COOK'S TIP
Fresh cranberries are available throughout the winter months and if you don't use them all, they can be frozen for up to a year.

NUTRITION NOTES

Per cake:	
Energy	1616kcals/6787kJ
Fat	47.34g
Saturated fat	6.14g
Cholesterol	0mg
Fibre	12.46g

PINEAPPLE AND CINNAMON DROP SCONES

Making the batter with pineapple juice cuts down on fat and adds to the taste.

INGREDIENTS

Makes 24
115g/4oz/1 cup self-raising (self-rising) wholemeal (whole-wheat) flour
115g/4oz/1 cup self-raising (self-rising) white flour
5ml/1 tsp ground cinnamon
15ml/1 tbsp caster (superfine) sugar
1 egg
300ml/½ pint/1¼ cups pineapple juice
75g/3oz/½ cup semi-dried pineapple, chopped

NUTRITION NOTES

Per portion:
Energy	15Kcals/215kJ
Fat	0.81g
Saturated fat	0.14g
Cholesterol	8.02mg
Fibre	0.76g

1 Preheat a griddle, heavy frying pan or an electric frying pan. Put the wholemeal flour in a mixing bowl. Sift in the white flour, add the cinnamon and sugar and make a well in the centre.

> COOK'S TIP
> Drop scones do not keep well and are best eaten freshly cooked. Other semi-dried fruit, such as apricots or pears, can be used in place of the pineapple.

2 Add the egg with half the pineapple juice and gradually incorporate the surrounding flour to make a smooth batter. Beat in the remaining juice with the chopped pineapple.

3 Lightly grease the griddle or pan. Drop tablespoons of the batter on to the surface, leaving them until they bubble and the bubbles begin to burst.

4 Turn the drop scones with a palette knife and cook until the underside is golden brown. Keep the cooked scones warm and moist by wrapping them in a clean napkin while continuing to cook successive batches.

CHEESE AND CHIVE SCONES

INGREDIENTS

Makes 9

115g/4oz/1 cup self-raising (self-rising) flour
150g/5oz/1 cup self-raising (self-rising) wholemeal (whole-wheat) flour
2.5ml/¹/₂ tsp salt
75g/3oz feta cheese
15ml/1 tbsp chopped fresh chives
150ml/¹/₄ pint/²/₃ cup skimmed milk, plus extra for glazing
1.25ml/¹/₄ tsp cayenne pepper

1 Preheat the oven to 200°C/400°F/Gas 6. Sift the flours and salt into a mixing bowl, adding any bran left over from the flour in the sieve.

2 Crumble the feta cheese and rub into the dry ingredients. Stir in the chives, then add the milk and mix to a soft dough.

NUTRITION NOTES

Per portion:
Energy	121Kcals/507kJ
Fat	2.24g
Saturated fat	1.13g
Fibre	1.92g

3 Turn out on to a floured surface and knead lightly until smooth. Roll out to 2cm/³/₄in thick and stamp out nine scones with a 6cm/2¹/₂in cookie cutter.

4 Transfer the scones to a non-stick baking sheet. Brush with skimmed milk, then sprinkle over the cayenne pepper. Bake in the oven for 15 minutes, or until golden brown.

RASPBERRY MUFFINS

These American muffins are made using baking powder and low fat buttermilk, giving them a light and spongy texture. They are delicious at any time of day.

INGREDIENTS

Makes 10–12

275g/10oz/2½ cups plain (all-purpose) flour
15ml/1 tbsp baking powder
115g/4oz/½ cup caster (superfine) sugar
1 egg
250ml/8fl oz/1 cup buttermilk
60ml/4 tbsp sunflower oil
150g/5oz raspberries

1 Preheat the oven to 200°C/400°F/ Gas 6. Arrange 12 paper cake cases in a deep muffin tin (pan). Sift the flour and baking powder into a mixing bowl, stir in the sugar, then make a well in the centre.

2 Mix the egg, buttermilk and sunflower oil together in a bowl, pour into the flour mixture and mix quickly.

3 Add the raspberries and lightly fold in with a metal spoon. Spoon the mixture into the paper cases.

4 Bake the muffins for 20–25 minutes until golden brown and firm in the middle. Transfer to a wire rack and serve warm or cold.

SPICED BANANA MUFFINS

These light and nutritious muffins include banana for added fibre, and make a tasty tea-time treat. If you like, slice off the tops and fill with jam.

INGREDIENTS

Makes 12

75g/3oz/²⁄₃ cup wholemeal (whole-wheat) flour
50g/2oz/¹⁄₂ cup plain (all-purpose) flour
10ml/2 tsp baking powder
pinch of salt
5ml/1 tsp mixed (apple pie) spice
40g/1¹⁄₂oz/¹⁄₄ cup soft light brown sugar
50g/2oz/¹⁄₄ cup polyunsaturated margarine
1 egg, beaten
150ml/¹⁄₄ pint/²⁄₃ cup semi-skimmed (low-fat) milk
grated rind of 1 orange
1 ripe banana
20g/³⁄₄oz/¹⁄₄ cup porridge oats
20g/³⁄₄oz/scant ¹⁄₄ cup chopped hazelnuts

1 Preheat the oven to 200°C/400°F/ Gas 6. Line a muffin tin (pan) with 12 large paper cake cases. Sift together both flours, the baking powder, salt and mixed spice into a bowl, then tip the bran remaining in the sieve (strainer) into the bowl. Stir in the sugar.

NUTRITION NOTES	
Per muffin:	
Energy	110Kcals/465kJ
Fat	5g
Saturated fat	1g
Cholesterol	17.5mg

2 Melt the margarine and pour it into a mixing bowl. Cool slightly, then beat in the egg, milk and grated orange rind.

3 Gently fold in the dry ingredients. Mash the banana with a fork, then stir it gently into the mixture, being careful not to overmix.

4 Spoon the mixture into the paper cases. Combine the oats and hazelnuts and sprinkle a little of the mixture over each muffin.

5 Bake for 20 minutes until the muffins are well risen and golden, and a skewer inserted in the centre comes out clean. Transfer to a wire rack and serve warm or cold.

OATY CRISPS

These biscuits (cookies) are very crisp and crunchy – ideal to serve with morning coffee.

INGREDIENTS

Makes 18

175g/6oz/1¾ cups rolled oats
75g/3oz/½ cup light muscovado (brown) sugar
1 egg
60ml/4 tbsp sunflower oil
30ml/2 tbsp malt extract

NUTRITION NOTES

Per portion:	
Energy	86Kcals/360kJ
Fat	3.59g
Saturated fat	0.57g
Cholesterol	10.7mg
Fibre	0.66g

1 Preheat the oven to 190°C/375°F/ Gas 5. Lightly grease two baking sheets. Mix the rolled oats and sugar in a bowl, breaking up any lumps in the sugar. Add the egg, sunflower oil and malt extract, mix well, then leave to soak for 15 minutes.

2 Using a teaspoon, place small heaps of the mixture well apart on the prepared baking sheets. Press the heaps into 7.5cm/3in rounds with the back of a dampened fork.

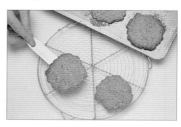

3 Bake the biscuits for 10–15 minutes until golden brown. Leave them to cool for 1 minute, then remove with a palette knife and cool on a wire rack.

COOK'S TIP
To give these biscuits a coarser texture, substitute jumbo oats for some or all of the rolled oats. Once cool, store in an airtight container to keep them as crisp and fresh as possible.

OATCAKES

Try serving these oatcakes with reduced fat hard cheeses, or topped with honey for breakfast.

────── INGREDIENTS ──────

Makes 8
175g/6oz/1 cup medium oatmeal,
  plus extra for sprinkling
2.5ml/¹/₂ tsp salt
pinch of bicarbonate of soda
  (baking soda)
15g/¹/₂oz/1 tbsp butter
75ml/5 tbsp water

1 Preheat the oven to 150°C/300°F/ Gas 2. Mix the oatmeal with the salt and bicarbonate of soda in a bowl.

2 Melt the butter with the water in a small pan. Bring to the boil, then add to the oatmeal mixture and mix to a moist dough.

COOK'S TIP
To achieve a neat round, place a 25cm/10in cake board or plate on top of the oatcake. Cut away any excess dough with a knife.

3 Turn the dough on to a surface sprinkled with oatmeal and knead to a smooth ball. Turn a large baking sheet upside down, grease it, sprinkle it lightly with oatmeal and place the ball of dough on top. Sprinkle the dough with oatmeal, then roll out to a 25cm/10in round.

4 Cut the round into eight sections, ease them apart slightly and bake for about 50–60 minutes until crisp. Leave to cool on the baking sheet, then remove the oatcakes with a palette knife or spatula.

─── **NUTRITION NOTES** ───

Per portion:

Energy	102Kcals/427kJ
Fat	3.43g
Saturated fat	0.66g
Cholesterol	0.13mg
Fibre	1.49g

SUNFLOWER SULTANA SCONES

INGREDIENTS

Makes 10–12

225g/8oz/2 cups self-raising (self-rising) flour
5ml/1 tsp baking powder
25g/1oz/2 tbsp sunflower margarine
30ml/2 tbsp golden caster (superfine) sugar
50g/2oz/⅓ cup sultanas (golden raisins)
30ml/2 tbsp sunflower seeds
150g/5oz/⅔ cup low-fat natural
   (plain) yogurt
about 30–45ml/2–3 tbsp skimmed milk

1 Preheat the oven to 230°C/450°F/
Gas 8. Sift the flour and baking
powder into a bowl and rub in
the margarine.

2 Stir in the sugar, sultanas and half
the sunflower seeds, then mix in
the yogurt, with just enough milk to
make a fairly soft, but not sticky dough.

3 Roll out on a lightly floured surface
to about 2cm/¾in thickness. Cut
into 6cm/2½in flower shapes or
rounds with a pastry (cookie) cutter
and lift on a lightly oiled baking sheet.

4 Brush with milk and sprinkle with
the reserved sunflower seeds, then
bake for 10–12 minutes, until well
risen and golden brown.

5 Cool the scones on a wire rack.
Serve split and spread with jam or
low-fat spread.

NUTRITION NOTES

Per portion:	
Energy	176kcals/742kJ
Fat	5.32g
Saturated fat	0.81g
Cholesterol	0.84mg
Fibre	1.26g

PRUNE AND PEEL ROCK BUNS

INGREDIENTS

Makes 12

225g/8oz/2 cups plain (all-purpose) flour
10ml/2 tsp baking powder
75g/3oz/⅓ cup demerara (raw) sugar
50g/2oz/⅓ cup chopped ready-to-eat prunes
50g/2oz/⅓ cup mixed chopped (candied) peel
finely grated rind of 1 lemon
50ml/2fl oz/¼ cup sunflower oil
75ml/5 tbsp skimmed milk

NUTRITION NOTES

Per portion:	
Energy	135kcals/570kJ
Fat	3.35g
Saturated fat	0.44g
Cholesterol	0.13mg
Fibre	0.86g

1 Preheat the oven to 200°C/400°F/
Gas 6. Lightly oil a large baking
sheet. Sift together the flour and baking
powder, then stir in the sugar, prunes,
peel and lemon rind.

2 Mix the oil and milk, then stir into
the mixture, to make a dough
which just binds together.

3 Spoon into rocky heaps on the
baking sheet and bake for 20 minutes,
until golden. Cool on a wire rack.

RYE BREAD

Rye bread is popular in northern Europe and makes an excellent base for open sandwiches. Add a low fat topping of your choice.

INGREDIENTS

Serves 16
350g/12oz/3 cups wholemeal (whole-wheat) flour
225g/8oz/2 cups rye flour
115g/4oz/1 cup strong white bread flour
7.5ml/1½ tsp salt
30ml/2 tbsp caraway seeds
475ml/16fl oz/2 cups warm water
10ml/2 tsp dried yeast
pinch of sugar
30ml/2 tbsp molasses

1 Put the flours and salt in a bowl. Set aside 5ml/1 tsp of the caraway seeds and add the rest to the bowl.

2 Put half the water in a jug or bowl. Sprinkle the yeast on top. Add the sugar, mix well. Leave for 10 minutes.

3 Make a well in the flour mixture, then add the yeast mixture with the molasses and the remaining water. Gradually incorporate the flour and mix to a soft dough, adding a little water if necessary.

4 Turn the dough on to a floured surface and knead for 5 minutes until smooth and elastic. Return to the clean bowl, cover with a damp dish towel and leave in a warm place for about 2 hours until doubled in bulk. Grease a baking sheet.

NUTRITION NOTES

Per portion:
Energy	156Kcals/655kJ
Fat	1.2g
Saturated fat	0.05g
Cholesterol	0mg
Fibre	4.53g

5 Turn the dough on to a floured surface and knead for 2 minutes. Divide the dough in half, then shape into two 23cm/9in long oval loaves. Flatten the loaves slightly and place them on a baking sheet.

6 Brush the loaves with water and sprinkle with the remaining caraway seeds. Cover and leave in a warm place for about 40 minutes until well risen. Preheat the oven to 200°C/400°F/Gas 6. Bake the loaves for 30 minutes or until they sound hollow when tapped underneath. Cool on a wire rack. Serve the bread plain, or slice and add a low fat topping.

SODA BREAD

Soda bread takes only a few minutes to make and needs no rising or proving. If possible, eat soda bread while it is still warm from the oven as it does not keep well.

INGREDIENTS

Serves 8
450g/1lb/4 cups plain (all-purpose) flour
5ml/1 tsp salt
5ml/1 tsp bicarbonate of soda
   (baking soda)
5ml/1 tsp cream of tartar
350ml/12fl oz/1½ cups buttermilk

1 Preheat the oven to 220°C/425°F/ Gas 7. Flour a baking sheet. Sift all the dry ingredients into a mixing bowl and make a small well in the centre.

2 Add the buttermilk and mix quickly to a soft dough. Turn on to a floured surface and knead lightly. Shape into a round about 18cm/7in across and put on the baking sheet.

3 Cut a deep cross on top of the loaf and sprinkle with a little flour. Bake for 25–30 minutes, then transfer the soda bread to a wire rack to cool.

COOK'S TIP
Soda bread needs a light hand. The ingredients should be bound together quickly in the bowl and kneaded very briefly. The aim is to get rid of the largest cracks, as the dough will become tough if it is handled for too long.

NUTRITION NOTES

Per portion:
Energy	230Kcals/967kJ
Fat	1.03g
Saturated fat	0.24g
Cholesterol	0.88mg
Fibre	1.94g

PEAR AND SULTANA TEABREAD

An excellent use for windfall pears.

INGREDIENTS

Serves 6–8
25g/1oz/¹/₄ cup rolled oats
50g/2oz/¹/₄ cup light muscovado
  (brown) sugar
30ml/2 tbsp pear or apple juice
30ml/2 tbsp sunflower oil
1 large or 2 small pears
115g/4oz/1 cup self-raising (self-
  rising) flour
115g/4oz/³/₄ cup sultanas (golden raisins)
2.5ml/¹/₂ tsp baking powder
10ml/2 tsp mixed (apple pie) spice
1 egg

1 Preheat the oven to 180°C/350°F/
Gas 4. Grease and line a 450g/1lb
loaf tin (pan) with baking parchment.
Put the oats in a bowl with the sugar,
pour over the pear or apple juice and
oil, mix well and leave to stand for
15 minutes.

2 Quarter, core and coarsely grate the
pear(s). Add to the oat mixture
with the flour, sultanas, baking powder,
mixed spice and egg, then mix together
thoroughly.

3 Spoon the mixture into the prepared
loaf tin and level the top. Bake for
50–60 minutes or until a skewer
inserted in the centre comes out clean.

4 Transfer the teabread on to a wire
rack and peel off the parchment.
Leave to cool completely.

COOK'S TIP
Health food shops sell concentrated
pear and apple juice, ready for
diluting as required.

NUTRITION NOTES	
Per portion:	
Energy	200Kcals/814kJ
Fat	4.61g
Saturated fat	0.79g
Cholesterol	27.50mg
Fibre	1.39g

GRANARY BAPS

These make excellent picnic fare, filled with cottage cheese, tuna, salad and low fat mayonnaise. They are also very good served warm with soup.

INGREDIENTS

Makes 8
300ml/½ pint/1¼ cups warm water
5ml/1 tsp dried yeast
pinch of sugar
450g/1lb/4 cups malted brown flour
5ml/1 tsp salt
15ml/1 tbsp malt extract
15ml/1 tbsp rolled oats

NUTRITION NOTES

Per portion:
Energy	223Kcals/939kJ
Fat	1.14g
Saturated Fat	0.16g
Cholesterol	0mg
Fibre	3.10g

COOK'S TIP
To make a large loaf, shape the dough into a round, flatten it slightly and bake for about 30–40 minutes. Test it by tapping the base of the loaf – if it sounds hollow, it is cooked.

1 Put half the warm water in a jug. Sprinkle in the yeast. Add the sugar, mix well and leave for 10 minutes.

2 Put the malted brown flour and salt in a mixing bowl and make a well in the centre. Add the yeast mixture with the malt extract and the remaining water. Gradually incorporate the flour and mix to a soft dough.

3 Turn the dough on to a floured surface and knead for 5 minutes until smooth and elastic. Return to the clean bowl, cover with a damp dish towel and leave in a warm place to rise for about 2 hours until doubled in bulk.

4 Lightly grease a large baking sheet. Turn the dough on to a floured surface, knead for 2 minutes, then divide into eight pieces. Shape the pieces into balls and flatten them with the palm of your hand to make neat 10cm/4in rounds.

5 Place the rounds on the prepared baking sheet, cover loosely with a large plastic bag (ballooning it to trap the air inside), and leave to stand in a warm place until the baps are well risen. Preheat the oven to 220°C/425°F/Gas 7.

6 Brush the baps with water, sprinkle with the oats and bake for about 20–25 minutes or until they sound hollow when tapped underneath. Cool on a wire rack, then serve with the low fat filling of your choice.

BANANA AND CARDAMOM BREAD

The combination of banana and cardamom is delicious in this soft-textured moist loaf. It is perfect for tea time, served with low fat spread and jam. No fat is used or needed to make this delicious loaf, creating a healthy low fat bread for all to enjoy.

INGREDIENTS

Serves 6

150ml/¼ pint/⅔ cup warm water
5ml/1 tsp dried yeast
pinch of sugar
10 cardamom pods
400g/14oz/3½ cups strong white
    bread flour
5ml/1 tsp salt
30ml/2 tbsp malt extract
2 ripe bananas, mashed
5ml/1 tsp sesame seeds

1 Put the warm water in a small bowl. Sprinkle the yeast on top. Add the sugar, mix well and leave for 10 minutes.

2 Split the cardamom pods. Remove the seeds and chop them finely.

3 Sift the flour and salt into a mixing bowl and make a well in the centre. Add the yeast mixture with the malt extract, chopped cardamom seeds and bananas.

4 Gradually incorporate the flour and mix to a soft dough, adding a little extra water if necessary. Turn the dough on to a floured surface and knead for about 5 minutes until smooth and elastic. Return to the clean bowl, cover with a damp dish towel and leave to rise for about 2 hours until doubled in bulk.

NUTRITION NOTES

Per portion:

Energy	299Kcals/1254kJ
Fat	1.55g
Saturated fat	0.23g
Cholesterol	0mg
Fibre	2.65g

5 Grease a baking sheet. Turn the dough on to a floured surface, knead briefly, then divide into three and shape into a plait (braid). Place on the baking sheet and cover loosely with a plastic bag (ballooning it to trap the air). Leave until well risen. Preheat the oven to 220°C/425°F/Gas 7.

6 Brush the plait lightly with water and sprinkle with the sesame seeds. Bake for 10 minutes, then lower the oven temperature to 200°C/400°F/ Gas 6. Cook for 15 minutes more, or until the loaf sounds hollow when it is tapped underneath. Cool on a wire rack.

COOK'S TIP
Make sure the bananas are really ripe, so that they impart maximum flavour to the bread. If you prefer, place the dough in one piece in a 450g/1lb loaf tin and bake for an extra 5 minutes. As well as being low in fat, bananas are a good source of potassium, therefore making an ideal nutritious, low fat snack.

SPIRAL HERB BREAD

An attractive and delicious bread which is ideal for serving with a salad for a healthy lunch.

INGREDIENTS

Makes 2 loaves
30ml/2 tbsp easy-blend (rapid-rise) dried yeast
600ml/1 pint/2½ cups lukewarm water
425g/15oz/3⅔ cups strong white bread flour
500g/1¼lb/5 cups strong wholemeal (whole-wheat) bread flour
7.5ml/3 tsp salt
25g/1oz/2 tbsp sunflower margarine
1 large bunch parsley, finely chopped
1 bunch spring onions (scallions), chopped
1 garlic clove, finely chopped
1 egg, lightly beaten
skimmed milk, for glazing
salt and ground black pepper

NUTRITION NOTES

Per loaf:

Energy	1698kcals/7132kJ
Fat	24.55g
Saturated fat	9.87g
Cholesterol	144.33mg
Fibre	30.96g

1 Combine the yeast with approximately 50ml/2fl oz/¼ cup of the water, stir and leave to dissolve.

2 Mix together the flours and salt in a large bowl. Make a well in the centre and pour in the yeast mixture and the remaining water. With a wooden spoon, stir from the centre, working outwards to obtain a rough dough.

3 Transfer the dough to a floured surface and knead until smooth and elastic. Return to the bowl, cover with a plastic bag, and leave for about 2 hours until doubled in volume.

4 Meanwhile, combine the margarine, parsley, spring onions and garlic in a large frying pan. Cook over a low heat, stirring, until softened. Season and set aside.

5 Grease two 23 × 13cm/9 × 5in loaf tins (pans). When the dough has risen, cut in half and roll each half into a rectangle about 35 × 23cm/14 × 9in.

6 Brush both with the beaten egg. Divide the herb mixture between the two, spreading just up to the edges.

7 Roll up to enclose the filling and pinch the short ends to seal. Place in the tins, seam side down.

8 Cover the dough with a clean dish towel and leave undisturbed in a warm place until the dough rises above the rim of the tins.

9 Preheat the oven to 190°C/375°F/ Gas 5. Brush the loaves with milk and bake for about 55 minutes until the bases sound hollow when tapped. Cool on a wire rack.

WALNUT BREAD

Delicious at any time of day, this bread may be eaten plain or topped with low-fat cream cheese.

INGREDIENTS

Makes 1 loaf
425g/15oz/3²/₃ cups strong wholemeal (whole-wheat) bread flour
150g/5oz/1¼ cups strong white bread flour
12.5ml/2½ tsp salt
550ml/18fl oz/2½ cups lukewarm water
15ml/1 tbsp clear honey
15ml/1 tbsp easy-blend (rapid-rise) dried yeast
150g/5oz/1¼ cups walnut pieces, plus more for decorating
1 egg, beaten, for glazing

NUTRITION NOTES

Per loaf:
Energy	2852kcals/11980kJ
Fat	109.34g
Saturated fat	12.04g
Cholesterol	77mg
Fibre	47.04g

1 Mix together the flours and salt in a large bowl. Make a well in the centre and pour in 250ml/8fl oz/1 cup of the water, the honey and the yeast.

2 Set aside until the yeast dissolves and the mixture is frothy.

3 Add the remaining water. With a wooden spoon, stir from the centre, incorporating flour with each turn, to obtain a smooth dough. Add more flour if the dough is too sticky and use your hands if the dough becomes too stiff to stir.

4 Transfer to a floured board and knead, adding flour if necessary, until the dough is smooth and elastic. Place in a greased bowl and roll the dough around in the bowl to coat thoroughly all over.

5 Cover with a plastic bag and leave in a warm place until doubled in volume, about 1½ hours.

6 Knock back (punch down) the dough very firmly and knead in the walnuts until they are evenly spread.

7 Grease a baking sheet. Shape the dough into a round loaf and place on the baking sheet. Press in the walnut pieces to decorate the top. Cover the dough loosely with a damp dish towel and leave in a warm place for about 25–30 minutes until doubled in size.

8 Preheat the oven to 220°C/425°F/Gas 7. With a sharp knife, score the top of the loaf and brush with the egg glaze. Bake for 15 minutes. Lower the temperature to 190°C/375°F/Gas 5 and bake until the base of the loaf sounds hollow when tapped, about 40 minutes. Leave to cool on a wire rack.

OATMEAL BREAD

A healthy bread, with a crumbly texture due to the inclusion of rolled oats.

— INGREDIENTS —

Makes 2 loaves
475ml/16fl oz/2 cups skimmed milk
25g/1oz/2 tbsp low-fat spread
50g/2oz/¼ cup soft dark brown sugar
10ml/2 tsp salt
15ml/1 tbsp easy-blend (rapid-rise) dried yeast
50ml/2fl oz/¼ cup lukewarm water
400g/14oz/4 cups rolled oats
450–675g/1–1½lb/4–6 cups strong white bread flour

1 Scald the milk. Remove from the heat and stir in the low-fat spread, sugar and salt. Leave until lukewarm.

2 Combine the yeast and lukewarm water in a large bowl and leave until the yeast is dissolved and the mixture is frothy. Stir in the milk mixture.

3 Add 275g/10oz/2½ cups of the oats and enough flour to obtain a soft pliable dough.

4 Transfer to a floured surface and knead until smooth and elastic.

5 Place the dough in a greased bowl, cover with a plastic bag, and leave it for about 2–3 hours, until doubled in volume. Grease a large baking sheet.

6 Transfer the dough to a lightly floured surface and divide in half.

7 Shape into rounds. Place on the baking sheet, cover with a damp dish towel and leave to rise for about 1 hour, until doubled in volume.

8 Preheat the oven to 200°C/400°F/ Gas 6. Score the tops of the loaves and sprinkle with the remaining oats. Bake for about 45–50 minutes, until the bases sound hollow when tapped. Cool on wire racks.

NUTRITION NOTES	
Per loaf:	
Energy	2281kcals/9581kJ
Fat	34.46g
Saturated fat	11.94g
Cholesterol	39mg
Fibre	24.11g

COURGETTE AND WALNUT LOAF

A wonderful combination of ingredients makes this loaf a real treat for the senses – this loaf looks, smells and tastes great.

INGREDIENTS

Makes 1 loaf
3 eggs
75g/3oz/6 tbsp soft light brown sugar
50ml/2fl oz/¼ cup sunflower oil
225g/8oz/2 cups wholemeal
    (whole-wheat) flour
5ml/1 tsp baking powder
5ml/1 tsp bicarbonate of soda
    (baking soda)
5ml/1 tsp ground cinnamon
2.5ml/½ tsp ground allspice
7.5ml/1½ tsp green cardamoms, seeds
    removed and crushed
150g/5oz/1 cup coarsely grated
    courgette (zucchini)
50g/2oz/¼ cup walnuts, chopped
50g/2oz/¼ cup sunflower seeds

1 Preheat the oven to 180°C/350°F/ Gas 4. Grease the base and sides of a 900g/2lb loaf tin (pan) and line with baking parchment. Beat the eggs and sugar together and gradually add the oil.

NUTRITION NOTES

Per portion:
Energy	3073kcals/12908kJ
Fat	201.98g
Saturated fat	26.43g
Cholesterol	654.5mg
Fibre	28.62g

2 Sift the flour into a bowl together with the baking powder, bicarbonate of soda, cinnamon and allspice.

3 Mix into the egg mixture with the rest of the ingredients, reserving 15ml/1 tbsp of the sunflower seeds for the top.

4 Spoon into the loaf tin, level off the top, and sprinkle with the reserved sunflower seeds.

5 Bake for about 1 hour or until a skewer inserted in the centre comes out clean. Leave to cool slightly, then turn out on to a wire cooling rack.

SAFFRON FOCACCIA

Makes 1 loaf
pinch of saffron threads
150ml/¼ pint/⅔ cup boiling water
225g/8oz/2 cups plain
  (all-purpose) flour
2.5ml/½ tsp salt
5ml/1 tsp easy-blend (rapid-rise)
  dried yeast
15ml/1 tbsp olive oil

For the topping
2 garlic cloves, sliced
1 red onion, cut into thin wedges
rosemary sprigs
12 black olives, pitted and coarsely
  chopped
15ml/1 tbsp olive oil

NUTRITION NOTES

Per loaf:
Energy	1047kcals/4399kJ
Fat	29.15g
Saturated fat	4.06g
Cholesterol	0mg
Fibre	9.48g

1 Place the saffron in a heatproof jug (pitcher) and pour on the boiling water. Leave to infuse (steep) until the saffron mixture is lukewarm.

2 Place the flour, salt, yeast and olive oil in a food processor. Turn on and gradually add the saffron and its liquid until the dough forms a ball.

3 Turn out on to a floured board and knead for 10–15 minutes. Place in a bowl, cover and leave to rise for about 30–40 minutes, until doubled in size.

4 Knock back (punch down) the risen dough on a lightly floured surface and roll out into an oval shape, 1cm/½in thick. Place on a lightly greased baking sheet and leave to rise for 20–30 minutes.

5 Preheat the oven to 200°C/400°F/ Gas 6. Use your fingers to press small indentations in the dough.

6 Cover with the topping ingredients, brush lightly with olive oil, and bake for about 25 minutes or until the loaf sounds hollow when tapped on the base. Leave to cool on a wire rack.

DATE AND NUT MALTLOAF

INGREDIENTS

Makes 2 x 450g/1lb loaves

300g/11oz/2 cups strong plain (all-purpose) flour
275g/10oz/2 cups wholemeal (whole-wheat) flour
5ml/1 tsp salt
75g/3oz/6 tbsp soft brown sugar
1 sachet easy-blend (rapid-rise) dried yeast
50g/2oz/4 tbsp butter or margarine
15ml/1 tbsp black treacle (molasses)
60ml/4 tbsp malt extract
250ml/8fl oz/1 cup lukewarm milk
115g/4oz/½ cup chopped dates
50g/2oz/½ cup chopped nuts
75g/3oz/½ cup sultanas (golden raisins)
75g/3oz/½ cup raisins
30ml/2 tbsp honey, to glaze

1 Sift the flours and salt into a large bowl, then tip in the wheat flakes that are caught in the sieve. Stir in the sugar and yeast.

NUTRITION NOTES	
Per slice:	
Energy	261Kcals/1104kJ
Fat	5.57g
Saturated fat	2.46g
Cholesterol	9.45mg

2 Put the butter or margarine in a small pan with the treacle and malt extract. Stir over a low heat until melted. Leave to cool, then combine with the milk.

3 Stir the liquid into the dry ingredients and knead for 15 minutes until the dough is elastic. (If you have a dough blade on your food processor, follow the manufacturers' instructions for timings.)

4 Knead in the fruits and nuts. Transfer the dough to an oiled bowl, cover with clear film (plastic wrap) and leave in a warm place for about 1½ hours, until doubled in size.

5 Grease two 450g/1lb loaf tins (pans). Knock back (punch down) the dough and knead lightly. Divide in half, form into loaves and place in the tins. Cover and leave in a warm place for about 30 minutes, until risen. Preheat the oven to 190°C/375°F/Gas 5.

6 Bake for 35–40 minutes, until well risen and sounding hollow when tapped underneath. Cool on a wire rack. Brush with honey while warm.

INDEX

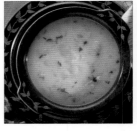